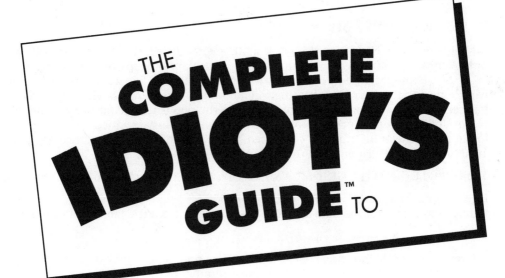

THE COMPLETE IDIOT'S GUIDE™ TO

Wills and Estates

by Stephen M. Maple

alpha books

A Division of Macmillan General Reference
A Pearson Education Macmillan Company
1633 Broadway, New York, NY 10019-6785

International Standard Book Number: 0-02-863597-3
Cataloging-in-Publication data available upon request from the Library of Congress.

99   8   7   6   5   4   3   2

Interpretation of the printing code: the rightmost number of the first series of numbers is the year of the book's printing; the rightmost number of the second series of numbers is the number of the book's printing. For example, a printing code of 97-1 shows that the first printing occurred in 1997.

Printed in the United States of America

Special custom-edition of THE COMPLETE IDIOT'S GUIDE® TO WILLS AND ESTATES.

Publisher
Kathy Nebenhaus

Editorial Director
Gary M. Krebs

Managing Editor
Bob Shuman

Development Editor
Carol Hupping

Production Editor
Mark Enochs

Cover Designer
Michael Freeland

Illustrator
Judd Winick

Designer
Glenn Larsen

Indexer
Cheryl Jackson

Production Team
Angela Calvert

Contents at a Glance

Contents

17 How Charitable Donations Can Save You Money 191

18 State Taxes: When and How You Can Be Hit 199

19 Keeping Your Wealth Within the Family 209

Foreword

There's one thing that we all can be sure of, and that's that one day we won't be here anymore. Unfortunately, we have no control over that certainty. But we do have control over what we leave behind for our families and loved ones.

In *The Complete Idiot's Guide to Wills and Estates*, Steve Maple gives us a good deal of valuable advice and information that makes estate planning understandable and doable for almost anyone. It's an enjoyable, readable, and instructive guide that's well-researched and thorough.

I compliment Steve Maple on this work and recommend it to anyone for interesting and informative reading on estate planning.

—Steven R. Nation, Judge
Hamilton Superior Court No. 1 Indiana

Introduction

Welcome to the world of estate planning.

You'll notice I didn't say the "wonderful" world or the "fascinating" world. I don't want you rolling your eyes and muttering "Come *on*." But I *do* want you to continue reading this book.

Okay, making your way through a guide about putting together an estate plan will probably not be as lighthearted as reading about how to select wines or start a rock garden. Still, I honestly believe you will find this book not only informative but also engrossing.

Why? Because it's very relevant to *you* and your life, and perhaps there are some important parts of estate planning that you haven't given much thought to before. Learning something new, especially when it's about ourselves, is *always* interesting.

I think you'll soon be absorbed in exploring just how you want to lay out an estate plan, which includes a basic will and a few other documents. You'll set planning goals for yourself, now and at different stages of your life ahead. You'll learn about professionals who can help you along the way. You'll read stories about others and their experiences, too—tales that will be informative, puzzling, amusing, and sometimes even touching. You'll learn from the mistakes some of those folks made—and from reading about the right steps others took at particular times in their lives.

So this book is about people as well as legal documents and tax talk. It's about how we *use* those papers, those directives, and even those taxes, to put ourselves in control of our financial destiny.

If you have an estate plan—and you will when you finish this book, or will at least have started the ball rolling—then obviously you have an estate. Trust me. No matter how small you may think your assets are, you do have an estate. You'll want to protect it, watch it grow, and even see it spent in exactly the ways you choose.

Having an estate plan will make you feel like a million dollars—no matter that your net worth may be missing a few of those zeros.

How This Book Is Organized

The chapters that follow are laid out to guide you through the estate planning process as it is likely to occur in your life, no matter what your age right now. Let me introduce you to the book's four parts.

Part 1, "Assets, Assets, Assets," introduces you to what an estate is and will acquaint you with the planning process. It will help you sort out your own assets, so that you know what you own and, in particular, *how* you own it.

Part 2 ,"About Wills, Trusts...and Probate," will take you into the heart of the book: preparing a will, and perhaps a trust if that can be useful to you. There are some cautions, too, about what happens when you *don't* have a will.

Part 3, "All in the Family—and Just a Little Beyond," talks about your nearest and dearest and how you will probably want to provide for them in some specific estate-planning situations. I'll tell you how to head off potential arguments and misunderstandings, too.

Part 4, "Taxes You Must Pay, and Those Maybe You Don't," will introduce you to the sometimes complex world of federal and state taxes and help you with terrific strategies for paying as little as possible on your estate, your income, and when making gifts.

Extras

To help you even further, and just for fun, you'll find small boxes with special items of interest in every chapter. You'll immediately see a clue to the subject matter of each box by the little cartoon at the top. Here's what you'll find:

Briefs

Intriguing stories about people in specific estate-planning situations.

Quote, Unquote
The words of the famous, from early history to the present day, speaking with humor or wisdom (and sometimes even both).

Watch Out
Steps to avoid, products to skip, when to be careful, and when to seek help.

Words, Words, Words
Definitions of legal terms and other words that may be unfamiliar to you.

Tip
How to find more information or learn a different way of doing things.

Special Thanks to the Technical Reviewer

The Complete Idiot's Guide to Wills and Estates was reviewed by an expert who double-checked the accuracy of what you'll learn here, to help us ensure that this book gives you everything you need to know about wills and estates. Special thanks are extended to George L. Smith.

George L. Smith is a partner in the Asset Planning and Probate Section of Robinson & Cole law offices in Greenwich, Connecticut. Mr. Smith practices in all areas of estate planning and administration. Mr. Smith is admitted to practice law in Connecticut, New York, and Florida, and is a member of the Bar Association in each of those states. Mr. Smith is also a member of the Executive Committee of the Estates and Probate Section of the Connecticut Bar Association, and of the Planned Gifts and Bequests Committee of the Archdiocese of New York.

Part 1
Assets, Assets, Assets

We're going to talk first about your estate and what it comprises. Makes you feel rather prosperous, doesn't it, to hear the words "your" and "estate" in the same sentence? You should feel that way. Your assets—all of your possessions acquired through the years—are valuable to you now for your own satisfaction and enjoyment and will matter one day to your heirs.

What exactly are those assets? I'll help you sort them out. You might find you have more than you think you do—always a pleasant discovery.

Chapter 1

You've Got to Have a Plan, Whether Simple or Deluxe

In This Chapter

➤ "Later," "Someday," "When I hit 40," and so on

➤ What comprises an estate

➤ The perils of having no plan

➤ Setting goals

➤ Your estate planning team

I don't believe in dying. It's been done. I'm working on a new exit. Besides, I can't die now. I'm booked. — George Burns, 1987

As you probably know, the much-loved comedian finally "exited" in 1996, at the age of 100. Burns also played God in two hit motion pictures. Neither of those accomplishments, of course, prevented him from eventually having to go on to meet his Maker (did He critique the actor who played Him?)—and having to leave behind a well-planned estate for his heirs. Did George Burns have a proper estate plan? I was not one of his attorneys, but I'd bet the farm he left an estate in A-1 condition, spelling out his wishes clearly and taking advantage of every legitimate tax break.

Sure, George Burns had a larger estate—a *lot* larger—than you or I are likely to leave, and so he should have worked hard on its intricacies. However, whether we are young or old, employed or not working, wealthy or just getting by, single, married, or in a long-term relationship with a "significant other," we need to plan for when we are not here or, because of illness, unable to speak for ourselves. Why on earth would anyone want someone else—perhaps, *Oh, God!*, the *state*—to make important, and very personal, decisions for him or her and the families left behind?

What IS an Estate?

"All right," you say, "I understand your point. But before you go any further would you tell me please, what exactly *is* an estate? And what's an estate *plan*? Of course I know what a will is, but what specifically goes into that document?"

Good questions. The area of wills and estates is likely to seem hazy if you have not given that subject area much thought. You certainly need to understand the terminology used in this book, so let's start with a few explanations right now.

Your Assets

The dictionary defines *estate* as the assets and liabilities left by a person at death. Well, that's true, but I'd extend that definition a little. If you are able to leave an estate at death, its ingredients are carried along by you through much of your life, too.

Those ingredients are assets—everything you own by yourself or jointly with someone else. If you're 18 years old you probably don't own very much. But as you grow older you begin to acquire possessions—a home, a car, a pension plan, perhaps some stocks and the like. All of that is valuable, first, because all of it becomes your assets (which are good for anyone to have) and second, because you can will those assets (according to various ownership styles that we'll get into in the next couple of chapters) to anyone you choose.

As you get older, your responsibilities increase, along with your assets. You will want to see that your spouse and children, especially young children, are taken care of if you die. You will want your debts to be paid, too. You might have elderly parents or an ailing sibling you're looking out for. Your wishes for after your death can be carried out with a proper estate plan. Which brings me to your next question.

Your Estate Plan

What is an estate plan? Well, that's an arrangement for the conservation and transfer of your wealth after your death. It's seeing that you keep the most money and other property for your heirs at the least cost to you during your lifetime, and to them when they inherit.

The minimum any estate plan should contain is a will. I'll touch on the contents of that document soon.

A good estate plan also includes a trust, if that is a better, or additional, choice for you. A trust is a written agreement that allows you to hold property and manage it for your beneficiaries in accordance with whatever instructions are in that trust agreement. It's a little like a will, but with a difference. We'll get to a fuller explanation of a trust later in the book, too.

Other documents you might want to add to an estate plan as you get older are a *durable power of attorney*, which legally gives someone you designate the right to make decisions for you even if you are incapacitated and cannot act on your own. You might eventually want a *health care power of attorney*, which gives the person of your choice the right to make decisions for you about your health care if you cannot make them yourself.

There are some other papers you may elect for your estate plan that I'll mention later in the book, but the most important component of an estate plan—the cornerstone—is the will.

Watch Out

If you move to another state during your lifetime, you will have to review your estate documents. Most states have their own requirements for those papers, and you might well need to have some of them drawn up again.

Your Will

Finally, to answer your last question, a *will* is a legal document setting forth your wishes for the disposition of your estate after your death. Yes, it's that "I, William Jefferson, of Smalltown, USA, being of sound and disposing mind and memory..." document you've heard and read about over the years. It can be as long or as short as you like. You can briefly leave every last thing you own to your spouse or someone else, and that's that. Or—and there is more than one elderly lady who has done this—bequeath every piece of property, including individual jewelry items and various collections, to different persons. And you can revise that will periodically, as relatives and friends rise and fall in your favor.

As you will see, you may leave anything and everything that is yours in your will, including your pets and requests for their future care.

A will might also include guardianship wishes for minor children. Keep in mind that what you are doing is essentially *nominating* the person or persons you choose. The appropriate court will ultimately make that guardianship decision.

What makes your will legal? Signing it in the presence of two witnesses who are not beneficiaries in the will makes it valid. But what makes it *effective* is its being

Tip

An estate plan is not carved in stone. Unfortunately, you can't complete your work and then forget what you've accomplished. You should review your papers every couple of years, certainly when there are major changes in your life: marriage, divorce, birth of a child, lottery win, etc.

filed in the appropriate state court after your death, and being recognized by the court as your valid will, revoking all previous wills and trusts.

Naturally we'll talk more about wills later in the book. A lot more.

That's it. Do you feel a little more comfortable now about the terminology I'll be using? Then let's move further into these topics and others in more detail.

Why Many of Us Don't Plan

Here's a statement that may ring a bell with you: "I think I'll see my lawyer next week, or certainly sometime this month, about drawing up a will. I'll *definitely* do it before the end of the summer (fall, winter, spring)."

Many of us who do not put off tasks in other important areas of our lives drag our feet when it comes to estate planning. Why is that?

Kim, a 26-year-old marketing executive says "What do *I* have to make a will for? I share a rental apartment, I don't have a car, and I have $2,000 in the bank. Where's *my* estate?"

Ah, but who would she like to inherit that $2,000? Instead of having the money turned over to her parents, which would probably happen if she dies *intestate* (or without a will, versus *testate*, which is having a valid will), she might prefer that it go to her younger brother. Kim could also have funds invested in a retirement fund. Has she already designated a beneficiary for them?

And what about that brooch of her great Aunt Mary's, the one she clips onto her lucky suit when she's preparing to make a major presentation at the office? If you ask her right now, she would say she'd like her god-daughter, her best friend's child, to have that favorite piece of jewelry.

Quote, Unquote
He is a fool that makes his doctor his heir.
—*Benjamin Franklin*

Quote, Unquote
Shrouds have no pockets.
—*Folk saying*

But no one is going to know, or carry out, Kim's wishes if those wishes are not set down in black and white in a will.

Then there is Frank, a 50-year-old telecommunications employee who shrugs off making a will, saying he wants his wife, Amy, to inherit everything of his and theirs. He says that's what will happen, even without such a document. It makes Frank uneasy to talk about a will, let alone take the first steps to having one drawn up for him. Why? Amy says she thinks it's because Frank's father died at the age of 47. Any mention of death or age or wills has spooked Frank since he himself passed that age.

Frank might not know that if he dies intestate the state will probably charge his wife a fee of a few hundred dollars, money that would not be levied against his estate if he had a valid will. Does Frank want her to pay that extra money? It's not likely. Besides a fee, property may go to children or Frank's parents, not just to Amy. With some advance planning, Frank could see to it that his estate is as large as it can be, with the least amount of taxes paid, through some clever investment and tax strategies.

Finally, there is Helen. She is 61 years old, manages a boutique and, aside from a few minor ailments, is in good health. Helen and her friends talk a good deal about a living will and a health care power of attorney. Helen has been quite vocal about not wanting to be kept alive "by extraordinary means" if she should fall seriously ill, a directive that is a major component of a living will. But she has not taken care of that aspect of estate planning. She keeps putting off the paperwork. If some day it does come to those extraordinary measures, Helen might not be able to communicate her wishes about medical treatment.

Kim, Frank and Helen are drifting along with what is usually called a head-in-the-sand approach, in this instance, to estate planning. They know what they should be doing, they read articles about wills and other components of a long-range plan but, for their own reasons, they refuse to take action.

The Importance of Looking Ahead

If you see yourself in any of the above scenarios you are not alone. As many as 50 to 70 percent of the population die without having made a will (and we won't even get into the numbers who do not have other important estate documents). For some, death is the only tragedy, but for others, the failure to plan an estate has catastrophic consequences for loved ones.

The state has made a will for you if you do not have one, and the heirs it decides upon might not be the ones you would have chosen.

Our trio above could have rather simple estates, at least monetarily, but many other people have more complicated situations. There might be quite sizable sums of money involved. Or there could be second marriages where there are children from that union, as well as from a previous marriage, to be considered. Or guardianship issues for minor children must be decided. Or perhaps there is a business that is part of an estate, and one with a partner or two at that.

Lack of planning by the deceased can keep the disposition of an estate on hold, sometimes for years. Then it could *still* not be disbursed the way that individual would have liked.

And let's not forget how poor planning—or no planning at all—can result in heirs being hit with higher federal and state taxes, and court costs for processing the will, that they would otherwise not need to pay.

Quote, Unquote
The palest ink is better than the best memory.
—*Chinese proverb*

The advice columns in newspapers and magazines are full of letters from frustrated readers whose parents didn't make a will or take the time to plan properly. As a result, the heirs were left with a financial mess, not to mention the stress of coping with sometimes incomprehensible paperwork and demands at a time of mourning and change in their lives.

Putting It All Together Can Be Enjoyable—Really

I can hear you saying "Good grief, what do you mean enjoyable? We're talking about my *death*." No, we aren't. How and when you leave this vale is, of course, beyond the control of either of us. However, seeing the pieces of your estate plan fall into place, knowing how well organized you are now and that your wishes will be carried out later, will bring you peace of mind and, yes, some pleasurable sense of accomplishment.

It might also give you the additional pleasure of knowing you're one up on many folks by being so farsighted.

(And, hey, come on, you did buy this book, so deep down, perhaps *way* down, you know you should be tackling at least some of these issues and are prepared to do so now, no matter how jolly or dreary the idea seems—am I right?)

As I said earlier in this chapter, planning ahead also means preparing for tomorrow, not just 10, 20, 30, or more years down the road. Judicious care of your current savings, and plans for anticipated income, can help your estate grow and bring you the comfort of knowing your money is working for you, working to make you even more comfortable in retirement. We're talking about a *life* plan here, with the opportunity to make wise choices and take advantage of perhaps unique opportunities from now on. Your aim should also be to build your assets and pay down your debts now so that you can retire to a pleasant, worry-free life later.

Look how many upbeat subjects we will touch on in this book that have to do with financial and lifestyle situations that could affect you in the years from now until…well, may you, too, live to be 100!

➤ An inheritance

➤ A salary increase, and/or a special bonus

➤ A marriage or remarriage

➤ A new job, perhaps your own business

➤ Real estate purchases

➤ Your pension

➤ Social Security

So you see, an estate plan doesn't talk only about wills and other mechanisms that swing into effect when you are no longer here.

What Should Your Goals Be?

Everyone will have his or her own priorities, of course, based on age range and individual family and financial responsibilities and interests. You will learn more about the various topics that fall under estate planning, and what you should strive for, as you read on. However, generally speaking, after reading this book and implementing its suggestions, you will have achieved these specific goals:

➤ You will have a will (or a trust, or both)

➤ You will have important auxiliary documents, such as a power of attorney

➤ You will know how to start saving money now

➤ You will be able to protect the assets you now have

➤ You can reduce your taxes

➤ You will be able to plan for retirement, securing the lifestyle you want in those years ahead

You don't have to do *everything* covered in this book. No doubt some suggestions will not even apply to you, at least not at this point in your life. You may not be divorced, for example, or even married, so advice in those areas will not be relevant. You may not have your own business. Your parents might be in their early 50s, quite hale and hearty, with no need for you to concern yourself as a caregiver quite yet.

Still, whether you are 25 or 65, the information you need today to set up a solid estate plan can be found within these pages.

Watch Out
Unmarried same-sex, or opposite-sex, couples in a long-standing relationship especially need careful estate planning. That should include funeral preferences, since a family can step in and perhaps carry out plans the deceased would not have wanted. Signed copies of funeral directions should be given to a friend or two, not locked in a bank's safe deposit box, which could be sealed immediately after death.

Starting Now

"What are your investments?" the broker asked.

I answered, "My sons, Ted, Josh, Ethan, and Zach."

That wasn't the reply the broker was looking for, of course, but he knew what I meant. You do, too. Still, while I am taking care of my children as they grow up, I must also, as mentioned above, tend to what is usually meant by the word "investments"—my home, my savings, a plan for retirement, and the like.

Are *you* as prepared as you think you are? Maybe yes, maybe no. To help you assess your particular situation right now I've created a planning quiz. After you've answered the questions, mark or fold over the corner of the page so that you can go back and refer to it again. By the time you finish reading this book, you'll know what you need to do to be able to answer yes to every question on that list.

Estate Planning Checklist

Yes No

❏ ❏ 1. Do you and your spouse have current, signed wills?

❏ ❏ 2. Have you discussed your estate plans with your family?

❏ ❏ 3. Have you consulted an estate-planning professional?

❏ ❏ 4. Have you reviewed the ownership of your assets to determine which are solely owned and which are co-owned?

❏ ❏ 5. Have you reviewed your life insurance needs?

❏ ❏ 6. Do you have a retirement plan?

❏ ❏ 7. Will your estate have enough cash to pay the bills, and enough left over to provide adequately for your family?

❏ ❏ 8. Do you know approximately how much you will receive in Social Security payments upon retirement?

❏ ❏ 9. Have you designated anyone to handle your affairs if you are no longer capable of doing so?

❏ ❏ 10. Have you made arrangements for your long-term care, or that of your elderly dependents?

❏ ❏ 11. Have you taken any steps to reduce income taxes now, and death taxes on your estate?

❏ ❏ 12. If you own a business, have you consulted a professional to plan for its future?

If you have checked a number of "No" answers, then this book is definitely for you.

Putting Together Your Estate Planning Team

Who can help define your needs, and then set you on the path toward setting up a valuable plan?

First, of course, *I* can. I won't hog the spotlight though. There are other professionals you may want to consult, either on a one-time or a fairly steady basis.

Your team will be made up of men and women with expertise in different aspects of estate planning. Their knowledge and guidance can be invaluable. However, do not forget for one moment that you are in charge. No one on your team should tell you what to do. He or she can offer options and discuss consequences, but only you can determine what your best estate plan is. So you will have to do some homework here, to be as competent as possible taking charge.

You may not need every member of this team, or at least not all of them at the same time in your life. The more complex your estate, however, the more likely you will be to call on a range of professional services.

Here are some of the people you should consider.

➤ **Life Insurance Underwriter.** Most of us are underinsured. Life insurance should be an integral part of most estate plans. Young families need term insurance to provide support for the family if a parent dies. You may need life insurance to make an estate more liquid—to pay the taxes without being forced to sell assets.

The life insurance underwriter can determine your needs and the amount and type of insurance that best meets those needs.

➤ **Trust Officer.** You may need a retirement trust to help manage your assets. Your children could require a trust to avoid wasting their inherited assets because of their immaturity.

The trust officer at your bank or other financial institution can discuss his or her services and fees. It is time well spent.

➤ **Accountant.** No one is likely to be more familiar with your financial situation than your accountant. Few details in life are more intimate than one's tax returns. If you have a business, this is the individual who knows the balance sheet. Use your accountant to help gather the information necessary to focus on your financial picture, so that you can prepare a good estate plan.

➤ **Financial Planner.** Your money can *always* be more productive. The financial planner's role is to advise you about appropriate investments that will meet your estate-planning goals.

"A financial planner," you say. "What exactly is that?" The profession of financial planner is rather new to the average consumer, and it is an unregulated pursuit. Do you want to be a planner? Hang out a shingle and voilà!, you're in business.

For some protection when shopping for this assistance, try to engage a financial planner who belongs to a national professional group. For more information about these folks, call the International Association for Financial Planning in Atlanta at

Tip
Try to attend a few free estate-planning seminars in your community, usually held in the evening and sponsored by brokerage offices and banks. You can learn about inheritance taxes and other estate matters as they apply specifically to your state, and you can probably ask questions of the speaker. Check your daily newspaper for news briefs or advertisements about upcoming seminars.

Quote, Unquote
I don't mind dying, I just don't want to be there when it happens.
—*Woody Allen*

(800) 945-4237, website: http://www.iafp.org; the Institute of Certified Financial Planners in Denver at (800) 282-7526, website: http://www.icfp.org, and the National Association of Personal Financial Advisors in Buffalo Grove, IL at (800) 366-2732, website: http://www.napfa.org. These groups can define their specific membership (they differ in requirements for joining and certification offered) and can send you free printed material about choosing a planner and a list of financial planners in your area who are members of their association.

➤ **Attorney.** The attorney drafts your will and prepares a trust, which you may also require. He or she also prepares all estate documents. You can try filling out your own documents from some form book or computer program, but you do so at your own risk.

Where to Find Team Members

"Psst, know a good doctor?"

Most of us pick physicians, dentists—and estate-planning professionals—rather haphazardly. Consulting the telephone directory or asking your brother-in-law or next-door neighbor, both of whom seem to know everything, is not the best way to proceed here.

A much better strategy is to talk with a number of friends and relatives whose opinion you value. Find out whom they have worked with and whether they would engage the same professionals again. Interview prospective team members. Discuss fees. Do they seem more interested in your money than your estate-planning goals? Do they appear to be in a hurry, too busy to talk with you, or do they take the time to answer your questions thoughtfully and completely?

Check with the licensing or professional association for those you are considering engaging. That might be a state office regulating that professional, located in the state capital, or the group's statewide association, comprising members throughout the state, usually located in the state capital or the largest city. Ask whether there have been any complaints lodged against that individual or firm. You might also ask that question of your local Department of Consumer Affairs.

Tip
Call your state Insurance Department, and/or Office on Aging, to see if they offer free printed material on estate planning. Many have a number of brochures they can send you about various planning topics. And sometimes these include things to watch out for, like scams to avoid.

You are doing the hiring here, and it's certainly a buyer's market. Take the time to assemble the best team at an affordable price.

Okay. You have some idea what you will accomplish by reading this book and then taking steps to implement good suggestions. You know that planning is an ongoing process, to be revisited time and time again as situations change in your life. You have your planning team in place.

Let's proceed to succeed!

The Least You Need to Know

➤ Everyone needs a will, at the very least, in estate planning.

➤ If you do not have a will, the state will decide your heirs for you.

➤ Planning needs differ; determine your own personal goals.

➤ There are professionals who can form your planning team, helping you achieve those goals.

MINE!
MINE!
MINE!

Chapter 2

What You've Got and How You've Got It

In This Chapter

➤ A close-up look at your assets

➤ Common ownership styles

➤ How property is classified

➤ Where to keep all your "papers"

Just what *do* you own? You boast of having the patent for a gizmo that's going to revolutionize life as we know it? Good for you. That's certainly a rare asset. You have a teeny island in the Caribbean? Again, congratulations, especially in January and February. That, too, is not on everyone's list of "haves." Most of us count the standard possessions, such as a home, a car, some savings, perhaps some art work and jewelry, maybe family heirlooms. Does that sound more like you?

Before we go on to consider your assets as part of your estate plan, you must know what those assets are. It's important to know, too, *how* you own them. Different ownership styles can be easier or more difficult to leave as part of an estate, as you will see throughout this book.

Taking Inventory

You might have—you *should* have—a household inventory you put together in case of fire or in the event you ever have a robbery at your place. That listing, which you could do as a videorecording rather than a written list, describes items of value and lists their serial numbers or other identifying marks. Your written list or videotape should be kept in a fireproof box at home, or perhaps with a relative or friend, or at your office. It will be helpful to the police and your insurance company in the unfortunate event your home is robbed or catches fire. In the former instance, serial numbers and, perhaps even better, photographs of special possessions, along with a written inventory, or that video, can help the police reclaim your property.

Tip
Since household possessions are a part of your total assets picture, by all means put together an inventory like the one described here if you haven't already done so. You can purchase inventory forms at a stationery or office supply store. Also, many police departments around the country lend residents etching tools for engraving names or numbers on bicycles and other possessions for identification.

It's reassuring to know you have such an inventory and, after you have put it together, perhaps surprising and nice to know, too, that you have so much. All those acquisitions over the years do add up, don't they?

In estate planning, a listing of your assets is also important. But here we are looking at a far broader picture than just household furnishings. Here we examine items like your home, automobile, retirement plan, and the like. It's just as important to have all of that itemized. Even more so, actually, since those belongings have a higher monetary value.

What will be included in *your* estate? Here is a form that will help you determine your assets. Take a few minutes now to fill it in, then keep it handy for easy reference as you read this book. (*Note:* Jot down everything. We'll be talking about insurance, pensions, and owning your business in the next few chapters, and about your other assets in this one.)

ESTATE PLANNING INFORMATION SHEET

Name _____ Birth _____ SS# _____
Name of Spouse _____ Birth _____ SS# _____
Residence Address _____
Names of Children _____
Age _____ Marital Status _____ Number of children _____

ASSETS

Real estate (residence and other land)

Description	Present value	Purchase price	Mortgage	How owned
_____	_____	_____	_____	_____
_____	_____	_____	_____	_____

Business interests (sole proprietor, partnership, corporation)

Form of business	Value of interest	Who owns
_____	_____	_____

Accounts (bank, brokerage, certificates of deposit)

Type of account	Account name	Value	Who owns
_____	_____	_____	_____
_____	_____	_____	_____

Stocks and bonds

Stocks/bond company	Market value	Cost	Who owns
_____	_____	_____	_____

Motor vehicles

Make	Model	Year	Value	Who owns
_____	_____	_____	_____	_____

Miscellaneous personal property (household goods, sporting equipment, jewelry, art, etc.)

Type of property	Value	Who owns
_____	_____	_____
_____	_____	_____

continues

continued

Life insurance

Insurance company	Face value	Cash value	Insured	Owner	Beneficiary
_____	_____	_____	_____	_____	_____
_____	_____	_____	_____	_____	_____
_____	_____	_____	_____	_____	_____

Retirement benefits (401(k), pension/profit sharing, IRA, Keogh, etc.)

Type of plan	Owner	Beneficiary	Value to date
_____	_____	_____	_____
_____	_____	_____	_____
_____	_____	_____	_____

Other assets (including possible inheritances)

Type of asset	Owner	Value
_____	_____	_____
_____	_____	_____
_____	_____	_____

Total Assets $ _____

LIABILITIES

Type of liability	Amount	Who owes
_____	_____	_____
_____	_____	_____
_____	_____	_____

Total liabilities $ _____

Total Assets minus Total Liabilities equals Net Worth: $ _____

One Man's Story—Something Like Yours?

Okay, you have finished your Information Sheet. Let's suppose that one John Fisher also filled out the form, and, in an abbreviated style, it looked something like this:

Property	Value	Ownership
Residence	$100,000	With wife, Ellen
Household goods	$20,000	With wife
Savings/checking account	$10,000	With wife
Automobile	$15,000	With wife
Corporate stock	$20,000	Solely
Family farm (inherited)	$125,000	With brother, George

I chose John because his estate shows the three most common ownership styles:

➤ **Solely.** John's corporate stock is in his name only. It's his to do with as he will. He can sell it or give it away. At his death it becomes part of his estate and passes to the beneficiary of his will, or to his heirs if he has no will.

Let's say at some point after filling out this form John decides to invest in U.S. savings bonds. If his name alone is on the bonds, they become part of his estate, too. But he may put a beneficiary designation on the bond. For example, they might read "POD (pay on death) to Jenny Fisher (John's 22-year-old daughter)." Jenny would then inherit the bonds.

➤ **As "joint tenants with right of survivorship."** If John dies tomorrow, his wife will own everything outright that was in both their names since they have those items as "joint owners with right of survivorship." That's an ownership style that is... well, pretty much just what it says. The property, usually a home, is in both their names. When one party dies, the other automatically takes over that co-owner's share, without the need for any mention of it in a will.

Words, Words, Words
Tenants, as used in the ownership styles discussed in this chapter, means owning and not renting. Of course, "tenant" more commonly refers to an individual or company that is leasing real property.

You do not have to be married to be joint tenants. However, that is the most common ownership style among married couples. The next chapter talks more about joint ownership in the context of spousal property.

However, there is an important point to keep in mind here: Right of survivorship takes precedence over property bequeathed in a will. In other words, John can't leave his sister anything that is already jointly owned by him and Ellen, or him and anyone else, for that matter.

➤ **As "tenants in common."** This is how the farm, which had belonged to John and George's parents, was deeded to the brothers. That means they equally co-own the property, but each can leave his share to anyone he chooses. Both chose their wives. They could, however, have owned as "joint tenants with right of survivorship."

Unrelated homebuyers usually buy as tenants in common. For example, if the Fishers and their friends the Blacks bought a ski home together, that's how they would likely take ownership.

Your Life Estate Lasts as Long as You Do

Here is another ownership style, although one not nearly as common as the three previously discussed:

Sarah owned her home and everything in it. She lived on Social Security and the small amounts of money her two sons gave her. One son, Herb, was concerned that Mom's small estate would be tied up in *probate court.* That is a special state office that handles the management of wills, of estates of those who have died without a will, and other similar estate situations, such as guardianships. Herb felt that once Mom's estate landed there, its monetary worth would go mostly to lawyers.

Herb read in a legal column of his daily newspaper that one could avoid probate by having an elderly homeowner deed over his or her property to a relative (or whomever else they wished to be the inheritor), but retain a *life estate* in it. That meant they could stay in it as long as they lived. The homeowner would continue paying expenses involved in maintaining that property, unless otherwise specified in writing.

Words, Words, Words

A life estate can be created with any form of property, but usually it is in real estate. Ownership is divided into two parts: the *life estate*, which is the length of that homeowner's life, and the *remainder interest*, which is willed to the heir and becomes his or her absolute ownership when the property owner dies.

Herb called his brother, Ed, and both suggested this to Mom. Sarah, trusting her boys, executed a deed that gave her the right to live on the property the rest of her days. At her death the title automatically would go to her sons as tenants in common.

The sons' goal of avoiding probate was accomplished. But was this best for Sarah?

Well, if Sarah needed, or wanted, to sell her home and use the proceeds to move into a retirement community, she would have to get her sons' consent, since they have an ownership interest in the property. Plus, there are gift tax consequences. If a son dies, leaving his interest to his wife, Sarah would need to get her daughter-in-law to agree to her plan. Relatives, and particularly in-laws, sometimes do not act kindly when someone wants to spend their "inheritance."

To avoid that potential trap, but still avoid the time and expense of probate, Sarah should read Chapter 9 of this book, on trusts, and create a *revocable living trust*. Among other features, this document will allow her to control her own property, and use it as she needs it for the rest of her life.

Homeowners with no mortgage and no children, or perhaps children they have provided for in other ways, might want to leave their home to a favorite charity, retaining a life interest in it. You do not have to own a mansion for a charity to accept your place. There are some tax benefits to this gesture as well. The home's value is determined by a formula that includes your life expectancy and that of anyone else on the deed, using an approved mortality table, and the appraised value of the residence.

Tip
You won't want to donate your home to charity when you are too young—there are too many changes life can bring you, in finances and housing. This is usually a practice for those in their sixties, seventies, and beyond.

Talk with your tax adviser, and keep in mind that an agreement between you and the charity can contain whatever specific arrangements you choose—the possibility you might want to move to a retirement community, for example. You could also agree that the charity will maintain the property, or maintain it *and* pay the property taxes. In a few cases it may be possible to secure a small income from the charity.

Is It Tangible, Intangible, or Real Property?

Lawyers are experts at classifying things. Take property, for example: You might own *real property*, *tangible personal property*, and *intangible personal property*.

John and Ellen Fisher's home is *real property*, or, more commonly, real estate. Real property is land, buildings, and things permanently attached to the land, such as trees. In some states there are special inheritance and probate rights attached to real estate.

The couple's jointly owned household goods and automobile are examples of *tangible personal property*. Other items under this heading include machinery, jewelry, sporting goods, and art works. These are possessions we can see and touch.

Stock certificates owned by John, and the savings account jointly owned with his wife, are examples of

Tip
By all means get duplicates of missing documents you need for your estate file. Contact your local government office, perhaps the Deeds Recording Bureau, or a similarly named office, for help with a lost house deed. Insurance and brokerage houses can supply you with copies of those mislaid documents, too.

intangible personal property. You can see it, but it's just paper, denoting ownership in something that also is represented by a piece of paper, like shares in a corporation. Other intangible personal property includes certificates of deposit, corporate bonds, patents, and copyrights. (The patent for that revolutionary gadget mentioned at the beginning of this chapter is intangible personal property, too.)

Inheritance laws, wills, and gifts distinguish among the three types of property. That's why you need to know *how* you own what comprises your estate, not just what's in it.

Okay, now it's time to attack those bureau drawers and rifle through cardboard files and anywhere else you keep valuable papers. Look to see how you own property. Check your deed(s), bank accounts, certificates of deposit, stock and bond certificates, title to your car—all should indicate which form of ownership you hold.

A Few Words About Condominiums, Cooperatives, and Timeshares

A home isn't always a single-family house on a half-acre lot, of course. Many millions of Americans live in condominiums and in cooperatives, or will be buying one in the years ahead. Does this apply to you? Then you might have special questions about estate issues and your home.

I've included timeshares in this section because owners of those vacation apartments also are frequently confused about just what they own, how they own it, and how they will pass it on to their heirs.

The Condo's Real

Condominiums were virtually unknown in the United States as recently as the early 1960s. My law professor told the class that this wasn't an important area for us to learn about in property law, so we'd skip it. So much for prognosticating profs.

A condominium is real property, or real estate. Your community might consist of one-story attached apartments, three-story townhouses, or even detached single-family houses. It's not the architectural style that determines a condo, but rather the joint ownership style. Each "unit" is owned separately. The rest of the property, known as the undivided common area, is owned jointly by all individual unit owners. That area consists of grounds, parking spaces, walkways and the like.

How does condo ownership affect your estate? Well, since you own your condo outright, you are free to leave it to whomever you choose, depending on the individual ownership style you have selected (solely, joint tenants, etc.). You do not need anyone's "permission" to sell your condo, and prospective buyers do not have to be approved by the condo association.

Keep in mind, however, that if you bequeath your condo to your son, Fred, and his wife, Julie, knowing as you do that they would love to live there, the couple will have to join the condo association and abide by its rules. Those regulations might say, for instance, no children are allowed (that is legal in some adult complexes), and Fred and Julie have two preteens. Or the condo association could have a clause prohibiting pets, putting little Fluffy's future on the line. Or the rules and regulations might have other clauses that make it difficult, if not impossible, for Fred and Julie to live there. They might have to sell or rent the property instead.

The Co-op's a Different Story

If you own, or plan to buy, a cooperative apartment, or co-op, you will, as you probably know, purchase shares of stock in the corporation that owns your building or complex. In your monthly maintenance fee, you pay for your share of the cost of running the building—utilities, mortgages, taxes, etc. Some states consider co-ops real estate, others say they are intangible property. (A co-op is intangible because ownership is your stock certificates, and not tangible property just because you can see the apartment.)

A cooperative may be co-owned or solely owned. If the latter, then the stock becomes part of a probate estate.

What Timeshares Are—and Are Not

Anyone who hasn't been living under a rock for the last decade or so knows what a timeshare is. It is, of course, a week (or two or more) that you buy and then own in a resort complex. You purchase the same week of the year for a specified period of time. That might be 25 or 40 years, or for as long as the complex is standing.

What you pay for your furnished timeshare apartment depends on its location, size and, most especially, the time of the year you choose to buy. "High season" in that resort will, naturally, cost you more than an off-season week.

The timeshare can be co-owned or solely owned, the same as all of the other assets mentioned in this chapter.

There are a couple of things to keep in mind about timeshare purchases as they apply to you and your heirs.

First, there are two styles of timeshares:

> ➤ **A Fee Simple Ownership.**
>
> If you bought under this type of ownership, you own your apartment as you would real estate. Your ownership is a percentage of that apartment's use. If you have one week, you own

Watch Out
Cooperatives often have important restrictions upon transfer, with the corporation retaining the right to veto a sale or, more accurately, veto the prospective buyer. You will want to check how your corporation handles inherited apartments. More of them these days are requiring heirs to qualify for entry as if they were new prospective buyers. That means conforming to the board's financial and other criteria.

1/50th of the year in Unit 240 (complexes usually keep two weeks open annually for cleaning and repairs). You also own an undivided share in the common areas.

You can leave your one-week real estate property in your will to anyone you choose, considering, of course, the ownership style you have adopted—joint tenants, etc.

➤ **A Long-Term Lease.**

Also known as *"right to use,"* this type of ownership means that you have personal property, not real estate. You can, however, leave this style of timeshare apartment to anyone you select, too, again depending on how you hold title to that unit.

Quote, Unquote
If all the year were playing holiday,
To sport would be as tedious as work.

—*Shakespeare, Henry IV*

Words, Words, Words
Illiquid means something not easily convertible to cash. A house, for example, is considered illiquid because even if you sold it the first day it was on the market, you would not have cash in hand from that sale for several weeks or more. Your timeshare apartment is likely to be illiquid, too.

Also, it's important to keep in mind that timeshares can be difficult to sell, unless your week is in the most glamorous of resorts in the most exciting geographic community in the high season. The reason: There are always new resorts opening up, not to mention resales in existing complexes, causing a flood of timeshare units on the market. "Right to use" apartments can be particularly difficult because you are selling less than the top number of years on your lease; for example, if you bought it with a 25-year lease, and held the timeshare for 10 years, you now have only 15 years to sell.

Your heirs, should they want to sell your timeshare, no matter what its style, may have trouble doing so, or might have to wait a longer time than they would like for a buyer. They may also have to sell at a price lower, sometimes a good deal lower, than what you paid for it.

But you can certainly adjust your view of a timeshare and your expectations from it. You might want to tell your heirs not to expect a windfall profit here. But, hey, they may not *want* to sell their week in paradise, so the potential problem of unloading a timeshare may never come up.

Papers Galore—Where Do You Keep Them?

Where are you storing deeds, no matter what ownership style you have chosen for your properties, and other important papers in your life? Is there room for the several more documents you will add to that file when you have finished this book and implemented many of its suggestions?

Some folks purchase a fireproof box to keep valuable papers at home. Others turn to a bank's safe deposit box. I know someone who put all his treasures in a safe deposit box, including his baby's first tooth, which, as the tooth fairy, he purchased for 25 cents. His daughter's first report card is there, too.

A safe deposit box is honored by the Internal Revenue Service, which will allow a tax deduction for its rental fee if you store investments, like stock certificates, there.

Besides the deed to your home, you might indeed want to keep investment certificates in the box, as well as papers like a power of attorney, birth certificate, and passport. Expensive, rarely worn jewelry could go into the box, rare coins and other valuable collectibles, and mementos like that baby tooth. One test of what to put there is gauging whether that item would be difficult, if not impossible, to replace and if it has considerable value. If the answer is yes to those questions you ask yourself, pop it in the safe deposit box.

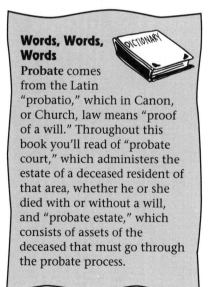

Watch Out
Did you know that if a bank robber steals the contents of your safe deposit box, you may not be insured by the bank for that loss? True! The bank guarantees the box is fireproof, but not theft-proof. Theft of safe deposit boxes isn't a frequent, or even occasional, occurrence, so you're probably quite safe leaving your belongings there. But do keep that point in mind when storing some items in a bank. You might want to see if your home-owner's insurance can pick up that coverage.

Don't Put Your Will in the Box!

Your will goes elsewhere. Some states seal the deceased's safe deposit box immediately at death, so that the state can determine taxes to be paid by that estate. In other states, if the spouse survives and is co-owner of the box, it is not sealed. And still other states don't seal the box no matter who the co-owner is. In any event, it is more practical to keep your will, and funeral instructions if you have them, more accessible to your next of kin, or whoever will be handling your affairs. A home safe or fireproof box will do just fine for those papers. Or you might want to leave the original with the lawyer who drew up the will (making certain his or her name is in your estate file). Losing the original document will cause significant delay and increase costs of probate.

Here's a story that shows how well-meaning people can use a safe deposit box, which is good, but then put something in it that turns out to be, well, not exactly *bad*, but not a smart move either.

James died, leaving a will naming his wife, Mary, as beneficiary, so she received his probate estate. They

Words, Words, Words
Probate comes from the Latin "probatio," which in Canon, or Church, law means "proof of a will." Throughout this book you'll read of "probate court," which administers the estate of a deceased resident of that area, whether he or she died with or without a will, and "probate estate," which consists of assets of the deceased that must go through the probate process.

had two daughters, Karen and Elaine. James had rented a safe deposit box in his own name at Trustworthy Bank. Among other items, he had placed two envelopes in the box, each containing $10,000, and each bearing a daughter's name. Mother and daughters were not on particularly good terms, and so they asked the estate lawyer to advise them about ownership of the cash.

The lawyer, after due deliberation and research, responded that since there was no actual delivery of the cash to the daughters, there could be no gift to them. Therefore, the cash became part of the probate estate.

This story does have a happy ending for the daughters, though. Mom gave them the cash anyway.

Quote, Unquote
The rich have heirs, not children.
—*Jewish saying*

Dad had tried to leave his girls something special, but he almost failed. He should have given them the money outright, or established a joint bank account for each daughter, or left them the money in his will.

Keep in mind that a gift of property requires (1) intent to make a gift; (2) delivery to the recipient, and (3) acceptance of the gift by the recipient.

The Least You Need to Know

➤ Get together an inventory of all your assets before you proceed with effective estate planning.

➤ There are several styles of ownership you can select. The form of ownership determines whether the property may be distributed through your will or go to the surviving co-owner.

➤ Your estate is divided into real, tangible personal and intangible personal property.

➤ Be careful to store important papers where they are safe as well as reasonably accessible; don't put your will in a bank's safety deposit box.

Chapter 3

Yours, Mine, and Ours: Marrieds and Property

In This Chapter

➤ Styles of buying together

➤ The famous "community property"

➤ Switching from one spousal style to another

➤ The prenuptial agreement

Marriage is a partnership, and like many partnerships, the marital couple owns property together and jointly manages it. This can be done in several legal ownership styles. If you are married, you are certain to recognize yourself and your spouse in one of these examples.

As I've pointed out throughout these pages, you need to know how you hold title to property in order to plan properly for its management in your lifetime, and its disbursal in a manner you choose through your estate. Maybe you want it to go directly to your spouse...or maybe not.

Jointly Speaking

You read briefly about buying property as *joint owners with right of survivorship* in the previous chapter. I said that anyone, single or married, could utilize that ownership style. Now I'll tell you about it in more detail, as it applies specifically to married couples.

If you are married and live in a non-community property state (a listing of community property states follows in the next few pages when we talk about that shared form of ownership), and you own real estate, such as a principal and/or a vacation home, you probably do have it as joint owners. That applies to your personal property as well—household goods, bank accounts, automobiles, and the like.

What I mean here is that if one party dies, the other automatically inherits that co-owner's share, without it having to be mentioned in a will. It's quick, no questions asked. That's why it is so popular.

As an example, let's take Hal and Wendy. Like many couples across this broad land, they live in a non-community property state, have been married several years, have two careers and two children.

Early in their marriage the couple were thrilled to be able to purchase their first house. They still live there 15 years later. The deed reads "...Hal H. Higgins and Wendy L. Higgins, husband and wife, as joint tenants with right of survivorship."

For purposes of this illustration we'll have to interrupt this pleasant life, and have Hal go to his heavenly reward. Upon his death, Wendy becomes the sole owner of all of the property they owned jointly. She takes the house because of that language in the deed: "...right of survivorship." The same terminology is on the savings account card she and Hal signed when they set up that account. The household goods go to Wendy because they are also owned in that style.

There are several benefits to this type of ownership.

➤ The ownership transfer is automatic.

➤ There is no probate (which means no delay, and no costly lawyers).

➤ There are no federal estate taxes.

➤ There are, in most states, no state death taxes.

Quote, Unquote
The truth is, I do indulge myself a little the more in pleasure, knowing that this is the proper age of my life to do it; and, out of my observation that most men that do thrive in the world do forget to take pleasure during the time that they are getting their estate, but reserve that till they have got one, and then it is too late for them to enjoy it.
—*Samuel Pepys, Diary, March 10, 1666*

Watch Out
With an estate of over $600,000, which is the beginning amount for having federal estate tax levied, joint ownership may have some tax disadvantages. Please turn to Chapter 15 for some suggestions here.

Let's look at a different scenario. Even more unfortunately, Hal and Wendy die in an automobile accident. Wendy survives a few minutes longer than Hal. Then Wendy's estate will include their jointly held property. If there is no evidence as to which one of the two survived the other, then the property is divided and one half is included in each person's probate estate. Using their house as an example, one half ownership of that residence would go into Hal's estate, the other into Wendy's.

"By the Entirety"

Here is another marital ownership style. This applies to Sam and Ann, to take one example, a couple who also purchased a home a few years back. The deed *they* received read "...to Sam R. Black and Ann Decatur Black, as husband and wife..."

Some states have spousal ownership in real estate that is known as *tenancy by the entirety*. Some recognize that form of spousal ownership in personal property as well.

If Ann dies before Sam, then Sam automatically becomes the sole owner of their home, because tenancy by the entirety transfers ownership to the surviving spouse. In other words, tenancy by the entirety has the same result as joint tenancy with right of survivorship, with the same advantages. This survivorship result applies no matter what the deceased's will provides because the house, because of the way it is owned, does not become part of the deceased's probate estate.

While joint tenancy with right of survivorship is in effect in every state, and can be used by married couples or single persons, tenancy by the entirety is not in all states and is confined to married couples. However, a state might have both styles.

I'd like to add a few words here about *palimony,* a term you hear occasionally these days. Palimony is usually money, although it can be other possessions, asked for by one half of an unmarried couple suing the other after the breakup of the union. The suit usually claims the plaintiff gave up work and other financial opportunities during the time the two were together, at the request of the other party. Now that individual wants to be recompensed for those lost dollars.

What's important to remember here is that palimony is not a legal marital relationship with those legal entitlements. It's an iffy process when it comes to the courts. Some folks win their cases, some don't.

Community Property: Not Just for Californians

Or should we say more specifically Hollywood? When we think of that form of marital property ownership, we almost always think of motion picture stars. Yet California doesn't have a lock on an ownership style that often makes headlines in front-page divorces. Besides the Golden State, other community property states are Arizona, Idaho, Louisiana, Nevada, New Mexico, Texas, and Washington. Wisconsin's law is similar to community property. Spouses whose legal residence is in any of these states are subject to community property laws.

What exactly are we talking about here?

Community property assumes that the husband and wife are in a marital partnership in which both contribute to the material success of the marriage and so both should share equally in the material acquisitions of that union. Essentially, community property consists of earnings of either spouse during the marriage, and property acquired through such earnings.

Would you like to see what a community property agreement might look like? Here is a sample form.

COMMUNITY PROPERTY AGREEMENT

This Agreement is made and entered into between _____ and _____ , husband and wife, residing at _____

WHEREAS, husband and wife during the existence of their marriage have acquired and now own property of various kinds:

NOW, THEREFORE, it is hereby mutually understood and agreed between husband and wife, as follows:

1. The following is the separate property of the wife under (state) law.

   [list property]

2. The following is the separate property of the husband under (state) law.

   [list property]

3. That all other property of every kind, nature, and description now owned or held of record title by said husband and wife in their names as joint tenants, or in joint tenancy, or in the individual names of either, at all times herein mentioned has been, now is, and shall remain community property of said husband and wife without regard to the form and record of ownership under which the same was acquired or is now held.

4. All property that may hereafter be acquired by said husband and wife, during the continuance of their marriage, except that acquired by either of them by gift, bequest, devise, or descent, shall remain the community property of said husband and wife without regard to the form and record of ownership under which the same may be acquired or held.

5. This Agreement shall remain in full force and effect until modified or revoked in writing by said husband and wife, and shall be binding upon them, their respective heirs, executors, administrators, and assigns.

IN WITNESS WHEREOF, the undersigned execute this Agreement this _____ day of _____ 19____, at _____.

_____   _____
Husband   Wife

Note to reader: This form applies to marital property acquired in a community property state. The couple is indicating what they agree is both their separate and community property.

Community property has these stipulations:

➤ One half of the assets are owned by each spouse. Upon the death of one, the survivor retains his or her half, and the deceased's half becomes part of that individual's probate estate.

➤ Income is considered community income, divided one half to each spouse.

➤ Pensions are treated as community property.

➤ Community property brings an income tax advantage not available with jointly held property.

➤ Upon divorce, courts usually divide the community property equally.

You've seen how fond I am of examples to illustrate certain points I want to make, or explanations to put forth. I'll use another one now for community property.

Quote, Unquote
Property has its duties as well as its rights.
—*Benjamin Disraeli*

Norman and Esther marry in California. Both are in the entertainment business. Esther is a huge star, but Norman is a struggling actor. Since this is only a story, we'll say they have no prenuptial agreement, although these days that might be unlikely given their vastly unequal incomes.

During the marriage Esther purchases a beach house in her name only, and then goes on to buy a condominium, with title in both her name and Norman's.

Quote, Unquote
Wedlock, a deadlock.
—*English proverb*

Norman, of course, is not earning anywhere near the major bucks Esther is bringing in. But "struggling" does not mean sacrifice for the young thespian. Thanks to Esther's income and generosity, his lifestyle is quite grand. He knows, too, that all of the property Esther purchases, no matter if titled in her name alone, is one half his under the state's community property laws. If it is sold, one half of the proceeds are his, too.

Of course, it should also be noted that one half of Norman's earnings come under the community property law and are Esther's.

While mulling his good fortune, and quite delighted with Esther and his present life, Norman gives the tiniest thought to all that he missed—monetarily—by not marrying the star sooner. He calls his attorney aside one day for an off-the-record chat. The lawyer informs him that whatever Esther acquired before the marriage is her separate property and Norman has no claim on it. But (always an important word in personal finance) if Esther were to use that separate property to purchase an asset in both their names, then Norman would have a one half interest in it.

What's This About "Separate Property?"

Well, *separate property* is whatever is owned by either spouse before marriage, as well as property acquired after marriage as a gift, or perhaps through an inheritance. What a spouse has or acquires as separate property belongs exclusively to him or her.

Separate property has these provisions:

➤ It becomes part of the deceased's estate.

➤ Income from the separate property—let's say rent from a small apartment building—can be treated either as separate or community ownership, depending on which community property state the couple claim as home. If there is any doubt as to whether property is separate or community, then there is a strong presumption that it is community property.

➤ If separate and community property are commingled in such a way that it is impossible to determine each source, then the commingled whole is presumed to be community property.

Does Community Property Last Forever?

It might not. The spouses may agree to convert it into separate property. That can be done with a written agreement signed by both parties.

Watch Out
Never enter into a conversion agreement without consulting an attorney. That agreement, whether going from separate property to community property, or vice versa, will affect your inheritance rights, and have income and death tax consequences.

On the other hand, husband and wife could agree to convert separate property into community property, tossing what they own by themselves into a communal pot. That would call for another written document, signed by the couple, of course.

Finally here, you should know that community property, once it is in effect as that style of ownership, and is not changed, continues as community property no matter where the spousal parties move. So if you purchase a valuable painting under a community property law, then you move to a non-community property state, the painting is still considered community property. Think about the confusion for those who move often!

About Those Prenuptial Agreements

If community property divorces make headlines, so too, do prenuptial agreements between celebrities. However, it isn't only the famous who scribble their names to these documents. It can be any two people about to marry who are, well, perhaps just a tad concerned about what will happen to what's theirs in the course of the marriage, and even in the event of a divorce one day. I say two people. Sometimes it is only one half of the couple that wants—demands—the "prenup." The other party goes along or there is no wedding.

This is a legal guide, so I will not get into who should and shouldn't have a prenup, and who should or shouldn't break an engagement over the request by the other party to sign one. That's for advice columnists. Obviously the best situation is when both parties want that document (or neither wants it). Let's get on with the other considerations of this arrangement.

Quote, Unquote
When poverty comes in at the door, love flies out the window.
—*Anonymous, 17th century*

A *prenuptial agreement*, signed by both parties, spells out any aspect of ownership in the marriage that the two can think of, and is a legally binding agreement. Unless a document is going to be recorded in a state office, most states do not require it to be notarized. And of course, to keep its contents confidential, neither half of a couple is likely to want to see a prenuptial agreement recorded. ("Recorded," by the way, means a document—a deed, for example—has been filed with a county recorder's office, putting everyone on notice of a legal agreement or relationship represented by those papers.)

A prenup can go into property ownership, salaries, pension plans, issues about existing children from prior marriages, specifically noting what belongs to whom going into the marriage, and perhaps for the duration of the marriage.

A prenup can take precedence over community property, and over joint ownership with right of survivorship, depending on the wording of the prenuptial agreement. However, prenups generally cover non-jointly owned property—that is the point of having one of these documents—so that does not often become an issue.

In case you have a prenuptial agreement in mind, or might some day, or are just plain curious about what is contained in such a document, a sample agreement for you to page through follows. This form is intended for a couple who have each been married before, and who both have children. That can make for a few extra pages. You will see there are even provisions, in the event of a divorce, for the distribution of the engagement and wedding gifts between the couple. A prenup can be quite thorough.

There is more about prenuptial agreement, especially how they are treated in contested wills, in Chapter 12.

A cautionary note here: If you are considering adopting this form for your own purposes, better check with your financial planner, accountant or attorney first. Different states have different requirements for legal documents to be effective within their borders. This warning holds true for most of the forms in this book you might want to use, but I'll remind you again when we come to those documents in upcoming chapters.

PRENUPTIAL AGREEMENT

THIS PRENUPTIAL AGREEMENT ("Agreement"), made in the City of _____, State of _____, this ___ day of _____, 199__, by and between _____, of _____ (City, State)_____, (hereinafter referred to as "Wife"), and _____, of _____ (City, State)_____, (hereinafter referred to as "Husband"), both of whom are also referred to herein individually as a "party" and together as the "Parties",

WITNESSETH THAT:

WHEREAS, the Parties intend to be married on _____; and,

WHEREAS, Husband has been previously married and has _____ children; Wife has been previously married and has _____ child. Each possesses or will possess wealth derived from their respective families or as a result of their respective employments.

WHEREAS, the Parties desire to clarify what their respective rights are to be in the property belonging to each other; to limit their respective rights in the property of the other during the marriage relationship and upon its termination by dissolution or death; and to accept the provisions of this Agreement in lieu and in satisfaction of all such rights; and,

WHEREAS, the Parties believe that this Agreement will enhance and encourage a harmonious marital relationship between them; and,

WHEREAS, the Parties have disclosed and discussed their mutual rights and obligations, in furtherance of which the Husband, through Exhibit A hereto, and the Wife, through Exhibit B hereto, have disclosed their respective assets, liabilities, and sources of income to each other, which disclosures each represent to the other to be substantially accurate and which include copies of their respective most-recently filed Federal Income Tax Returns; and,

NOW, THEREFORE, for the reasons stated in the Recitals hereof and in consideration of the promises and acts to be exchanged as set forth herein, the Parties agree as follows:

1. Property Covered. The property of the Parties as listed in their respective exhibits, and property of business, tangible or intangible, real, and personal, which they have inadvertently omitted therefrom, and all interest, rents, profits, and increased value which may in time accrue or may result in any manner, or any other property owned or to be owned by each party, shall be owned as separate property of each party during the marriage, except as elsewhere provided herein. Each party hereby waives, discharges, and releases all right, title, and interest in and to the property of the other party presently owned, or hereafter acquired, except as elsewhere provided herein. Each party shall have the absolute right to sell, transfer, convey, or otherwise dispose of his or her property as he or she sees fit. Each realizes that although the other now has property, there may be an increase or a decrease in the value thereof, or ultimately, there may be no property at all. From time to time, each party shall, if requested, join in the conveyance or other transfer of the other's property to third person, but shall not be required to assume personal liability in connection with any such transaction.

   Joint use of separate property shall not give rise to joint ownership of that property, unless the Parties agree otherwise in a writing signed by each of them and executed in a manner which would entitle a deed to be recorded in _____. Notwithstanding the provisions of this

Agreement that allow the Parties to maintain their separate income and assets, the Parties recognize that it is possible, through accident or intent, for their respective separate income or assets to become, or appear to be, commingled. It is the Parties' intention that such commingling or pooling of assets not be interpreted to imply abandonment of the terms and provisions of this Agreement and that the provisions contained herein addressing the Parties interest in separate property be applied so that each party be determined to be the owner of that proportion of the total fund or value of the assets in question which reflects the proportionate amount deposited or invested by him or her, respectively. Jointly owned property shall be deemed to be owned by the Parties as tenants in common, in proportion to the source of funds used to acquire and improve such property when determining the Parties' respective ownership interests in said property, except as elsewhere provided herein.

The fact that the Parties may file joint state or federal income, shall not be interpreted to imply an abandonment of the terms and provisions of this Agreement.

2. Claims Covered. Except as otherwise provided herein, each party with respect to the other party's property and estate now hereby waives, renounces, relinquishes, and releases all rights as surviving spouse, heir, distributee, survivor, or next of kin, whether by common law or by statute, state or federal, now in effect or hereafter enacted to all claims, interest, estate, title, dower, curtesy, whether inchoate or otherwise, right to elect against the will, homestead, statutory widow's allowance, or statutory widow's family allowance nor to the property, real and personal or mixed, or distributive share of the other party. Each party shall, on the demand of the other party of his or her heirs, devisees, administrators, executors, or assigns, execute any and all acquittances, assurances, deeds, releases, instruments, receipts, and other documents that may be necessary to accomplish the foregoing. The rights of each party herein described as released and renounced are hereby assigned to the other party, his or her heirs, devisees, legatees, administrators, executors, successors in the interest, guardians, and assigns.

3. Provisions for Each Other. Except as elsewhere provided herein, each party shall make no provision for the other unless he or she voluntarily elects to do so. Each party may in his or her sole discretion, make additional provisions for the other, whether by lifetime gift, by future will or codicil, by joint or community property, by insurance, or otherwise.

4. Income Tax Refunds. Any federal or state income tax refunds or obligations with respect to a joint return, and any interest on any such refund or penalty on any tax obligation, shall be divided between the parties in proportion to their respective monetary contributions to the tax that is being refunded or that is owed.

5. Marital Residence. Husband owns the real estate located at _____, _____, _____, individually. Upon the death of either party, or divorce, Husband or his estate shall become the sole owner of the real estate. The household furnishings located therein shall be divided equally between the parties in the event of divorce. Upon the death of either party, the survivor shall become the sole owner of the household furnishings.

6. Adequate Provision. The Parties hereby agree that the provisions made herein by each party for the other are fair and equitable under the circumstances.

continues

continued

7. Gifts. Husband and Wife may make annual exclusion gifts to their respective children, and each party consents to make available to the other his or her annual exclusion gift exemption for gifts to each other's children.

   Either party may make a gift to the other party, which gift shall be the separate property of the other party.

8. Divorce and Dissolution. The Parties, in the event of marital discord resulting in the dissolution of this marriage, whether absolute or limited, renounce and release, except as elsewhere provided herein, all rights, present and future, each may have with respect to the other's assets now owned, including all business ventures and property owned by the Parties, as well as any inheritance they may acquire during the marriage. Each party renounces and releases all rights he or she may have with respect to the other party for spousal support, alimony, property settlement, attorney's fees, and court costs.

9. After Acquired Assets and Liabilities. The Parties agree that if either party should file for dissolution, all assets and liabilities acquired or incurred by either party in joint name during the marriage shall be shared equally between the parties, but not including: any inheritance; and increase in the value of the Parties' pension funds; or any other increase in the value of other property owned by either party prior to the marriage (including, but not limited to, increases in net value attributable to the retirement of any outstanding indebtedness with respect to such property during the marriage).

10. Wedding and Engagement Gifts.

    A. Death. If either party dies while the Parties are married, then all wedding and engagement gifts received by the Parties from third parties shall belong to the surviving party.

    B. Divorce. In the event of a divorce, said wedding and engagement gifts shall be distributed between the Parties so that each party receives wedding and engagement gifts which, in the aggregate, have a value which is as close as reasonable to being equal to the value of all the wedding and engagement gifts to be distributed to the other party.

11. Employee Plans and Employee Benefit Rights. Except as may be otherwise provided herein, each party (as "Releasee") hereby elects, and the other party (as "Releasor") hereby consents to a waiver and release of any and all benefits, including without limitation, the qualified joint and survivor annuity benefit form of benefit and the qualified pre-retirement survivor annuity form of benefit under all pension, retirement, death benefit, stock bonus, or profit-sharing plans, systems, or trusts (hereinafter collectively called "Employee Plans") of which the Releasee is, or may become, a participant, beneficiary, or member. This waiver and release is meant, without limitation, as a waiver pursuant to Internal Revenue Code Section 417(a). If requested, the Releasor shall consent in writing, in any form requested by the Releasee, to any such election. The spousal consent of the Releasor set forth herein is irrevocable. Each party acknowledges that he or she has received an explanation of a qualified pre-retirement survivor annuity in accordance with the Internal Revenue Section 417(a)(3)(b) and the effect of this consent to the Releasee's election is to deny Releasor any right, interest, or annuity in or from the Releasee's benefits under any employee benefit plan, now or in the future.

Except as otherwise provided herein, the Releasor acknowledges and hereby consents to the Releasee's election that upon the Releasee's death benefits under any employee plan of the Releasee will be paid to such person as the Releasee may have designated at any time before the execution of the Agreement or may designate from time to time hereafter, in Releasee's sole and unfettered discretion.

If the Releasor shall receive any part of or benefits from the Releasee's account or accrued benefit in any employee plan, other than pursuant to a beneficiary designation executed after the date hereof by the Releasee which designated expressly names the Releasor as a beneficiary, the Releasor shall promptly turn same over to the Releasee (or if the releasee is not then living, to his or her designated beneficiaries under said employee plan, if any, or if there is no designated beneficiary, to the Releasee's estate).

The Parties intend that this Agreement be accepted as a spousal consent by each of them as Releasee to a waiver of a qualified pre-retirement survivor annuity pursuant to Internal Revenue Code Section 417(a). The Parties understand that certain laws and regulations [Internal Revenue Code Sec. 417(a) and Treasury Regulation Sec. 1.401(a)-20] require that, in order to be considered effective, the waivers and releases contained in Article must:

(1) Be consented to by a spouse;

(2) Designate a beneficiary other than the spouse; and,

(3) Acknowledge the effect of the waiver for the spouse.

In order to make the waivers and releases contained in this Article effective, the Parties agree that, within a reasonable period of time after their marriage ceremony (but no later than thirty (30) days after the date of their marriage, or with respect to any plan in which they commence to participate after their marriage, the date on which they commence to participate in such plan), they will sign a separate document which contains the waivers, releases, and acknowledgments set forth in this Article.

12. Spousal Support and Maintenance: Debts and Obligations. Each of the Parties acknowledges that, taking into consideration, among other things, each spouse's private estate, education, work experience, health, age, and ability to work and earn a living, each is fully capable of being self-supporting. Accordingly, if a Dissolution of Marriage occurs, each of the Parties waives, relinquishes, and releases any and all rights and claims as against the other and their respective successors to receive support, alimony, maintenance, or any other payment of a similar nature whether permanent or temporary.

13. Property Settlement. The amount of the property and support settlement Husband shall pay to Wife shall be based upon the length of the Parties' marriage and equal to _____ Dollars for the first year of the Parties' marriage, and _____ Dollars per year for every completed year thereafter of the Parties' marriage, with no maximum, and determined as follows:

Length of Marriage   Total Settlement Amount

_____   _____

continues

continued

The first installment payment of the property and support settlement shall be in the sum of $_____ and made on the 30th day after the dissolution occurs. The balance of the property and support settlement shall be paid yearly in $_____ increments. If, when Husband dies, there are remaining installments of the property and support settlement owed to Wife, then the remaining payments shall be accelerated and paid to Wife within a reasonable time after the settlement of Husband's estate. If Wife predeceases Husband, then any remaining installments of the property and support settlement shall be paid to Wife's estate as the installments come due. The property and support settlement will be made as and for a tax-free property transfer under Section 104l of the Internal Revenue Code. Husband shall not deduct said payments or any part thereof on his income tax returns, and Wife shall not be obligated to include such payments or any part thereof in her taxable income on her income tax returns.

14. Vacating Residence. Wife acknowledge that Husband owns the residence located at _____, _____, _____, where she and Husband expect to reside immediately after their marriage. In the event one of the Parties files for separation or dissolution, within thirty (30) days after the filing for said separation or dissolution, Wife shall remove herself and her property from the _____ residence and give Husband all keys thereto, and consents that thereafter Husband shall have exclusive use and possession of all other rights pertaining to such residence. In the event of Husband's death, Wife shall be allowed to remain in the residence for her lifetime (a life estate) or until she remarries. Husband's Estate shall be the owner of the residence upon Husband's death.

15. Liability for Debts. The debts contracted by each party hereto prior to their marriage are to be paid by the party who shall have contracted the same, and the property of the other party shall not in any respect be liable for the payment thereof, except as elsewhere provided herein.

16. Representation of Parties by Counsel. The Parties hereto both stipulate that they, and each of them, were advised to be and have been represented by legal counsel of their choice in the preparation and execution of this Agreement; they were advised to and have read this Agreement and have had its contents explained to them, by such counsel. In addition, the Parties were advised not to and did not execute the document until they fully understood the terms, provisions and legal consequences of this Agreement.

17. Child Support. Nothing in this Agreement shall be construed to limit or in any way decrease any child support which might be awarded pursuant to a dissolution of the marriage, should a child or children be born to or adopted by the Parties together.

18. General provisions.

    (a) This Agreement shall become effective upon the date of the marriage.

    (b) This agreement and the provisions hereof may be asserted as a bar and estoppel in any court of law or equity to the claims of the surviving party in the estate of the first to die.

    (c) The parties may amend, revoke, or rescind this Agreement only by written mutual agreement.

(d) The Parties hereto and their respective heirs, devisees, delegatees, administrators, executors, guardians, successors in interest, and assigns, shall be bound by the provisions of this Agreement.

(e) The domicile of the Parties at the time of the execution of this Agreement is the state of _____, and the law of such state shall govern. The Parties recognize that they may change their domicile to another jurisdiction by agreement. The Parties agree that all questions arising under or with respect to this Agreement and its interpretation or enforceability shall be governed by the substantive laws of the state of _____, state where Husband and Wife are presently residing and the state where the Parties expect to reside after their marriage.

(f) At those places in this Agreement, including this sentence, except Exhibits A and B, where there appears a recitation of property, ownership rights, survivorship rights or interests, or otherwise which list shall be by way of illustration and not by way of limitation.

(g) In the event a provision of this Agreement is held to be unenforceable for any reason, it shall be considered severable from all other provisions of this Agreement and the Agreement shall be binding upon the Parties in the same manner as it otherwise would have been, had the unenforceable provision not be inserted herein.

(h) The Parties acknowledge and agree that it is difficult to value equity interest, agree to accept the valuation of such interest as set forth in this Agreement, and waive any right to secure an independent valuation thereof and to otherwise present any challenge to the values as set forth herein.

(i) The Parties hereby agree, and state their intentions that, this Agreement shall be followed by, and considered binding upon, any judicial or quasi-judicial proceeding in any way concerning a dissolution of this marriage or death of one or both of the parties.

19. Complete Agreement. The Parties hereby agree, represent, and warrant that this Agreement comprises the entire understanding of the Parties regarding this matter and no promise or inducement not contained in this Agreement has been offered to either of them by anyone and that this Agreement is executed without reliance upon any statement or representation not contained in this Agreement by either the Wife, the Husband, their attorneys, or any other person or entity.

IN WITNESS WHEREOF, the Parties have executed this Prenuptial Agreement on the day and year first above written.

_____   _____

Witness   "Wife"

_____   _____

Witness   "Husband"

Briefs

It was said the document signed by Jacqueline Kennedy and Aristotle Onassis before their 1968 wedding was quite hefty, providing weeks of work for both parties' lawyers (and bringing in an okay to the agreement by Jackie's brother-in-law, Ted Kennedy). It was rumored there were even clauses about where each would maintain a permanent residence, and how often the two would spend time together. But then there was a good deal of property, real and personal, involved on both sides of this famous union. There was a business owned by Onassis, and children from previous unions to be considered.

Did John Kennedy Jr. and Carolyn Bessette have a prenup? If they did, no doubt bits and pieces of *those* clauses will eventually surface.

The Least You Need to Know

➤ Most couples hold property as "joint tenants with right of survivorship."

➤ In community property states, what couples earn, buy, etc., individually during the marriage becomes property that belongs to them equally.

➤ It is possible to switch from separate property to community property ownership styles, and vice versa.

➤ A prenuptial agreement can take precedence over some forms of property ownership.

Chapter 4

Life Insurance: You Need It!

In This Chapter

➤ How insurance can help your estate grow

➤ A term or whole life policy?

➤ How much you will need?

➤ Your beneficiary(ies)

Do you have enough life insurance? No, no, come back, I'm not trying to sell you a policy. I ask because life insurance is an integral part of estate planning.

So force yourself to read this chapter and give the subject some thought. Then you will almost certainly want to take steps to make sure you (a) know what your own coverage entails and (b) beef it up in areas where it needs emphasis, or perhaps buy insurance in the event you have none.

What Life Insurance Can Do For You

You are probably underinsured. Remember, I am not an insurance broker, and have no stock in any insurance company, so I have no vested interest in making such a statement.

Sadly, many of us view life insurance like a bad lottery: If we win, we're dead. We often have little regard for life insurance salesmen as well (although I believe they still rank slightly higher than lawyers). Still, there are those folks who wisely look and plan ahead and do buy insurance. Take a look at this graph, which will give you an idea of the growth of life insurance over the last dozen years or so.

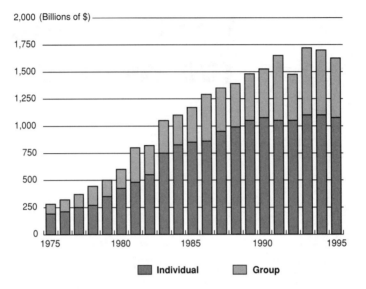

Life Insurance Purchases in the United States

There are several reasons why coverage is a worthwhile expenditure.

Life Insurance:

➤ Increases your estate, building wealth with a relatively small outlay of cash in the form of premiums;

➤ Provides ready cash for loved ones upon your death;

➤ Is received by its beneficiary free of income tax;

➤ May be owned by someone besides the insured and not be subject to death taxes;

➤ Can be used to fund a business buy-out plan; and

➤ Could serve as a savings account, if it is whole life insurance.

Let's look at these statements in more detail.

Building Wealth

Most of us would like to have as substantial an estate as possible so our loved ones can live comfortably after our death. Unfortunately, most of us, me included, don't have a rich relative about to pass away and leave us her fortune—or rich relatives eager to share their wealth during their lifetime through generous gifts. We have to build up an estate the old fashioned way: by earning money and saving it, or by investing it very wisely.

Your estate can be substantial with the inclusion of life insurance. Take me, for example. I am 52 years old. My 401(k) pension and the house are my biggest assets. When I die, my wife will own both. But I am concerned that she and our children will not have enough to live comfortably, so several years ago I bought term life insurance (I'll talk about this in detail in the next page or so) with a face value of $350,000. That's in addition to the group term life insurance I have at work. I know that my family will be financially more secure because of that insurance.

Quote, Unquote
Lack of money is the root of all evil.
—*George Bernard Shaw*

I pay approximately $300 in quarterly premiums for my coverage. I hope my wife and I have many years together, and I'm certainly content with the insurance company keeping the premiums. That's a small investment for my family's financial future.

Ready Cash

Life insurance people like to emphasize that your estate may not be "liquid." That is a genuine concern, and one that some form of insurance protection can address.

Let's take Ed and Eve as an example here. The couple, in their mid-thirties, have two young children. They own their own home, have a small savings account, a little invested in stocks and mutual funds, and each has a small contributory retirement plan through their jobs. Ed earns considerably more than Eve, although it could be the reverse with other couples.

If Ed suddenly dies, his salary would end, but bills wouldn't stop coming in. The IRS in particular isn't all that patient if you owe them money. The cost of a funeral might be around $5,000, and funeral directors want to be paid, too.

Ed could solve those immediate problems with life insurance, at very little expense. Since he is young, the premium for coverage similar to my policy will be

Watch Out
Beware of skimping in this area. Two-income couples with children should each have an insurance policy. Look at it this way: If one party's death would result in a serious financial hardship for the family, then both husband and wife should carry insurance.

considerably less than what I am paying. Eve can deal with her grief and not have to worry about where the money is going to come from—it's in the mail from the insurance company.

Not so incidentally, single people and couples without children can make use of an insurance policy, too, and for the same reasons: immediate cash for beneficiaries, money to pay funeral expenses and that individual's other bills—repayment of loans, credit card balances, and other debts that would have to be satisfied from the estate.

Taxes

The beauty of life insurance is that the beneficiary receives the proceeds free of income tax. Eve, for example, does not have to pay a cent to the IRS. With proper planning—and I'll tell you how later in the book—the proceeds may also escape federal estate tax.

Business Plans

If you are the owner, or part owner, of a business, you also need to consider life insurance. The business could purchase insurance on the life of the owner, and the proceeds could be paid to the business and/or the owner's next of kin. The business that has an owner or key employee who dies suddenly might experience a financial crunch for a short time, or perhaps even longer. That could be alleviated by the insurance proceeds. The owner's family may need cash, but can't sell his business interest to generate the necessary money. Life insurance can be an answer there too.

Tip
Some folks purchase a life insurance policy as a gift, perhaps to a grandchild, making that individual the beneficiary. Others make a favorite charity a beneficiary. Money left in this manner goes directly where you want it to after your death, and is not held up as part of your estate.

Savings

If you choose whole life insurance—explained in detail in a couple of pages—your premiums are divided into two parts. One part pays for the insurance coverage, while the other becomes a savings account. If you have trouble saving money, this feature can help you build a small nest egg. Of course, the savings amount of the premium could be used to purchase more term insurance, which would increase that coverage.

Which Policy Is Best for You?

There is life insurance coverage to fit practically every reader of this book, and at a variety of costs too. You just need to determine the type of policy best for your purposes.

We can divide most policies into two categories: term and cash value.

Term Policies

Term policies have one common feature: there is no cash value built up by your premiums. This is simple life insurance, offering the most coverage for the least cost. You can select whatever that amount will be, perhaps $50,000, maybe $500,000, or any other number. You pay an annual premium. If you die while you own the policy, your beneficiary receives the money.

You cannot borrow against a term life insurance policy because, of course, there is no cash value.

Briefs

Life insurance is one of the staples of the mystery novel (another is the will). When police investigate a murder, the first question they ask is "Who benefits from this crime?" Why, the murderer, of course, and that's rarely the butler. It's often the insurance beneficiary. Timing the purchase of life insurance may allay or enhance suspicion about that buyer.

There is the serial wife killer, who takes out an insurance policy on each new bride. Sadly, too, there is also the bomb exploding on an airline flight. Investigation leads to a relative of one of the passengers, who had purchased a large policy of flight life insurance before the departure—or straight life insurance back home. So much havoc and heartache caused by a few pieces of paper.

The premium you pay is based on the amount of insurance you purchase, your general health and your age when you first buy the policy. The premium rises as you grow older. Also, Insurance costs vary the way prices of other products do, so it pays to shop around to find the best, safest coverage with a company offering the lowest cost to you. As a gauge, keep in mind my age and the fact that I pay $300 a quarter for a $350,000 policy.

Here are some varieties of term policies:

Annual Renewable. This offers one year of insurance, usually renewable every year with an increased premium (because you are growing older). This has the advantage of giving you the greatest coverage at the lowest cost to you. Read carefully any policy you are considering to see what your renewal rights are.

Level. Coverage here is for a guaranteed term, such as 3, 5, 10 or 20 years, with level premiums. That means they reach a certain plateau and stay "level" until the next change, or the premium remains the same but the coverage decreases from one level to another. Some insurance companies will allow cost-of-living increases at proportionally the same premium.

Decreasing. Coverage decreases over a set period of time, but the premiums remain the same. One plus of this program is it provides greater coverage when most of us need it, early in our family lives.

Mortgage or Credit. With this style, coverage decreases as the debt you are insuring is paid down, but with a level

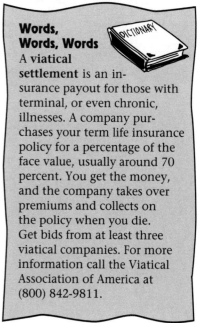

Words, Words, Words
A **viatical settlement** is an insurance payout for those with terminal, or even chronic, illnesses. A company purchases your term life insurance policy for a percentage of the face value, usually around 70 percent. You get the money, and the company takes over premiums and collects on the policy when you die. Get bids from at least three viatical companies. For more information call the Viatical Association of America at (800) 842-9811.

Tip
You might want the free booklet "What You Should Know About Buying Life Insurance," offered by the American Council of Life Insurance, a trade association of some 600 life insurance companies. Call (800) 338-4471.

premium. This is expensive, so you will want to consider purchasing another form of term insurance if you want that debt paid off at your death. Buy this only if you are otherwise uninsurable.

Group. Many employers carry group term life insurance policies for their employees. It's a great fringe benefit because the premiums for the first $50,000 of coverage are income tax free, and the employee pays a low rate of income tax on the policy beyond that coverage. My advice is to get as much group term life insurance as you possibly can.

Cash Value Policies

Tip
If you have child support obligations under a divorce decree, you might want to consider a life insurance policy, payable to the children for their financial future should you pass away.

Another option, *cash value life insurance* is sometimes referred to as *whole life insurance*. Most of these policies have, as mentioned earlier, a savings account feature, with variables in investment returns. Here are some cash value policy styles.

Whole (ordinary). Coverage is guaranteed at a fixed amount, with level premiums. Part of each premium goes into a savings account at a predetermined amount and investment return. You can borrow against the cash value of the policy.

Universal. The term and cash value portions are split into two accounts. Depending on the insured's allocation, the insurance can increase or decrease. It does have the flexibility of changing coverage as needs alter, but is more expensive than term if the insured uses most of the premium for insurance coverage.

Vanishing Premium. Here, premiums are overpaid in the early years so that the cash value can accumulate more quickly. Then the later premiums are partially paid from the cash value, or the coverage could be reduced or lost.

Joint First-to-Die or Second-to-Die. This is life insurance coverage for two persons, usually spouses. It is less expensive than buying two separate policies. The proceeds are payable according to the first- or second-to-die provisions.

Discuss policies you are considering with your financial adviser. (Remember, you are going to call often on your estate planning team.) He or she can probably be more objective than a life insurance agent. Have your advisor read the fine print of policies. What the large print giveth, the small print often taketh away.

How Much Coverage You Need, and Where to Find It

First, you need to determine how much insurance coverage is sufficient for you. A life insurance company and your financial advisor can help you here. After your purchase, you will want to review your calculations periodically, perhaps once every year or two, to be sure your coverage matches current needs.

These things are quite subjective, but usually the main purpose of life insurance is to provide a lump sum amount that will replace the deceased's income. If you want a quick calculation, here's a suggestion, keeping in mind your future income may vary considerably from these guesstimates.

Step 1. Calculate your annual income (reduced by personal expenses for you alone, such as clothing, lunches, etc.)

Example: You earn $45,000 after taxes and spend $5,000 on yourself = $40,000.

Step 2. Divide that amount by your expected rate of return from investing the life insurance proceeds.

Example: $40,000 divided by .05 = $800,000.

Step 3. Subtract your current total savings and investments.

Example: $800,000 minus $30,000 = $770,000 your life insurance needs.

The rough method I used for *my* life insurance was to add up all my debts—and don't think that's not a depressing experience—then determine how much money, when invested, would be needed once all those debts were paid.

Example:

Debts to be paid	$100,000 plus
Investment need (at 5% return for family —$30,000)	$600,000
Total needed	$700,000

With this kind of need, term life insurance is your best buy.

Tip
Do you have more questions about insurance? You can call the National Insurance Consumer Hotline at (800) 942-4242. This is a consumer service sponsored by a number of insurance industry trade associations. Besides life policies, you can ask about home and auto insurance. The Helpline operates from 8AM to 8PM, Eastern Time, Monday through Friday.

Watch Out
Naturally, you'll want to choose an insurance company in good health for your policy. Some are in better shape than others. Company financial strength ratings are published by A.M. Best, Standard & Poor, Moody's, Duff & Phelps, and Weiss Research. Your public library's reference department can help you access those reports, or you can check with your financial planner.

Yes, I know the $700,000 I list above as what I need is far from the $350,000 term life insurance policy I carry. I do have another policy, though—group life insurance through my place of business. However, I concede I'm still a little underinsured.

Don't forget if you have college expenses coming up for one or more children, those costs could considerably alter the amount you will need.

Who Owns the Policy? Who Is the Beneficiary?

If the insurance is on *your* life, then probably you own the policy. It works that way for most of us. We can control premium payment and beneficiary designation because it is our policy.

Your spouse might own your policy, or perhaps one of your children does. The proceeds are payable to them or anyone they designate. That way, the policy is not subject to federal estate taxes. If someone else owns your policy, they may look to you to pay the premium, but need not consider your wishes as to who will benefit from its proceeds after your death. Tax concerns may, or may not, override this. There is more about this in Part 4.

Quote, Unquote
I have enough money to last me the rest of my life, unless I buy something.
—*Jackie Mason*

Watch Out
Don't transfer a life insurance policy without consulting with your estate planning team. The potential tax savings may not be as important as the insurance coverage payable to the beneficiaries of your choice.

If you are married, you probably have named your spouse as primary beneficiary of the policy and, if you have children, have named them as alternate beneficiaries.

You ought to review your beneficiary designation at regular intervals, especially if your family needs and life situations change. Always make sure that you have an alternative beneficiary, because if the primary beneficiary dies before you do, without an alternative named, the proceeds become part of your probate estate. That is generally not desirable because it will delay distribution of the proceeds, and be subject to probate costs. You can change your beneficiary designation by using the insurance company form provided for that purpose.

If you have minor children, then consider establishing a trust for them to receive the proceeds, and to manage the assets until they become more mature. Chapters 8 and 11 talk about trusts for minors.

Easy Go the Taxes

Keep in mind that life insurance proceeds paid to a beneficiary because of the death of the insured are exempt from income tax.

There may be several pay-out options for insurance proceeds, such as a lump sum or a periodic payment over a number of years. For example, if my wife chooses the latter, part of each check will include interest on the amount left with the insurance company. The interest portion is taxable.

If you own a policy at your death, or the proceeds are payable to your estate, then the insurance will be subject to federal estate tax, which begins with an estate valued at $600,000. You can avoid this by transferring ownership to another person, such as an adult child, even if he or she is also the beneficiary. Then the proceeds will no longer be included in your estate. However, if the policy has a cash value, the transfer may be subject to a gift tax.

Is There Anyone Who Should Not Carry Insurance?

Empty nest couples, both of whom are reasonably healthy, *and* own their home free and clear *and* have sufficient investment income to survive fairly well financially if one or the other dies, *might* want to drop their life insurance coverage, or not take out a policy in the first place.

If you do some number crunching here and see that you can do without your term life policy, all you have to do is notify the company that you are canceling and not continuing payments. Dropping a cash value policy is more complicated, because while those policies are part death benefit, they are also part savings. Check with your financial planner or accountant to see if this is a wise step for you. If you are in poor health, for instance, it might be wise to keep the policy in effect. You could be considered uninsurable if you go to purchase another one some day.

If you want to stray outside your estate planning team, you can send your cash value policy to the Insurance Group of the Consumer Federation of America. They will analyze your rate of return and give you an idea of what you would have to earn investing to better it. The service costs $40. For more information, call the CFA at (202) 387-0087.

Where does your insurance dollar go, anyway, once you've sent in a premium? As an aside I thought you might like to know how your money is spent, and so I have included this pie chart to show you that disbursement.

Where Your Life Insurance Dollar Goes

U.S. Life Insurance Companies —

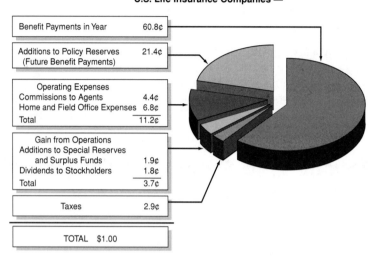

Benefit Payments in Year	60.8¢
Additions to Policy Reserves (Future Benefit Payments)	21.4¢

Operating Expenses	
Commissions to Agents	4.4¢
Home and Field Office Expenses	6.8¢
Total	11.2¢

Gain from Operations	
Additions to Special Reserves and Surplus Funds	1.9¢
Dividends to Stockholders	1.8¢
Total	3.7¢

Taxes	2.9¢

TOTAL	$1.00

Think about it, though. You pay a reasonably small amount in premiums for insurance, and the return on investment can be very large. In my case, with term life insurance, for example, my policy will pay my wife over $350,000 when I die; so far I have invested approximately $5,000 in premiums. Of course I prefer not to think about the downside for me personally should that happen, but at least I know the money will be there for her if I'm not.

The Least You Need to Know

➤ Life insurance can significantly increase your estate at very little expense.

➤ Work the numbers to determine what your specific coverage should be.

➤ Term insurance is straight insurance, payable at death, with a low cost compared to the coverage offered.

➤ Whole life insurance is a combination of term insurance and a savings account.

➤ Insurance proceeds paid to a beneficiary at the death of a policy holder are exempt from income tax.

Chapter 5

Will You Have a Pension?

In This Chapter

➤ Typical pension plans

➤ Other ways to save for retirement

➤ Deferring distribution—and taxes, too

➤ Borrowing from your pension

We're all certainly trying. A recent survey by the accounting firm of KPMG Peat Marwick LPP, found 91 percent of employers with 200 or more employees offer some kind of retirement plan. Many smaller employers have specific savings programs for workers, and some employees make contributions on their own for retirement.

We look to our future with some concern. No one wants to rely solely on Social Security after retirement, but many of us have trouble saving on our own. Fortunately, a variety of pension plans have been developed, with attractive tax incentives as well. This is a complex area, but after you've read this chapter you'll better understand your own choices, and have more confidence in building savings for your—let us hope—"golden years."

Qualified Pension Plans

A *pension plan* is simply an employee compensation program where the worker receives his or her benefits upon retirement.

What does *qualified* mean in the context of pensions? That's a pension plan in which the employer's contribution will not be taxed to the employee in the year it is contributed.

Quote, Unquote
Who hath so entire happiness that he is not in some part offended with the condition of his estate?
—*Boethius (AD 470–525)*

The accumulated income and contribution will be taxed only upon distribution, which is usually a monthly payout to the employee after retirement. Those payments are *tax-deferred*, a term you'll read often in this chapter. In the context of pensions, that means taxes on that money are not due and payable until the employee has retired, when he or she is presumably in a lower tax bracket and will have to pay less than when employed.

There are three styles of qualified retirement plans I'll talk about: defined benefit pensions, profit sharing, and stock bonus plans. Let's take them in that order.

Defined Benefit Pension Plan

The *defined benefit pension* is one in which the amount an employee will receive at retirement is specified. So if Joann walks into her company's Human Resources Department, or Plans Benefit Office, and asks how much she will be entitled to at retirement, the staff will do some calculations and perhaps tell her $2,000 a month for as long as she and her husband live.

Joann is enrolled in a defined benefit pension plan because it clearly states her retirement income. It might have some variables, such as a cost-of-living adjustment, or a reduction equal to her Social Security benefit when that kicks in. But essentially Joann can count on that $2,000 coming to her each month at retirement.

Tip
Government employees and some others might have pensions not discussed in this chapter. If that applies to you, check with your Plans Benefit office for information about *your* retirement program.

Joann's husband will receive her pension benefits if she dies before him because she has a joint-with-survivor pension. If her husband had waived his right to that money, then her pension would be larger, but only for her life rather than paid over two persons' lives.

Generally, a husband or wife has a right to at least a 50 percent survivor benefit in the other spouse's qualified pension, unless that right is waived in writing in a pre-scribed form. (A prenuptial agreement won't ensure that a spouse has waived his or her pension rights.) If spouses agree to a waiver to those rights, then an employee can ask to fill out an employer waiver form, which can be given to him at his place of work.

Defined pension benefits are determined by years of employee service and average compensation during that work time, based upon a formula set into the plan. The employer is supposed to set aside enough money to fund your benefits, using actuarial calculations of how long you and your spouse are expected to live. There are limits to annual benefits ($120,000 in 1996), but you probably won't have to worry about that unless you are a retiring senior executive with a Fortune 500 company—or a pro athlete.

Defined Contribution Pension Plan

In this plan what's fixed is not the amount of money you'll get out at retirement, but how much money— usually determined as a fixed percentage of your income—you put in before retirement. In a *defined contribution pension*, benefits are based solely on the amount contributed by the employee and employer, and the account's accumulated income. Each plan participant has his own account, which is much like a savings account. Usually the employer makes a contribution as determined by the plan. Upon retirement, the employee's amount available for retirement living is easily determined, and usually will be reported on a quarterly basis.

For example, Ken is employed by Medium Company. He is enrolled in a defined contribution plan and contributes 4 percent of his salary, which is matched by his employer. The quarterly statement on his retirement account shows his contribution, his employer's contribution and the accumulated income. Neither his nor his employer's contributions are taxed when he earns the money, nor is the accumulated income. Ken only starts paying taxes on the money when he begins receiving retirement payments.

Profit Sharing Plan

A *profit sharing plan* is just what it sounds like: a program where employees share in any profits the company makes. It's set up by the employer, who contributes part of the

Tip
The Employee Retirement Income Security Act (ERISA) gives you the right to get information from your employer about your company's pension plan. Ask what type of plan it is, how it works, your options for collecting benefits, rules for participation, etc. ERISA also gives you the right to your individual benefits statement. Request a statement at least annually.

Tip
Some companies offer employees no say at all in how they invest pension funds. But yours might allow you to select the type of investment you prefer. For growth you might want a selection of stocks, while bonds could be your choice for a fixed return. Discuss your options with your financial advisor. Your choice will depend on factors in your personal and financial life.

company profits to separate employee accounts, as determined by the plan and those profits. The law generally treats a profit sharing plan like a defined contribution pension, although it could also be used to fund accident, health, or disability programs. When the profit sharing plan makes a distribution to the employee, then the employee is taxed on the money he or she receives.

Watch Out
Since the retirement account in a stock bonus plan consists of the employer's company stock, there is no diversification of portfolio. With this plan, market fluctuation in that stock will have an impact on your retirement benefits. In other words, your eggs are all in one basket, and that basket is your company.

Stock Bonus Plan

In a *stock bonus plan,* the employer establishes and maintains a program of contributing shares of its company stock to employees. The plan is subject to most of the same requirements as a profit sharing plan. When the employee receives the stock, he or she is taxed on its worth.

Quite similar to stock bonus is an *employee stock ownership plan* (also known by its initials, *ESOP*). In such a plan, the employer contributes its company stock to a qualified trust, which manages it for both employer and employee. The employee is taxed upon distribution.

Vesting Requirements

In pension language *vesting* means you have met the particular plan requirements for the legal right to receive pension benefits, based on your years of service. Your benefits start at retirement age, which is usually 65. In most plans, an employee is vested after contributing to the plan for x months. Once vested, the employer begins to contribute to the plan as well as the employee.

To use the jargon, you are 100 percent vested in, or own, what you contribute to that plan.

Your right to your employer's contribution is another matter. If, according to your plan, you are entitled to all of the employer's contribution upon completion of five years' service with that company, that's called *cliff vesting*. Or your plan might have *graded vesting*, which is a staggered ownership style likely to look like this:

What You Are Allowed to Keep of Employer's Contribution

Years of Service	Nonforfeitable Percentage
0-2	0%
3	20%
4	40%
5	60%
6	80%
7 or more	100%

Amy has worked for her employer for six years. Her retirement plan has five-year cliff vesting, so 100 percent of her accrued benefits are hers. Tommy has been employed by his company for the same six years, but his employer has graded vesting, structured as in the table above, so Tommy is 80 percent vested in employer contributions.

If you leave the company, the employer's contribution that is not vested remains in the pension plan. You take with you whatever you put into the plan.

Check your own retirement plan, and consult with the appropriate office at your place of employment if you have any questions.

Distribution Requirements

Distribution, or payment, from any qualified retirement plan *must* begin no later than April 1 of the calendar year following the calendar year in which you reach age $70^1/_2$. So if your birthday is January 1, then your half-birthday is July 1. If your $70^1/_2$ birthday is July 1, 1997, then you must receive a distribution no later than April 1, 1998.

Wait, there is more to this complicated formula. You must have a required minimum distribution each year for as long as those benefits are available to you. Here's how you can compute that amount:

Step 1: Determine how long you are supposed to live.

Yes, really. The IRS can lend you a hand with this. Take a look at their life expectancy table on the following page. It can give you an idea of a figure to put down in working this step.

Step 2: Find out what your retirement account balance will be in the year prior to your becoming $70^1/_2$. (Your Plans Benefit report tells this.)

Step 3: Divide the amount in Step 2 by the figure in Step 1.

Let's use Bart as an example. Bart must receive his first distribution in 1997. According to the IRS table, his calculated life expectancy is 15.3, which means 15.3 years from the starting point of distribution of his retirement money. The amount in his retirement account is $120,000. Therefore, Bart must receive $7,843 each year ($120,000 divided by 15.3).

Generally, you can't take any distribution prior to reaching age $59^1/_2$, but there are exceptions to this rule that I'll discuss later in this chapter.

> **Quote, Unquote**
> When I was young I used to think that money was the most important thing in life; now that I am old, I know it is.
> —*Oscar Wilde*

> **Words, Words, Words**
> COLA is not for sipping, at least not when you're speaking pension talk. It stands for Cost Of Living Adjustment. Check to see if your pension plan provides automatic or periodic COLAs. Or, too bad for you, no COLAs at all.

Estimating Life Expectancy

Age	Multiple	Age	Multiple	Age	Multiple
5	76.6	42	40.6	79	10.0
6	75.6	43	39.6	80	9.5
7	74.7	44	38.7	81	8.9
8	73.7	45	37.7	82	8.4
9	72.7	46	36.8	83	7.9
10	71.7	47	35.9	84	7.4
11	70.7	48	34.9	85	6.9
12	69.7	49	34.0	86	6.5
13	68.8	50	33.1	87	6.1
14	67.8	51	32.2	88	5.7
15	66.8	52	31.3	89	5.3
16	65.8	53	30.4	90	5.0
17	64.8	54	29.5	91	4.7
18	63.9	55	28.6	92	4.4
19	62.9	56	27.7	93	4.1
20	61.9	57	26.8	94	3.9
21	60.9	58	25.9	95	3.7
22	59.9	59	25.0	96	3.4
23	59.0	60	24.2	97	3.2
24	58.0	61	23.3	98	3.0
25	57.0	62	22.5	99	2.8
26	56.0	63	21.6	100	2.7
27	55.1	64	20.8	101	2.5
28	54.1	65	20.0	102	2.3
29	53.1	66	19.2	103	2.1
30	52.2	67	18.4	104	1.9
31	51.2	68	17.6	105	1.8
32	50.2	69	16.8	106	1.6
33	49.3	70	16.0	107	1.4
34	48.3	71	15.3	108	1.3
35	47.3	72	14.6	109	1.1
36	46.4	73	13.9	110	1.0
37	45.4	74	13.2	111	.9
38	44.4	75	12.5	112	.8
39	43.5	76	11.9	113	.7
40	42.5	77	11.2	114	.6
41	41.5	78	10.6	115	.5

401(k)s, IRAs, and Other Great Ways to Save

You've got several choices if you don't have a pension plan, or you want to put away for retirement more than what your company is providing.

401(k)

This is a defined contribution plan for retirement, named after the section of the IRS Code numbered (you guessed it) 401(k). It has several attractive features that have made it popular with lots of folks:

➤ Contributions can be made by deducting money automatically from your pay (through a salary reduction plan). You're less likely to miss money you never see; even better, you don't pay taxes on the money deducted from your salary.

➤ Your employer might make a matching tax-deferred contribution.

➤ You're taxed upon distribution of the employee and employer tax-deferred contributions, plus the accumulated earnings, but that tax is when the retiree's income bracket is lower than it was when he or she was working.

➤ Plan distributions can be delayed until age $70^1/_2$, when you may be in a lower tax bracket.

You can take your 401(k) plan with you if you leave your present employer. However, the employer contributions may have vesting requirements similar to a defined contribution plan, above.

403(b)

This plan is similar to a 401(k), except that it applies to not-for-profit companies. There are some slight differences in income limitations and investment opportunities here, too.

An Individual Retirement Account (IRA)

An IRA allows working people with no company pension to contribute up to $2,000 to it annually. A married couple can have two IRAs, each for up to $2,000, including a spouse who does not work outside the home.

There are heavy financial penalties for early withdrawal here, and also income and employment pension plan limits for tax deductibility of the contribution. There

Watch Out

If you leave your company, you are entitled to all employee contributions to your pension and, depending on plan vesting requirements, the employer contributions. To avoid a tax upon distribution, you must invest the distribution within 60 days of receipt in another qualified plan or in an Individual Retirement Account (IRA). A direct rollover payment from your ex-employer's pension to your IRA avoids the IRS requirement of a 20 percent withholding on the pension check if paid directly to you.

are some limitations on your choice of investment vehicles, but you still have plenty to choose from, including mutual funds. For more information about this popular investment, call the IRS at (800) 829-3676 and ask for publication number 590 titled, of course, *IRAs*.

Words, Words, Words

Keogh is a name, not a word. That pension plan was named after U.S. Representative Eugene James Keogh, who first suggested the benefits program in the House.

The deductible contributions and the accumulated earnings of an IRA are taxable when distributed. That distribution may begin as early as age 59^1/$_2$ but no later than age 70^1/$_2$.

A Keogh Plan

Self-employed individuals are eligible to receive qualified retirement benefits under a *Keogh plan* (pronounced *key-oh*). Keoghs cover partners and sole proprietors, and can include employees. The coverage requirements, contribution limitations, and taxability upon distribution are similar to defined benefit or defined contribution plans, depending upon which form is used in the Keogh plan.

Or Is There an Annuity in Your Future?

Here's another way to save for retirement. Whether through your place of employment or on your own, you can put as much money as you like each year into an annuity. An *annuity* is an investment vehicle that brings a fixed, periodic return for a specified number of years, or for a lifetime (or, if desired, the lifetime of a spouse). The annuity grows without taxation. But the amount you deposit is not deducted from your reported earnings.

Joe purchased an annuity from an insurance company for $20,000 in 1996. The company promised him that he will receive $3,000 a year for 10 years (a fixed term), beginning in the year 2006, when he is retired and in a lower tax bracket.

Each one of Joe's annual payments starting in 2006 will include income earned from his premium. His investment was $20,000, with an expected return of $30,000. His annual payment will be $3,000, but because $2,000 of that will be considered one-tenth of investment and not earnings on that investment, only $1,000 will be taxable to him each year.

The advantage of the annuity is, as you've read so often here, to defer payment of income earned until the future, when your tax rate is likely to be less. Contrast that with Joe putting his $20,000 into a Certificate of Deposit. Each year the interest earned from the CD will be taxed, while the income from the annuity will be tax deferred until payout begins.

Annuities are considered safe for future needs, but with limited returns. That should appeal to the conservatives out there.

Variable Annuity

You say *you* want something a bit more daring? There is also what is known as the *variable annuity*, which puts your principal into the stock market. Now your annuity has become as responsive to the current economy as the performance of any stock or mutual fund. And any earnings are tax deferred.

Building Wealth at the IRS's Expense

April is a very trying month. I'm trying to keep my money and the IRS is trying to take it away.
—Stephen M. Maple

You have been very patient in reading through this complex subject area. For that you are to be commended. But the bottom line, you are probably saying about now, is "Just tell me how much all of this will save me."

The answer is "Well, that will depend." For one thing, it depends upon how much you can afford to put into your retirement plan. Of course, there are limits. With an IRA, for example, you can contribute only $2,000 a year.

Here are the tax deductible limits for each year for some plans.

➤ A defined contribution plan and a Keogh plan allow contributions up to $30,000 per year, or 25 percent of your compensation if that is less.

➤ A 401(k) plan permits you to contribute up to $9,500 annually, to an overall limit of $30,000 or 25 percent compensation if combined with other retirement plans.

All of the above is income that is tax deferred. Here is an example of how one employee is working her pension to her advantage.

Hope has a 401(k) plan at work. She earns $50,000 annually, and has agreed to contribute 5 percent of her salary to her plan through a salary reduction plan. Her employer agrees to match her contribution. Hope's taxable salary for a year will then be $47,500 ($50,000 salary minus her $2,500 salary contribution, which is 5 percent of her income). Into her 401(k) goes her $2,500 contribution, which is tax deferred, and her employer's $2,500, which is also tax deferred. Thus Hope has $5,000 put away for retirement *and* has reduced her taxable income by the $2,500 she herself contributed. If she wanted to, she could make an additional contribution from her salary, which could also be tax deferred.

When Hope retires and starts receiving distributions from her 401(k), they will be taxable, but by then she will be making less money, so her tax rate will be less.

Compare the results in Hope's 401(k) account with her putting her contribution into a savings account. If she is taxed at a 20 percent rate, then she will have to earn $3,125 to save $2,500 (since the savings account is funded with after-tax dollars), and any interest earned each year would be taxed. She is, therefore, saving at the IRS's expense. And you would, too, if you had a 401(k). And as a bonus, her employer kicked in another $2,500!

What you save in your retirement account is tax deferred, and the income earned by the account is tax deferred. I don't know about you, but I personally prefer paying taxes sometime in the future—when I retire, but certainly not now!

Other Deferred Compensation Plans

I like to get paid up front. The IRS prefers that I make money that way, too, and pay tax on it right away. However, most of us have some form of retirement plan that pays us later—after that magic 65 or 70 years of age, or whenever we officially leave the 9-to-5 world. Our money is tax deferred until those payouts begin. A few folks have other deferred compensation plans I haven't talked about yet that deserve mention.

Note to readers: If you are not in the 39.6 percent or higher income tax bracket, you can skip this section.

Tony "Tiger" Templeton is a running back for the Indianapolis Horses. Tony signed a four-year contract with the team for $500,000 per year. Actually he is only going to receive $250,000 each of the four years. The other $1 million will be paid beginning in the year 2010 in 10 annual installments of $100,000 each, quite a few years after Tony's knees will have started giving way. Tony's taxable compensation this year and for the next three years is $250,000. The rest will be taxed when he receives it, beginning in 2010 and each year after that, when he is in semi-retirement signing autographs, and is in a lower tax bracket.

Quote, Unquote
Life does not begin at the moment of conception or the moment of birth. It begins when the kids leave home and the dog dies.
—*Anonymous*

If you are an employee in a high tax bracket, you may be able to contract with your employer for a deferred compensation arrangement, with part of your salary to be paid when you begin retirement. It would likely be taxed at a lower rate than it would be now, since your income then will have dropped. Besides deferred compensation plans, you may also want to investigate stock options with your employer. They also receive favorable tax treatment, with taxes often hitting when you're retired and in a lower tax bracket.

Early Withdrawals from Your Pension Plan

Most of us look at our assets and see that a big chunk of money is sitting right there in a retirement plan, doing absolutely nothing. What a crime! If we are short of cash, there is the temptation to withdraw some money to pay off debts.

You just might be able to borrow from your retirement plan. There are a number of restrictions in this area, and you need to consult your Plans Benefits administrator to do it correctly. Keep in mind, though, that the amount you borrow, if not paid back, may seriously deplete your retirement fund.

Early withdrawals (that usually means before age $59^1/_2$) from qualified pension plans are subject to a 10 percent penalty tax. In addition, you must report the tax-deferred amount you withdrew to the IRS as income in the year withdrawn.

There are several exceptions to this withdrawal penalty:

➤ Employee separation from employment after age 55.

➤ Distribution to a beneficiary after the employee's death.

➤ Distribution to the employee due to a disability.

➤ Distribution to pay medical expenses.

➤ Distribution to a divorcing spouse.

Uh-Oh Department: Will Your Company Pension Be There When You Need It?

Well, we certainly hope so. During the coming few decades the baby boomers (those born between 1946 and 1964) will earn larger and larger incomes, rack up more years with their company and, as all of us must, approach retirement. Employers will have to make larger and larger contributions to their pension funds. Some experts fear that some companies will cancel that benefit when faced with the increased amount they must spend.

Quote, Unquote
There are two times in a man's life when he should not speculate: when he can't afford it, and when he can.
—*Mark Twain*

"Gee," you say, "Can they do that?" Yes, I'm afraid they can. A company does not have to file for bankruptcy, or even be in financial trouble, to justify terminating its pension plan. Actually, more than 30,000 American companies have done just that since 1980. However, most have replaced it with some form of employee contribution plan.

Whatever the future holds for you—and your company—your pension is probably safe, although its benefits might be frozen at the date the plan was terminated. You can thank an act of Congress, which in 1974 set up the Employee Retirement Income Security Act (ERISA) that now governs pension plans. (You read a little about ERISA earlier in this chapter). It in turn established the Pension Benefit Guaranty Corporation (PBGC), which acts sort of like the FDIC does for banking.

For example, if Acme General Company wants to terminate its pension program, PBGC requires it to prove that it has enough money to pay all the scheduled benefits for retired and vested employees. If PBGC is satisfied, the company in question usually purchases an annuity from an insurance company to pay pensions.

If a company declares bankruptcy and has an underfunded pension plan, PBGC will take on the responsibility for paying its pensions. Broadly speaking—and there are a lot of

Quote, Unquote
Those who work too much do not work hard.
—*Henry David Thoreau*

"whereases" in this operation—as a retired Acme employee, you would likely be paid some, if not all, of your money.

Note: What we are talking about here is private company pensions. PBGC's role does not include government employees, not-for-profit groups, and professional associations, such as doctors or lawyers.

So the answer to the question "Will my pension be there for me when I'm ready?" is "Very likely it will." But not knowing absolutely for certain, coupled with nailbiting about Social Security and whether *that* system will be around for us when we retire, should get all of us busy putting away as much as we can in savings and investments—just in case.

The Least You Need to Know

➤ A company retirement plan can sometimes be tailored to fit your own particular needs.

➤ If your company does not provide a pension, you can set up your own.

➤ Money you put into your pension doesn't get taxed until it's distributed to you at retirement, when you're probably in a lower tax bracket.

➤ Your company pension will probably be alive and well when you hit retirement age, but it still makes lots of sense to save as much as you can for retirement.

Part 2
About Wills, Trusts... and Probate

Now we come—ta-da—to one of the most important parts of this book. In the pages that follow you'll learn all about what should go into your will, and you'll see how to examine your family and financial situation so that you can prepare a solid document. You say you've never heard of a trust, at least not for those who don't have incomes somewhere up there in the stratosphere? You may be surprised to find that not only is that not true, but also that a trust is just what you need right now. Or, perhaps not right at the moment, but that it is something to consider down the road, when you've built up your assets a bit more.

Probate is what happens to your will once your heirs have it in hand and turn it over to the state to be acknowledged as your last will and testament. It's also what happens to your estate if you don't have a will. Probate is an interesting, and to many a mysterious, process that transfers your assets from your estate to your heirs or beneficiaries. What exactly goes on here? I'll tell you. The mystery will be gone, but I'll replace it with a few interesting, sometimes quirky, probate stories.

Chapter 6

No Will? No Good!

In This Chapter

➤ How your property is distributed

➤ Guardianship issues

➤ Who administers your estate

➤ Remarriage and children

If you're with me so far you're making good progress in your planning. You have just analyzed and recorded what you own and how you own it, giving you a clear idea of exactly what constitutes your estate. We're coming soon to one of the most important parts of this book—having a will prepared.

Are you at all reluctant about making your will, perhaps because you're put off by all the decisions and details that it entails, or maybe because you just don't like to even *think* about the inevitable? You're not alone; many people feel that way. But by the end of this chapter, I guarantee you'll feel differently.

As you will see, when you don't have a will things can get pretty sticky, with a string of complications that could some day, if you'll excuse the expression, have you spinning in your grave.

Dying Intestate Is About as Bad as It Sounds

If you do not have a will when you die (that's what dying "intestate" means), you may have given your family another reason to mourn your loss. Without a will they must turn to state statutes to determine who your heirs are and how much of a share in your estate they are entitled to inherit. The state poking its nose into your family affairs? Yes indeed, that's exactly what they will do, down to your last penny.

Watch Out

Just as bad as having no will is having an outdated one. If there has been a marriage, death, birth, and maybe a divorce or two in your family since you wrote yours, then get thee to a lawyer for a new one. Otherwise, the old one will be honored (although the rights of children born since that document was made are protected).

When you don't get around to making a will, you give up the right to:

➤ Select the beneficiaries of your estate

➤ Make gifts to close friends

➤ Name the executor of your estate

➤ Designate a guardian for your minor child

Here are a few other complications you may leave behind if you die intestate. All will be covered in depth in upcoming chapters.

➤ Federal estate taxes could be higher without the full marital deduction you could be entitled to.

➤ State death taxes take a larger share of your estate.

➤ Income savings may be lost.

➤ Probate expenses are higher.

Ah, Probate

There's that word you often hear in the same breath with "wills" and "estates." It's usually said with a shudder. What does it mean, and can it really be that terrible?

Probate is commonly defined as a state court procedure administering the estate of a deceased resident, whether that individual died with a will or without one.

It is designed to apportion your estate according to your own wishes if you have a will, or according to how the state sees fit if you don't. Naturally, it is also created to see that your creditors are satisfied and that any legitimate taxes due on your estate are paid before assets are disbursed to your family and friends.

If an individual dies with a will, the presumed beneficiaries bring it to the probate office. If he or she dies intestate, again heirs come in, this time with a list of the deceased's (or decedent's, in legal parlance) assets that comprise an estate, in order to begin probate administration. They file a "petition for probate," a simple form that contains essential information needed by the court, such as name and address of the deceased, and names and addresses of relatives and likely heirs.

Most times the family member or other individual petitioning an intestate estate to be settled through probate must post a bond, to cover any loss to the estate caused by their negligence or malfeasance. That might be, oh, let's say a bond of $17,000, for which the executor might pay a fee, or a premium, of maybe $100 a year until the estate is settled (and most estates are settled in less than a year). That cost varies, however. The executor would go to a local insurance company that has bonding power to purchase the bond, and then would return with it to the court. The premium cost comes out of the estate, not the executor's pocket.

(You'll find out more about probate court in Chapter 9. I thought you needed to know a little about the process right now, in the context of dying intestate.)

Estate Exceptions

There seem to be exceptions to almost every explanation. There is one with probate, too.

A *probate estate* is defined as property a probate court has to administer. But there is property that *doesn't* go through probate. That's what you own jointly with right of survivorship, which I discussed in Chapter 3. Also, if you have a life insurance policy, a pension fund and other investments with a named beneficiary, then those assets also skip probate and go directly to the person named.

As a matter of fact, what with the above-named exclusions, sometimes there is little that *is* subject to probate these days. That might be done on purpose by the deceased, to avoid having his or her heirs spend time and money in probate court. Sometimes, though, it's just a coincidence on the part of the deceased.

Speaking of heirs, I'll digress a little here for a brief explanation. Technically, the word *"heirs"* is used for those who inherit in an intestate estate, *"beneficiaries"* for those who inherit from a legitimate will. Sometimes the terms are used interchangeably. I'll try to keep them separate throughout these pages, but once in a while you'll probably find I've just used one word or the other.

Quote, Unquote
When it comes time to divide an estate, the politest men quarrel.
—*Emerson, Journals (1863)*

How the State Determines Your Heirs

Once your assets—minus a will—land in probate court, the process of settling the estate begins. Here is an example of how that court's thinking might proceed, again noting there are slight differences among states.

Let's use a typical family as an example. Albert is married to Susan. They have three adult children: Ken, Betty and Clark. Ken has one child, Alice; Betty has no children; Clark has two, Chloe and Charity. Albert's father is deceased, but his mother is alive.

Albert dies without a will. Who inherits his probate estate?

In many states, that estate would be divided as follows: One half to Albert's wife, and one half divided equally among each of his children.

Some states give everything to the spouse, while others would give the spouse a specified amount of money from the estate, plus one half of the rest of it.

Albert's mother and his grandchildren would receive nothing.

Let's vary Albert's situation a little. Here are some other lifestyle possibilities for him.

Quote, Unquote
Once in every half-century, at longest, a family should be merged into the great, obscure mass of humanity, and forget all about its ancestors.
—*Nathaniel Hawthorne, The House of the Seven Gables*

Quote, Unquote
Nothing is more difficult, and therefore more precious, than to be able to decide.
—*Napoleon Bonaparte*

➤ Let's say Susan is his second wife, and the children are all from his first marriage.

Susan may receive only one-third of the probate estate and Albert's children share the balance. Some states give the subsequent spouse, who had no children with the deceased, less than half the estate.

Once again, Albert's mother and his grandchildren receive nothing.

If there is no surviving spouse, but there are children, then the children receive the entire probate estate.

Grandchildren inherit their deceased parent's share. So if Clark were deceased at the time of Albert's death, his two girls Chloe and Charity would inherit Clark's share of his father's estate.

➤ If Albert were single—there is no surviving spouse and no surviving children—then most state intestate laws divide the probate estate among the parents and siblings. If the parents are deceased, then it is just among the siblings. If Albert had no brothers or sisters, the estate could be divided among his grand-parents, if they are living, and aunts, uncles and cousins.

➤ If Albert were single but had been in a 10-year, live-in relationship with Lee, then since Albert died without a will Lee would come in for no portion at all of Albert's estate. (There is more about "living together" outside of marriage in Chapter 13.)

If you're preparing a will, you can apply all of the above family situations to your own position, and discuss with your attorney just who you want your heirs to be.

Here is a chart to help you see at a glance how states typically divide the estate of a resident who dies without a valid will.

Dying Without a Will: How the State* Is Likely to Divide Your Estate

If you are:	Your property will go:
unmarried with no children, parents alive	to your parents and possibly brothers and sisters as well
unmarried with no children, parents dead	to your brothers and sisters; if an only child, to other next of kin: grandparents, aunts, etc.
unmarried with children	to your children, but not step children. The court also appoints a guardian for minors.
unmarried with no relatives	to the state
married with children	often divided between spouse and children
married with no children	usually to the surviving spouse, or part to the spouse and part to your parents, perhaps even siblings

State laws vary slightly regarding intestate property distribution.

The State Specifies the Guardian, Too

If you have minor children (under the age of 18), and your spouse survives you, then you won't need a guardian. However, if the other parent is not alive, or is not capable of caring for the minor children, or a child of any age with special needs, then a guardian is necessary for them if you die.

Naturally, parents of young children should appoint a guardian for them in the event they both die at the same time. Naming a guardian is especially important in a one-parent situation.

Let's consider Jane's situation. It is a potential guardianship nightmare because there is no will. Her husband passed away several years ago. Jane has two minor children, Jason and Joan, both in their early teens. Since Jane doesn't have a will designating who will be guardian, then state law takes over.

Whom would the state appoint? Well, grandparents and siblings are usually in line for that appointment. If they agree on who will care for the child, fine. But if they cannot, then a court battle may ensue.

It's bad enough to have relatives fighting over child custody. Worse yet is when *no* family member wants the child or children. Perhaps both sets of grandparents in Jane's situation define their golden years as not including child rearing. And Jane's siblings might have

Watch Out

It's trendy, but is it legal? If you'd like to try 'shooting' a video will, which is a videocassette of you reading your will out loud—and probably with comments from you throughout—you ought to consult a lawyer to see whether your state law permits a video will to substitute for a proper written one. The video might only be considered a supplement to a written will.

children of their own and say quite frankly they don't want to be responsible right now for a couple of teenagers.

What happens then?

Jane could have a close friend who would be competent, and quite capable and willing to serve as guardian. But the friend might not be able to take on that role without being nominated in Jane's will. Can Jane's kids recommend that friend? Sure, and since they are older children, the judge is likely to listen to their recommendation and seriously consider that nominee.

But if there is absolutely no one to take Jane's kids—and surely if the situation became that desperate one would hope that a set of grandparents or a sibling would step forward—the kids become a ward of the state, and are then placed in a foster home. They are, after all, orphans.

If you have a will, name a primary and alternate guardian to be sure that one will serve. Always get that family member's or friend's permission before naming him or her as guardian. A guardian is not required to serve just because you name that individual.

You can see that a will matters with property, but that it is absolutely vital when it comes to the welfare of your children. There is far more about guardianship when I talk specifically about kids and your estate in Chapter 11.

The Administrator: It Could Be a Stranger

The *executor* of an estate is a person nominated to handle the disposition of that property according to the wishes of the deceased. We'll get into that role in more detail in Chapter 9.

Tip

Here's another good news/bad news reason for having a will. The good news: If you die in an accident of some kind, a court could bring in a sizable judgment, payable to your estate. You'd certainly want that money to go to specific loved ones. (The bad news? You're not around, of course, to enjoy the windfall.)

The *administrator* of an estate is an individual appointed by the probate court to handle that function for the deceased who dies intestate.

While you are apt to ask a relative or friend to be your executor, if you die without a will there could be a stranger handling your estate, and dealing with your family on estate-related, certainly personal, matters. The judge has quite a bit of leeway in appointing an administrator, and could even name a friend of his to that position.

The administrator usually is paid for his or her services. Fees run quite a wide range. I hesitate to offer even a ballpark figure because so much depends on the size of the estate and the amount of work facing the administrator. But I'd say perhaps that fee could be as much as 5 percent of the estate's worth. It is paid from the estate before any part of it is disbursed to heirs.

The administrator handles the paperwork of an estate, such as composing a list of the deceased's assets, hearing from likely heirs, processing claims from creditors, and the like.

Divorce, Remarriage—and No Will

There are complications here, too, as you might imagine.

Consider Hank and Wanda. The couple both work outside the home. Wanda had been previously married and has one child from that union, Willie, who is under 18. Hank likewise had had an earlier marriage, and he has two minor children: Hank Jr. and Karen. Hank and Wanda have one minor child, Holly.

Wanda has custody of Willie; Hank does not have custody of his children from the prior marriage.

Wanda dies suddenly. She does not have a will. Let's look at possible consequences:

➤ **Inheritance** Wanda owned the house where she and Hank lived, and she had a substantial investment in stocks and bonds in her own name, all of which is in her probate estate. What happens to that property?

In most states the surviving spouse, Hank, will have to divide ownership of the house and investments with Wanda's child of her previous marriage, Willie, and his and Wanda's daughter, Holly, as follows: half to the spouse, and one quarter to each child.

Whether Hank can continue living in the house is a question; he may have to pay rent to the children for their share, or the estate may have to sell the house. Is this what Wanda would have wanted?

➤ **Probate Administration** The surviving spouse is usually, but not always, appointed administrator. If Hank is named to that position, very likely his administration will be closely scrutinized by the child from the prior marriage (Willie) and/or his supporters (his biological father, for example, or a maternal aunt). Because of a potential conflict there, a simplified probate provided for by many states might not be available, so estate expenses could be considerably higher than they would have been if Wanda had had that will.

➤ **Guardianship** Hank and Wanda's child will have Hank around to serve as her guardian. Wanda's son from her prior marriage may have his father appointed as guardian. If the father has been out of Willie's life for years, that may not be a viable option. Hank could be the seemingly likely choice, but he might not be chosen by the court, which could favor the biological father. This could be quite a lengthy, even messy, issue.

71

An additional worry: The guardian manages the minor's money until he or she is 18 years old. What if Wanda's previous spouse had made a career of maxing out credit cards?

➤ **Death Taxes** The tax situation will be worse for Wanda's estate since she has no will. We'll get into tax unpleasantries in detail in Part 4 of this book.

Tip
A written (typed/ computer-printed) will is best. However, some states will recognize an *oral* will or a *holographic* will—handwritten and unwitnessed. A few states have will forms where blanks can be filled in, which is not likely to be useful if you have a large or complicated estate. Check with your state's probate office to be sure what you have in mind is acceptable.

Watch Out
Stepchildren have no inheritance rights under state intestate laws. Children inherit from you if you are the biological parent or the adopting parent. If you want to make provision for your stepchildren, that's another good reason for making a will.

➤ **Simultaneous Death of Spouses** Finally with this couple, we must consider what could happen if both Hank and Wanda died at the same time, in a boating accident, say, or a car or plane crash. Of course neither has a will. All of the problems we just discussed remain, or are magnified. Now we also have an orphan—their child, Holly.

The state would likely split the house and investments that Wanda owned solely as follows: $1/2$ to Willie and $1/2$ to Holly.

Any property that Hank owned solely at his death (which in this example is simultaneous with Wanda's, remember) would likely be shared by Hank Jr., Karen and Holly. However, those children may or may not have a claim for child support from the estate during the rest of their minority, so they may be in financial distress. Children in some states can make a claim for child support from an estate, sometimes until they are 17 or 18, sometimes up to age 21, which can include college expenses. Naturally, Wanda's son Willie could make the same claim against Wanda's estate.

Any property the two owned jointly as spousal property would be equally divided and put into each estate.

For example, Hank's estate would be distributed this way: $1/3$ each to Hank Jr. and Karen (children of a previous marriage) and $1/3$ to Holly (child of a current marriage).

Wanda's share would be divided equally between Willie and Holly.

You'll learn more about simultaneous death of spouses, both with and without a will, in Chapter 10.

Adoption

Adopted children inherit from their adopting parents. In most states the adopted child will not automatically inherit through the biological parent, unless that parent is married to the adopting parent.

So let's look at Al, who adopted Ally, the daughter of his wife, Tracy, from a prior marriage. He and Tracy have a child of their own from their marriage, a son, Cory. Al has no will. If he dies, his probate estate will be divided like this: $1/2$ to his wife and $1/2$ divided equally between the adopted child (Ally) and the biological child (Cory). If he had not adopted Ally, she would have received nothing from his estate.

And Children Born out of Wedlock

Social Security, child support, survivor's rights and inheritance are but a few heavy legal issues swirling around these youngsters.

Clearly, a child born out of wedlock can inherit automatically from his or her mother. What is less certain is the child's inheritance (not to mention support) rights from the father.

Most state laws provide that the child may inherit from the father if paternity is established in court or the father marries the mother and acknowledges the child born out of wedlock as his child.

A *paternity suit* is a court action to have it acknowledged that a man is the father of a specified child and, usually, to secure financial support for that child by that father.

Paternity actions require the assistance of the mother, who is often reluctant to bring the lawsuit for a variety of reasons. The mother may deem the father unfit to fulfill his parental role, or the father could simply have left the scene. If a paternity action is initiated, today's blood tests will disclose whether that man is the biological father.

If there is no paternity action, or marriage between the biological parents, then the child will not be able to inherit automatically from the father or the father's parents without a will.

Have I motivated—or perhaps scared—you into writing a will yet? Good. Now you're ready for the next chapter, in which I'll explain to you just how to go about it.

> **Quote, Unquote**
> Go not in and out in the court of justice, that thy name may not stink.
> —*Ancient Egyptian writing, circa 900 BC*

The Least You Need to Know

➤ If you die without a will, state law specifies who inherits your probate estate.

➤ If you are married when you die and there's no will, your spouse will usually receive half of your probate estate and your children divide the other half.

➤ The court appoints a probate administrator, and a guardian for your children if you have no will.

➤ Adopted children do inherit automatically from the adopting parent, but stepchildren do not when there is no will.

Chapter 7

WILL
I ___ BEING
NAME
OF SOUND MIND
AND BODY, HEREBY
BEQUEATH ALL MY
WORLDLY GOODS
TO ___ NAME/NAMES
(USE BACK IF NEEDED)

X - ___
SIGNATURE

The Basic Will, and a Few Extras

In This Chapter

➤ Identifying yourself

➤ Bills and taxes get paid first

➤ How to determine who gets what

➤ Avoiding snags

Now we come to the most important element of your estate plan: your will. Here you will decide (a) who will inherit your property (beneficiaries); (b) who will administer your estate (executor); and (c) who will take care of your children (guardian).

For the person with an average estate (certainly under $600,000, sometimes several hundred thousand dollars under) and a rather uncomplicated business and family life, this is not difficult work, and the document needn't be long, as you'll see. Short, but important. Let's start.

First, Do You Know Where You Live?

That's certainly a silly question. Or is it? Some of you might have a home here and another one there, perhaps a vacation home—or two.

For purposes of your will, you must clearly designate your legal residence. That is likely to be your voting address, where you have your driver's license and where you file tax returns. It is important to use that address—and have evidence backing it up in the form of those documents—to determine the county and state where your will will be submitted to probate court administration.

If there is no clear evidence of your legal residence, each state where you have a home could claim death taxes against your estate. (There's more about which state to make your legal residence as that decision applies to tax matters in Chapter 18.)

Words, Words, Words
Lawyers use the word **domicile** a lot. In legal documents it means your permanent residence.

Another complication might be that one state in which you own property is a community property state and the other is a common law property state (any state that is not a community property state), so that confusion about your legal residence could provide a nice fee until the retirement of the lawyer hired to sort through the conflicting evidence upon your death.

Incidentally, you may not know that if you own real estate in a second state, probate proceedings are required in that second state to transfer title to your beneficiary. This means that if, for instance, you are a legal resident of New Jersey, and have a second home, say, in Florida, probate will occur in New Jersey for all of your estate except that Florida house. There will be a limited probate, or *ancillary administration*, for the Florida property.

Tip
You can pay anywhere from around $100 to $250 for a will. The fee depends on how complicated the will is, and price ranges of individual law firms.

You should look to a Florida financial institution, or a trusted relative living in Florida, to be your ancillary executor for the property located there. A Florida bank or Florida attorney can help you.

The Simple Will

It helps to see what's being described in text, so I've reproduced here a sample will for you to follow along with me. It's a basic, very brief document that I call "bare bones." It's for a woman who is rather typical in that she leaves everything to her next of kin, which in this case are her spouse and children. There are no other bequests.

You will see from time to time in this chapter and in a few others, that I suggest clauses that should be added to any will. Heed my advice. They are not in the will reproduced here because, as I said, this is a bare bones document just to show you what absolutely must go into a will, not necessarily what also should or could.

I'll explain this will practically line by line so that it's crystal clear to you. Immediately following the will you'll see another document called "Self-Proving Provision." It is attached to a finished will, and I'll explain its purpose after discussing the bare bones will.

First, though, I'll issue the caution you're expecting when you come across a legal form in this book that you or anyone else can fill in: Since state laws vary with regard to an enforceable will, do not adopt this as a will form for yourself without being certain it is valid where you live.

Introduction

This seems clear enough. It introduces the name and residence of the person making the will, and—very important—revokes any prior wills and codicils by that individual. A *codicil* is an amendment to a previous will. (*A warning here*: If you begin re-arranging assets and beneficiaries in a codicil, you're running the risk of having your will challenged, or contested, by a beneficiary or whomever. If you need to make a codicil, keep it short and simple, such as changing your executor from one person to another.) If it's much more complicated, then write a new will.

Use your legal name on your will, of course. That is the name that should appear on all your official papers, such as deeds to real estate, stock certificates, insurance policies and the like. Problems for your estate *could* arise if, for example, you were to refer to yourself on a legal document as Biff Hanover instead of Barton T. Hanover.

Tip

Do you have legal fees you paid for tax advice in connection with writing your will? You're entitled to a federal tax deduction. Ask your lawyer to itemize your bill. I know what you're probably thinking now, but no, you can't deduct an attorney's bill for preparing a will document.

LAST WILL AND TESTAMENT OF

_____

I, _____, of _____, being of sound and disposing mind and memory, do make, publish, and declare this to be my Last Will and Testament, and I hereby revoke all Wills and Codicils heretofore made by me.

I. Identification, Definitions, Comments

    A. I am married to _____. I have _____ children: _____

    B. A beneficiary must survive me by thirty (30) days to be entitled to receive a devise.

    C. "Issue" is to be construed as lawful lineal descendants, and include adopted persons.

Issue shall receive any devise by representation.

II. Debts, Expenses, Encumbrances, Taxes

    A. I direct that my enforceable debts, expenses of my last illness, and funeral and administrative expenses of my estate shall be paid by my personal representative from my residuary estate. In his or her discretion, my personal representative may continue to pay any installment obligations incurred by me during my lifetime on an installment basis or my prepay any or all of such obligations in whole or in part, and my personal representative may, in his or her discretion, distribute any asset encumbered by such an obligation subject to the obligation.

    B. I direct that all inheritance, estate and succession taxes (including interest and penalties thereon) payable by reason of my death shall be paid out of and be charged generally against my residuary estate without reimbursement from any person.

III. Specific Devises

I devise all my personal effects and household goods, such as jewelry, clothing, furniture, furnishings, silver, books, pictures, motor and recreation vehicles to_____. If he does not survive me, I devise said property, in equal shares, to_____. If a child does not survive me, then his or her share devolves to the deceased child's issue, or if none survive me, then the share devolves, equally, to the surviving children.

IV. Residuary Estate

I devise my residuary estate to_____. If he does not survive me, I devise my residuary estate, in equal shares, to_____. If a child does not survive me, then his or her share devolves to the deceased child's issue, or if none survive me, then the share devolves, equally, to the surviving children.

V. Personal Representative

I hereby appoint_____ as personal representative. If he cannot serve, I appoint _____ as personal representative. I authorize unsupervised administration of my estate. I request that the personal representative serve without bond, or if a bond is required, that a minimum bond be required.

My personal representative shall have all powers enumerated and granted to personal representatives under the Indiana Code, and any other power that may be granted by law, to be exercised without the necessity of Court approval, as my personal representative determines to be in the best interest of the estate.

VI. Miscellaneous

If my spouse and I executed Wills at approximately the same time, this Last Will and Testament is not made pursuant to any contract or agreement with my spouse.

I have signed this Last Will and Testament in the presence of the undersigned witnesses on this day of _____, 199__

_____

testatrix

The foregoing instrument, consisting of two typewritten pages, this included, was at _____

(city, state), this _____ day of, 199__, signed, sealed, published, and declared by the testatrix to be her Last Will and Testament, in our presence, and we, at her request and in her presence and in the presence of each other, have hereunto subscribed our names as attesting witnesses.

residing at _____.

Self-Proving Provision

UNDER PENALTIES FOR PERJURY, We, _____ , and _____ ,
the testatrix and the witnesses, respectively, whose names are signed to the foregoing instrument,
declare:

(1) that the testatrix executed the instrument and signified to the witnesses that the instrument is her will;

(2) that, in the presence of both witnesses, the testatrix signed this will;

(3) that the testatrix executed this will as her free and voluntary act for the purposes expressed in it;

(4) that each of the witnesses, in the presence of the testatrix and of each other, signed the will as witness;

(5) that the testatrix was of sound mind when the will was executed; and

(6) that to the best knowledge of each of the witnesses, the testatrix was, at the time the will was executed, eighteen (18) or more years of age.

Date: _____ , 199 _____ ,

_____ , testatrix

_____
Witness

_____
Witness

I. Identification, Definitions, Comments

The document in Paragraph "A" asks for your spouse's name, if you are married, and the number and names of your children, if you have them.

Careful identification of your beneficiaries by name avoids possible confusion. Fathers and sons often have the same name as cousins. There is a boxer who has given all of his sons the same first name as his. In his will he will probably have to label them by order of birth for separate designations.

Words, Words, Words
The word **testament** means a disposition, or distribution, of personal property to take place after the owner's death, according to his desire and direction. It is used, of course, in the expression "last will and testament."

Paragraph "B" seems self explanatory, until you get to the word *devise*. In legal terminology, that means gift. The first sentence in Paragraph "I.C" is understandable. But what is that legalese in the second sentence? (Could it, by chance, have been written by a lawyer?) Essentially it means that *issue* (or children) shall receive any gifts by taking their deceased parent's share that happens to pass on to them through the will.

II. Debts, Expenses, Encumbrances, Taxes

In Paragraph "II.A," that first sentence seems clear. *Residuary estate* means what is left in an estate after debts, taxes and other expenses are deducted and other gifts or bequests made. You'll see that term often in the next chapter. *My personal representative* is your executor. Here you are asking your executor to keep paying installment bills, such as a mortgage, perhaps until the estate is settled.

Let's say you own a cabin by the water, or a cabin cruiser in the water. You leave it to your son. It has a mortgage or other lien, or financial obligation/debt, perhaps a bank loan, against it. In many states your son inherits that property subject to that mortgage or lien. If you want him to have the property free of debt, then you need to specify in your will that the estate pay off that debt.

Tip
You can forget about awarding a family member $1 in your will so that he or she cannot contest that document, and claim the right to more. That $1 business is the legal equivalent of an old wives tale.

Paragraph "B" directs that all due taxes be paid from the estate. I'll get into what those taxes are likely to be in subsequent chapters.

III. Specific Devises

Watch Out
It's best not to make a separate list for special gifts to be attached to your will. If you want specific items to go to certain individuals, then specify that in the will. Many courts do not consider the separate list as part of the will, and do not allow the executor to honor the list.

Here we talk about particular gifts you want to make. This can be almost the fun part of a will, where you look at your possessions and, like royalty, proclaim "I bequeath my stamp collection to..." and so on and so on. You will read more about some different kinds of specific devises later in this chapter.

Listing their current home address after the names of your beneficiaries is not necessary with family members. Believe me, if someone is in your will they will hear about it and will be there to come forward for their bequest. Besides, people do move frequently and addresses become outdated. Friends might be another matter. If you are leaving your sterling silver tea set to a good friend, you might include her address. It will give an executor a place to start with a search, since the family might not know your friend, or have kept up with her moves over the years.

IV. Residuary Estate

This seems pretty clear. In the third line, the word *devolves* means goes to.

Remember, no one can be awarded anything from your will until your debts and taxes have been paid.

Words, Words, Words
Alas, legal terminology remains politically unfashionable in some ways. For example, **executor** is used for a male in that position, **executrix** for a female. A **testatrix** is woman signing her will, a **testator** a man. For ease in reading, I'm using "executor" and, if the occasion arises, "testator" throughout this book.

V. Personal Representative

Here's another section that seems pretty obvious. I'll talk more about executors in Chapter 9.

VI. Miscellaneous

What does that first sentence mean? Briefly, it is there so that no one interprets the survivor's will as unchangeable, written with the spouse as a two-will package. Her spouse's will, if he has one, is a separate document. And this woman *can* write another version of her own will at any time she chooses.

Your lawyer will bring in two witnesses from his office. They must not stand to inherit from the will, and they must "witness" your signing that document in their presence. (If you worry about strangers seeing your will, there is no need. The lawyer can cover all but the signature lines for the witnesses.)

Finally here, there is the document titled "Self-Proving Provision" filed along with this woman's will. A similar form is reproduced here. It is a common page that goes along with a will these days. It avoids the need for witnesses to come to court to identify the signature of the deceased on the will, otherwise usually mandatory.

How to Distribute Your Worldly Goods

In Part 1 you have read how to list your assets, and how you own them. What you need to do now is see in black and white what property you can leave in a will, and exactly what you'd like to bequeath to family and friends before making out that document.

Take a look at the Estate Planning Information Sheet you prepared in Chapter 2. You know that property owned jointly with right of survivorship goes automatically to that other owner and need not be mentioned in a will. Property that names a beneficiary, like a life insurance policy, also skirts probate.

However, if you have any of the following:

➤ Solely owned property

➤ Property held as tenants in common

➤ Your share of community property

➤ Life insurance, retirement plan or employee death benefits or any similar asset with no named beneficiary

then those assets are distributed in your will. Here's a worksheet to fill in that will help you sort out what you can bequeath, and whom you would like to receive that property. You might want to work this out in pencil—you could change your mind a few times before deciding on final dispositions.

Will Worksheet

Here's some homework. Doing it will help you see what assets you have to leave in a will and, if you bequeath them to anyone at all, whom you would choose. This is just a scratch sheet to help you in thinking about bequests, so mark it up as much as you like and perhaps use pencil so that you can easily erase and make changes.

In column one, "Assets," you might, for example, list your condominium. In column two, you could jot down 'solely.' In the third column you might write 'no.' Then, under 'I'll leave it to:' in column four, you can name the person you'd like to inherit the property if you do not own it jointly, or if you have already named a beneficiary.

Asset	How I own it	Does anyone automatically inherit?	I'll leave it to:

Who Gets What

If you are single, you will probably leave assets owned by you alone to anyone you choose—parents, siblings, a significant other, friends. There is no usual "order" here.

If you are married, then you probably want your spouse to inherit, and can so specify in your will. Your children are likely to be next in line. Who receives what and in what percentage is up to you—or almost. Please read Chapters 11 and 12 about spousal and family rights before finalizing your disbursements to see if the information there must affect your decisions.

How They Get It: The Specific Devise

You usually provide for the distribution of tangible personal property, such as household goods, automobiles, antiques and collectibles, tools, jewelry and sporting equipment in the specific devise section of your will.

Tip
You've read about a video will. Can you present your will out loud, just by speaking it? An oral will, usually in the presence of witnesses, is recognized by a few states. Usually it is limited to those on their deathbed, and those in military service. It may dispose of personal property only, and is limited to no more than $1,000 of that property.

I once had a client who owned an extensive collection of Hummel figurines. She bequeathed each one to a different family member or friend, a list that ran two single-spaced legal size pages. That was her prerogative, of course, and many do leave specific items that do not necessarily have monetary worth, but perhaps have heirloom value. Or perhaps pass along a particular memento to close friends.

Specific devises may be for specific property, for a sum of money, or from a specific source. For example, you could say:

> I devise my diamond wedding ring to...

> I devise the sum of Five Hundred Dollars to...

> I devise one half of my Trustworthy Bank savings account to...

Often you will have several beneficiaries sharing in your specific devises, such as children. You should consider how amicably they will divide that property. If you believe amicable won't enter into it, then your will should carry a provision specifying a method of selection, such as rotation among the children, with specific dollar limits for each rotation.

That could work like this. Sandy, Ginger, and Toni are each allowed to select $1,000 of personal property from your estate. They can make their selection in whatever

Tip
If you have keepsakes or family heirlooms, consider asking your children now if they wish one day to inherit specific items that might have special meaning for them.

order you like, perhaps with Sandy, the oldest, going first, then Ginger, and finally Toni, the youngest, choosing. The next $1,000 of property is rotated, with Toni now having first dibs on the remainder of the property, with Ginger next and Sandy following her. That should keep everyone happy and not bickering over the tea towels.

Oops: When Beneficiaries Die Before You

You need to consider that the person given the specific devise might not survive you. The provision "I bequeath my Rolex watch to my cousin, Fay Summersby, if she survives me" is preferable to just bequeathing the watch to Fay. If you don't name an alternative to Fay, the watch will go to the residuary beneficiary.

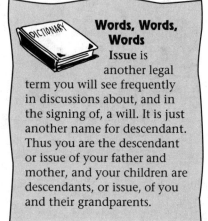

Words, Words, Words
Issue is another legal term you will see frequently in discussions about, and in the signing of, a will. It is just another name for descendant. Thus you are the descendant or issue of your father and mother, and your children are descendants, or issue, of you and their grandparents.

Many states—and you can ask your lawyer if yours is one—have an *anti-lapse law* which provides that another of your descendants will receive the specific devise from your will if the descendant you named did not survive you.

Here's how that works. Suppose that this chart represents your family:

You and Your Spouse

Your Daughter, Debbie

Your Daughter's Child, Geraldine Carole

Your Daughter's Grandchild, Georgia Gloria

In your will you left a specific devise of your grandmother's ruby ring to your daughter, Debbie. If your daughter predeceases you and you haven't made a new will, then the anti-lapse statute would automatically provide that her child, Geraldine Carole, your grand-daughter, would receive the ring.

The anti-lapse statute only applies to descendants. For example, if in your will you leave me $1,000—for which I truly thank you—and if I die before you do, since my descendants aren't yours, they receive nothing. If no one is alive to receive that ring, it goes to the residuary beneficiaries in the will.

Or When You No Longer Own What You've Willed

Let's leave the anti-lapse statute, and consider another potential problem with wording in a will. Let's say you leave your collection of baseball cards to your friend, Mickey. But then your mother, in a cleaning frenzy, tosses them out at some point (an often-told tale of woe). Or you sell the collection to George Steinbrenner. And you die without changing your will.

Common sense (not always applicable in the law!) would dictate that Mickey gets nothing. Your will only distributes what you own at your death, and the cards are now long gone. But more than one court has held that the equivalent amount in cash should be distributed to that beneficiary.

You might want to put in the will the phrase

"...if I own the collection at my death."

That should take care of that.

Here's still another occasion for misunderstanding. Let's suppose you want to leave "100 shares of Brewski Co. to my friend, Ted Foster." In these days of mergers and business tremors, strange things have happened to corporate stock. Perhaps the best solution is to word this as follows: "I devise to Ted Foster the amount of stock I own in Brewski Co., or its corporate successor, at my death." That's better.

> **Watch Out**
> Be very careful to identify beneficiaries specifically. No one receives anything from your will unless he, she or it (such as a pet, which we'll get into later in this chapter) is named: Joseph Carl Turner, Spot or the American Heart Association. You can identify a person as "child" or "my aunt," if you have only one of each, but if there are others, use the specific name.

Finally here, add up all your specific devises to determine if they significantly reduce what the residuary beneficiaries receive under your will. After all, they are the persons you want to receive the bulk of your estate. Don't shortchange your family by being too generous to others in specific gifts.

How They Get It: The Residuary Devise

You may have an extended family of the yours, mine, and ours variety. You and your spouse each have children from a prior marriage, as well as children from this union.

Let's consider the possibilities here. Remember that the residuary beneficiary receives the balance of the estate after your special devises, and, of course, after debts have been satisfied.

Perhaps you want everything to go to your spouse. Fine, just say that in the will. What about the children? Therein might lie some difference of opinion between spouses (but remember, your will can be different from your spouse's). If you name your spouse as residuary beneficiary, but don't specify further, then you have a problem. Your estate could go intestate since you do not have a surviving beneficiary by name. It's best to name an alternate beneficiary to your residuary estate. That might read like this:

> ...if my brother, Seth A. Baker, does not survive me, then his share devolves to his children who survive me.

Do you think you might have more kids one day? Then you should provide for them in your will, too. State laws vary here, but most allow a child born after you make your will to inherit through the will even if he or she is not named. The safe practice, though, is to specify that possibility with a phrase like this:

"to my daughter, Rose, and to any afterborn or adopted children of mine…"

Here's a reminder in passing: Children *can* be cut out of a will (except in Louisiana, where they have something called forced heirship). I tell my college students they had better be *very* nice to their parents.

Also here, you may choose to divide the residuary estate into several shares going to different persons or institutions. For example:

> I devise my residuary estate as follows: 45 percent to my brother, Seth A. Baker; 45 percent to my sister, Charlene C. Dewey; 10 percent to the Sierra Club.

Briefs

Jack Kelly, self-made Philadelphia millionaire and father of the actress Grace Kelly, wrote his own will. "For years," it went, "I have been reading Last Wills and Testaments, and I have never been able to clearly understand any of them at one reading. Therefore, I will attempt to write my own will in the hope that it will be understandable and legal. Kids will be called "kids" and not "issue," and it will not be cluttered up with "parties of the first part," "per stirpes," "perpetuities," "quasi-judicial," "to wit," and a lot of other terms that I am sure are only used to confuse those for whose benefit it is written. This is my Last Will and Testament and I believe I am of sound mind. (Some lawyers will question this when they read my Will; however, I have my opinion of some of them, so that makes it even.)"

Hey, What About Rover?

Oh, yes, your pets. I wouldn't think of forgetting them. If you are married, your spouse will probably take over caring for Fluffy and Spot. But if you are single, you'd had better give some thought to who *will* care for those animals after you're gone.

Remember, if you die intestate, a judge will decide who gets the animals. If you have a will, you have more control over their fate.

It's smart to ask the person you'd like to be responsible for your pets before including him or her in your will as "beneficiary," if you will, of the animals. Even smarter is to name an alternate in the event your first choice is unable to come through. You might want to include a small (or larger, if you can afford it) sum of money as a gift to that individual for taking over the care of your pet. If you have a quite sizable estate, you probably have a trust and can authorize payment to that person periodically for Pywacket's care.

If you find no one willing to take your animal(s), you might look into humane societies in your area that accept household pets, giving them a home there for the remainder of their lives. Ask your veterinarian about places like that in your region, then give them a call.

If there's any doubt about who will care for a beloved pet, resolving that concern can bring you as much peace of mind as having a will made. Perhaps more.

Now you know what a simple, and slightly more complex, will is. But before you run out to have one prepared—a quite commendable step—you will want to read the next chapter, about trusts. A trust could serve you better than a simple will. Also, there is more information in upcoming chapters that could have some bearing on the contents of your will. So continue reading and gathering information before having that document drawn.

Incidentally, it's best not to keep your will in a bank's safe deposit box since that could be sealed on your death. Keep a will in a fireproof box or safe in your home. Or at your lawyer's office.

The Least You Need to Know

➤ A will can be the simplest of documents, or as complex as your needs and wishes require.

➤ You have quite a bit of latitude in leaving what you solely own to anyone you choose.

➤ Wording is important in seeing that your gifts go to the beneficiary you select.

➤ Don't write your will just yet—continue reading.

A Trust and a Will (The Best of Both Worlds?)

In This Chapter

➤ How a trust works

➤ Who's a trust for

➤ Living and testamentary trusts

➤ Selecting a trustee

➤ But you also need a will

Depending on the size of your estate, and what you would like it to accomplish for you, a trust can be an excellent financial tool.

A trust will see that your estate directives are carried out now, or that your assets are passed along to your beneficiaries. It can save you money, through your own funding of it and in tax strategies. And it has some other pluses that you'll learn about a little later in this chapter. Drawbacks? Well, of course there are a few. I'll talk about them as we go along, too.

Definition, Please

A *trust* is a legal instrument to hold and manage your real property, and your tangible and intangible personal property. Putting all of those assets into a trust transfers them from your ownership to the ownership of that entity known as the trust. That trust will hold the property for your benefit, or for that of anyone you name.

Trusts can be set up and run while you are alive, or you can prepare a trust as you would a will, to take effect upon your death. For example, in this chapter I'll talk about a *living (or inter vivos) trust* and a *testamentary trust*. Generally speaking, as you can pretty much determine from their names, one is set up for use in your lifetime, the other (the testamentary trust) comes into existence after your death, when your will is probated. More about them later.

Quote, Unquote
Money, big money (which is actually a relative concept), is always, under any circumstances, a seduction, a test of morals, a temptation to sin.
—Boris Yeltsin, *The Struggle for Russia (1994)*

A trust used to be just for the very wealthy, or at least that's what most of us thought. But in the last decade or so the use of trusts has grown significantly in popularity as more and more folks of less than millionaire means take advantage of their benefits. However, the workings of a trust are still not that well known by the average person. How a trust can help in estate planning is also a mystery to many.

What a Trust Offers That a Will Does Not

A trust has several advantages over a will. It:

➤ Manages property for you while you are alive.

➤ Can reduce your taxes, depending on how it is written and on laws in your state.

Tip
You can, if you like, skip generations in your trust, with income going to your children, and the principal secured for future grandkids.

➤ Easily transfers your assets to beneficiaries after death.

➤ Could allow you more flexibility in how you dispose of your assets—for example, passing your money on to your children from a prior marriage while omitting your present spouse.

➤ Avoids probate, and its time and expense.

➤ Protects your privacy; it is not filed and open to public scrutiny the way a will is.

Who Would Want or Need a Trust?

People establish trusts for a number of reasons, but these are the main ones:

➤ **Minor children**. Parents might use a trust for minors after their death, or for the special-needs child of any age throughout his or her life. You'll read about trusts for kids in Chapter 11.

➤ **Spendthrift children**. A trust can be set up for a child of any age thought to be unable to manage money prudently. I'll talk about a trust for the adult child (sounds like an oxymoron, doesn't it?) in this chapter.

➤ **Retirement management**. If you want a trust to manage your funds during your retirement, no problem. It can take care of you and your spouse when you can no longer look after your affairs, too.

➤ **Tax planning**. A trust can help you in a number of ways here, not the least of which is legitimate tax avoidance, always a welcome benefit of any estate plan. If your estate is over $600,000, then you can certainly make use of a trust for tax savings.

➤ **The charitable trust**. You may be philanthropically inclined, and want to establish a trust, perhaps for worthy college students attending your old alma mater. Or you might have a pet charity you'd like to contribute to in an ongoing way. Or you could participate in a trust already established by your favorite charity. The choice is yours. I'll explain charitable trusts in Chapter 17.

Who Does NOT Need a Trust

Would a trust be right for you? That would depend on the size of your estate, and your plans for it. If you have few assets right now—say you're young and single, or newly married and just starting out—you can skip a trust for a while. If none of the earlier-mentioned family or lifestyle situations quite fits your needs at the moment, you do not need a trust.

Keep in mind that a trust is likely to be more expensive to set up than having a will drawn. You might have to pay around $1,200 for a trust versus a couple of hundred dollars, or less, for a will. So a trust's cost alone might put off some, which could be another good measuring device for deciding whether or not you need one.

(Speaking of cost, by all means comparison shop when looking for a lawyer to set up a trust for you. You should be able to do better than that high-end figure cited above.)

Words, Words, Words
Boilerplate is a slang word for standard paragraphs and clauses you'll find in legal documents—wills and trusts, for example.

Here's the Lingo

More words! Each area of the law has its terminology, of course. You've been introduced to many terms so far in this book. Here are a few more—words having to do with trusts that I'll be using in this chapter, with an explanation of each, to help you as you read on.

➤ **Creator.** This is the person who establishes, or sets up, the trust. That's you in other words. The creator can also be called the grantor, donor, settlor or trustor.

➤ **Beneficiary.** You probably have a handle on this term by now—it's the person who receives property, in this instance from the creator, according to the provisions of a living trust.

➤ **Trustee.** This is the individual or institution entrusted to carry out the terms of the trust. So it's the person, (or institution) who turns property owned by one person (you) over to another, in accordance with your wishes as creator. A trustee also invests property for the beneficiary's benefit. A trustee can be a relative, friend, lawyer or bank; these are—the most common choices.

➤ **Successor Trustee.** This is the second-string trustee, also known sometimes as the surviving trustee. He or she continues to manage assets in the trust should the primary trustee die or become incompetent.

➤ **Trust Estate.** All the property legally transferred to the trust by the creator for the benefit of the beneficiary or beneficiaries.

➤ **Trust Agreement.** This is the legal document itself, spelling out the terms of the trust and how it is to be administered.

Briefs

The Roman Emperor Augustus (63 BC–AD 14) is said to have instituted trusts. They first appeared as a method of apportioning assets, for the most part to family members other than the oldest son, who otherwise was always the sole inheritor. There are records that credit Augustus with using a trust to try to make inheritance fairer for younger sons, who often suffered financially from that custom.

And Thomas Jefferson set up a trust to avoid passing his estate to his bankrupt son-in-law, who would control Jefferson's daughter's property (those were the days before women could own property in their own name).

One Choice: The Testamentary Trust

A *testamentary trust* is a directive established in a will and is effective when the will is probated. It isn't a separate document, it's incorporated in that will. Your assets are just transferred to the trustee as if that trustee were the beneficiary of the will (which he is in a way because he's holding your property for the real beneficiary). For example, the wording might be "I devise my residuary estate to ABC Company as trustee for my sons, John and Jeffrey."

The trust survives probate and goes on to exist as long as you, the creator, have designated. A standard will, of course, is wrapped up and the assets distributed after probate proceedings.

Downside to This Kind of Trust

Well, with a testamentary trust your assets have to go through probate, and are subject to creditor's claims. So if your goal is to avoid probate, you'd be better off setting up a living trust.

Another Choice: The Living Trust

The client was reluctant to sign her will, thinking it her death warrant. The sagacious attorney suggested she might sign a "living trust." She signed.

The terminology is simple here. A *living trust* is a legal instrument established during its creator's life. It might serve as a partial substitute for a will. At the death of the person creating the trust, his or her assets are distributed to beneficiaries according to the terms specified in the trust.

You designate a trustee, who can be your spouse, another person, or a financial institution, like a bank's trust department. It's your choice (you'll read about determining a choice later).

Tip
Keep in mind a trust may not exist forever. It can last until a date you specify in the trust document, or upon a particular event—the date a young child reaches a particular age, for instance. Many states limit a non-charitable trust to 90 years.

Watch Out
Don't confuse a living trust with a living will. The latter relates specifically to health matters.

A living trust would also be a choice for what I referred to earlier in this chapter as your adult child who perhaps spends too freely. Or you might have an older child who, at the moment, is involved in drugs or alcohol. The umbrella term for a solution in those situations is known as the *spendthrift trust*, and is set up to prevent that child from spending a legacy foolishly. With this trust, specified amounts of money are released periodically to the beneficiary rather than a lump sum as in the case of most bequests. There are other restrictions, too, to that child's access to his or her inheritance.

A living trust can be established in either of two styles. You must determine which you want at the time the trust is set up.

Revocable Living Trust

This type of trust gives you the freedom to sell, spend or give away your assets while you are still alive. You can change any of the trust's conditions, too.

A revocable living trust may be an important part of your estate plan. It isn't for everyone, but it does have some features that warrant your attention:

Tip
If you act as your own trustee, you are likely to specify that the alternate trustee begin serving when you become incompetent. Who makes that decision? You might put into the trust agreement a clause stating that there will be medical evidence of incompetence from your own physician. A lawyer can help you with the wording, in accordance with your wishes.

➤ Assets in the trust pass to the trust beneficiaries outside of probate

➤ Creator(s) can serve as trustees or select another to serve

➤ The alternate trustee can serve when the creator/trustee is no longer capable

➤ The trust can receive assets from the creator and the creator's estate

The revocable living trust does not have any special tax advantages, since all income is taxed to the creator, and the assets are subject to federal estate taxes upon the creator's death.

On the following pages is a sample of such a trust, to give you an idea what such a document can contain. Again, be careful, if you want to use it yourself, that it is all right to do so where you live.

Irrevocable Living Trust

This trust, which is not as popular, allows you to make a gift of property while you are still alive. That gift is then subject to federal gift tax, paid by the donor, which is discussed in Chapter 16. Here, however, you forfeit all control of it in order to receive an exemption from federal estate taxes. So you'd better be careful: Once this trust is established, it is impossible to revise.

The irrevocable trust is often used to minimize estate taxes for the wealthy who can afford to give away assets to others, such as children or grandchildren.

REVOCABLE TRUST AGREEMENT

This Trust Agreement is made this _____ day of _____, 199_____, at _____, between _____, the Creator and _____ also serving as the Original Trustee under this Agreement.

The Creator desires to establish a Trust for the purposes outlined in this Agreement, and has enumerated the terms and conditions that the Trustee shall follow in administrating the Trust corpus.

Article I

The Creator has delivered to the Trustee the property indicated in Exhibit A attached hereto, receipt of which is acknowledged by the Trustee of the Trust by signing and dating Exhibit A.

That property and any other property that may be received by the Trustee from the Creator as additions to this Trust, shall be held and disposed of by the Trustee in accord with the terms stated in this Agreement. Property other than cash may be added to the Trust and any property added to the trust shall be acknowledged by the Trustee by signing and dating additional exhibits, and any such property added to the trust shall be retitled in the name of the Trustee designating that they are holding the asset in their capacity as Trustee.

Article II

Creator may, by signed instrument delivered to the Trustee, revoke this Agreement in whole or in part or amend it, but no amendment changing the powers, duties, or compensation of the Trustee shall be effective unless approved in writing by the acting Trustee.

An individual Trustee may resign by giving the Creator written notice thirty (30) days in advance of the effective date of the Trustee's resignation. If there is no Successor Trustee designated, then the personal representative of the estate of _____ shall designate a Successor Trustee.

Article III

During the life of the Creator, the Trustee shall pay all the net income of the Trust estate, and such portions of the principal as the Creator may from time to time direct in writing. However, during any period in the Creator's life in which he is deemed mentally and/or physically incapacitated pursuant to a medical statement obtained from the Creator's physician, wherein said physician is of the medical opinion that _____ is unable to handle his financial affairs or make financial decisions, then the Successor Trustee shall proceed with the administration of this trust and shall, in their sole discretion, use so much of the net income and any portions or all of the principal to maintain the lifestyle of the Creator. Disbursement of such amounts may be made by the Successor Trustee as they deem desirable, including to the Creator, to a qualified legal representative of the Creator, to some relative or friend who has care or custody of the Creator, or by the Successor Trustee using such payment directly for the benefit of the Creator. The receipt of any such party shall release the Trustee from any liability for its expenditure. After the death of the Creator, the Successor Trustee shall continue to administer the trust estate as set out in Article IV and V of this Trust Agreement.

Article IV

The Successor Trustee shall continue to hold title to all assets in the trust until appropriate distribution can be lawfully made.

continues

continued

A. In the event that the Creator's probate estate is insufficient to satisfy the deceased Creator's legal debts and obligations, then the Successor Trustee may collect the Creator's bills, debts and expenses incurred as a part of the Creator's last illness and may proceed to pay all legitimate debts of the deceased Creator and may process all medical claims prior to the distribution of the residuary trust estate as provided in Article V.

B. The Successor Trustee may prepare or supervise the preparation of all tax returns that are due as a result of the Creator's death. These returns include the federal estate tax return, any state death tax return, the Creator's personal federal and state income tax returns and federal and state fiduciary tax returns that are required as a result of this Trust. After the appropriate tax returns are filed and the taxes paid, then the Successor Trustee shall proceed to distribute the residuary trust estate as outlined in Article V.

Article V

After satisfaction of the Creator's legal debts, obligations, death taxes, personal and fiduciary income taxes, then the Successor Trustee shall distribute the remaining balance held in the Trust as follows:

If the Creator's spouse, _____ ("spouse") survives the Creator, the Trustee is directed to pay the net income from the trust estate to her at least annually and to use any portion or all of the principal necessary to maintain her lifestyle. At the death of the spouse, the Trustee shall distribute the entire trust estate, in equal shares, to _____ and _____ ("child"); however, if one child is not then living, her share shall be distributed to her issue, and if the predeceased child has no issue then her share shall be distributed to the surviving child, or to her issue if she is not then living. If none of the foregoing survive the spouse, the then Trustee shall distribute the trust estate to the intestate heirs of the Creator who are surviving at the time of this distribution. After the distribution, the trust shall terminate. In no event shall the trust continue in violation of any _____(state)_____ law limiting the term of its existence.

Article VI

_____ as the Original Trustee and all Successors as Trustees under this Agreement shall have all powers enumerated under the (state) Code and any other power that may be granted by law, to be exercised with the necessity of Court approval, as my Trustees, in their sole discretion, determine to be in the best interests of the beneficiaries. Said powers are to be construed in the broadest possible manner and shall include the following and shall pertain to both principal and income, but shall in no way be limited thereto:

A. To retain any property received from the Creator without liability for loss due to lack of diversification or non-productivity.

B. To invest and reinvest the Trust estate in any kind of real or personal property without regard to any law restricting investment by Trustees and without regard to current income.

C. To sell any Trust property, for cash or on credit, at public or private sales; to exchange any Trust property for other property; and to determine the prices and terms of sales and exchanges.

D. To take any action with respect to conserving or realizing upon the value of any Trust property, and with respect to foreclosures, reorganizations, or other changes affecting the Trust property; to collect, pay, contest, compromise, or abandon demands of or against the Trust estate, wherever situated; and to execute contracts, notes, conveyances, and other instruments, including instruments containing covenants and warranties binding upon and creating a charge against the Trust estate.

Article VII

The following provisions govern the administration of this trust as established by the Creator.

A. Any named Trustee of this Trust is relieved from any requirement as to routine Court accountings that may now or may hereafter be required by the statutes in force in any jurisdiction, although it is not precluded from obtaining judicial approval of its accounts. The Trustee shall be required to account on at least an annual basis to the income beneficiary of the trust.

B. This instrument and the dispositions hereunder shall be construed and regulated and their validity and effect shall be determined by the laws of the State of _____.

C. Any Trustee shall be entitled to reasonable compensation for services rendered in administering and distributing the trust property which shall be paid in accordance with an hourly rate if the Trustee is an individual. If the Trustee is a corporate fiduciary, it shall be compensated in accordance with its current fee schedule. During the administration of this Trust, the Trustee shall be entitled to reimbursement for expenses.

D. No person paying money or delivering property to a given Trustee need see to its proper application by the Trustee.

E. In the event that _____ dies, resigns, or is unable to serve as Trustee of this Trust, then _____ is nominated to serve as Successor Trustee under this Trust Agreement. The Successor Trustee shall automatically assume his position as Successor Trustee upon the signing of an oath without the necessity of any Court order or approval of the same.

IN WITNESS WHEREOF, I, _____, have hereunto signed my name as Creator and as the Original Trustee of this Agreement on the day of ____, 199____.

_____, Creator   _____, Trustee

WITNESSES: _____

_____

Funding the Living Trust

Watch Out
Putting your money in a trust *could* jeopardize a homestead exemption, which is a local or state government reduction in your property taxes, or cause your property to be reassessed for real estate tax purposes. You'll want to look into those possibilities, or ask your lawyer for the answers in your situation.

You might want to *fund* the trust, which simply means putting some assets in it to begin with. Once a trust does exist you can add to it if the document allows you to do so. In some states you can set up a fund with just $1 to get it going. Trust language calls this the trust *res* or *principal* (depending on whether you prefer the Latin or English version).

A living trust can have contingent funding, such as a life insurance policy payable to it, or be partially funded at the time it is established, with later additions. A trust can also be funded at the creator's death from his or her probate assets through the will.

The trust principal is invested and generates income, which the IRS likes to see because it can tax that money (the state might tax it, too). That principal may be used by you if you have established a revocable living trust and made yourself a beneficiary. Similarly, you can use that income.

Retiring? How a Trust Can Simplify Your Life

Let's look at an example of a couple who could make good use of a living trust. Reed and Shirley are in their late sixties. They own their home, have household goods, cars, retirement plans, and significant investments in stocks and bonds. They have two adult children who are both married and have children.

The couple have assets worth over $100,000, not counting their home. They truly want someone else to handle their estate so they can enjoy retirement days in other pursuits. Their trust could have the following features:

➤ Reed and Shirley as joint trustees

➤ Trustworthy Bank as the alternative trustee if the two become incompetent or choose to resign as trustees

➤ Trust income paid to Reed and Shirley

➤ Trust principal possibly used by Reed and Shirley as they determine

➤ Assets added or withdrawn by Reed and Shirley

➤ Trust revoked by Reed and Shirley at any time, except after the survivor becomes incompetent or dies

Reed and Shirley may choose to put some or all of their property in the trust. If one of their goals is to avoid probate upon the death of the last of them, they can put their assets, such as their home, household goods, cars and investments into their trust. If they have retirement plans such as 401(k)s and Keough accounts that they want to keep out of probate, they can add successor beneficiary designations, such as their children, to these plans.

If the house is put into the trust, then a deed must be prepared to reflect the trust as holding legal title. Household goods and the cars placed in trust have to be accounted for if sold, exchanged or abandoned. Those complications should be considered before the couple contribute real or tangible personal property to a trust. Certainly putting their liquid *investments*—stocks, bonds, mutual funds and the like—in the trust would be simple.

Quote, Unquote
Cessation of work is not accompanied by cessation of expenses.
—*Cato the Elder*, "De Agri Cultura" *(2nd c. BC)*

Downside to a Living Trust?

Well, one "down" is the foregoing paragraph—all that personal property in the trust could cause a lot of record keeping, too much for some. For instance, would you want to keep records of household items sold at every garage sale you hold? And file paperwork to the trust every time you buy and sell a car? Some assets, like these, can well be kept outside the trust.

Watch Out
You may come across living trusts sold door-to-door, or over the phone by telemarketers. You pay a high fee here for a document that might not be valid where you live. It's wiser to pay a lawyer to answer your questions and draw up a trust document.

How to Select the Right Trustee

If you establish a trust, you name the trustee. His or her duties are specified in the trust and by state law. Naturally you will want to be sure your choice is willing to serve in that capacity.

A trustee's duties may include:

➤ Administering the trust according to its terms

➤ Managing trust property, which can include reinvesting assets

➤ Investing the trust principal

➤ Maintaining trust accounting records

➤ Making tax decisions and filing tax returns for the trust

➤ Distributing assets to various beneficiaries

➤ Terminating the trust at the time specified by the trust agreement

If you are creating a revocable living trust, then you and/or your spouse, if you are married, may be the logical choice for trustees.

Or you might consider appointing co-trustees where one would be a person who understands what you intend the trust to accomplish, *and* an institution. The institution is going to be around, while the individual may retire, become disabled, or die. Review the trustee duties. Do you have a relative or friend who would be capable of and willing to perform them?

Watch Out

It's smart to provide in the trust a way to replace the institutional trustee if the beneficiaries are not satisfied with his or her performance, because of poor investment return or other problems. The replacement should be another institutional trustee.

Since most trusts are not supervised by a court, there is always a danger of misappropriation. If you decide on an individual as trustee, I would suggest at the minimum an annual accounting to the beneficiaries, and a bond taken out by the trustee to protect you from wrongdoing.

If you elect to name an institution as your trustee, investigate the various trust departments at area banks. Discuss their fees (usually a small percentage of the trust assets, probably no more than 5 percent). Inquire about their investment policy and who in the department is likely to invest your assets. Be wary of a trust department that assigns inexperienced employees to your size of trust, or has a high rate of employee turnover. You want continuity and sound investments.

"So I Need a Trust Instead of a Will?"

No, no, no. You almost certainly need a will, even if you have a trust. For one thing, as you have read in this chapter, you probably don't want all your assets placed in a trust. It can be a nuisance to do that with some personal property. There are also items you may inherit or receive as a gift after the trust is established that you elect not to put into it.

So those assets remain outside the trust, even if one day they are subject to probate. You need a will to cover that residue. Probate, as you will see in the next chapter, is not the money gobbler it used to be (and there are legitimate ways around that expense).

Be wary of anyone who suggests that all your problems will be solved by establishing a trust. That just isn't so. On the other hand, if it's right for you, a trust can be an excellent ingredient in a comprehensive estate plan.

Don't forget, though: You still need a good old reliable will.

The Least You Need to Know

- ➤ You don't have to be very wealthy to set up a trust.
- ➤ A testamentary trust is part of a will.
- ➤ A revocable living trust gives you the most freedom; it allows you to change your mind. An irrevocable living trust, on the other hand, is etched in stone, so to speak.
- ➤ Even with a trust you need a will.

All About Probate

I gave you a brief overview of probate and probate court in Chapter 6, pointing out what happens if you have no will (and you won't let that happen, will you?).

There's more to probate than that concise explanation, of course; quite a bit more to this frequently puzzling and misunderstood judicial arena.

Let's Bring This Court to Order

As you learned in Chapter 6, probate provides for an orderly transfer of property from the deceased to his or her beneficiaries.

Let's go on from there.

Laws governing probate procedures vary slightly from one state to another, and so can the court itself. Probate court is under a state's Judicial Department. In some states there is a special court to handle probate and guardianship issues only, while in other states and jurisdictions within a state, a specific court will handle other legal issues along with probate.

There is always a judge presiding at probate court, to oversee proceedings, review various documents—a will, inventory of assets, petitions from possible heirs (we'll get into that later)—and make decisions where necessary. However, this is basically a supervisory role, the only adjudication—handing down of a decision—coming in when a will or claim is contested, or when a guardianship issue must be decided.

Quote, Unquote
Let giving and receiving all be in writing.
—*Apocrypha, Wisdom of Ben Sira 42:7*

Is It Really That Formidable?

Of course not. You may have read or heard over the years that folks seem to run from probate or even the mention of it. The court has had a reputation for being time consuming when reviewing an estate, and expensive, because federal and state governments take a chunk of that estate in the form of taxes. The message you may have picked up in your general reading has been "avoid probate at all costs."

Well, let's see.

If you die without a will, it's true that probate can be longer and more costly for your heirs than if you had had that document.

On the other hand, some folks easily avoid probate because all of their property consists of jointly held assets, life insurance, pensions, and other assets with named beneficiaries, which ordinarily are not subject to probate. You'll recall that from my explanations over the last few chapters. Other people use a trust, which also does not go through probate. So, you see, not everyone makes use of probate court.

Probate really isn't a problem for the average estate, and especially where practically all the decedent's worldly goods go to his or her spouse. There might be a few bequests to other family members, and to friends, but then the estate is closed, usually within three or four months after the time for creditors to file claims has elapsed. That's about four or five months after probate opens. That means most estates should be closed within eight or nine months of death. State laws do vary, and complications arise, particularly if there is no will, numerous heirs, complicated property holdings, business interests, will contests, or complex tax issues.

Quote, Unquote
Let us endeavor to live so that when we come to die even the undertaker will be sorry.
—*Mark Twain*

The probate process is fairly simple to describe, although again, each state varies its system a little.

When a person dies owning solely owned property, or other property that will be in his or her probate estate, someone—usually a relative—contacts the court and asks to open the estate. If there is a will, the family will have read it, and usually it is the executor named in that document who files the petition, and requests the court to open the will to probate.

If there is no will, the court will, as you might recall from Chapter 6, appoint an administrator. (Since an executor and an administrator serve the same function, I'll use the term executor from now on to avoid confusion and save ink. You might want to keep in mind, though, that some courts use the generic "personal representative" for that individual. I'll still stick with executor.)

Simply put, the executor collects the assets of the estate (a written list), pays the estate's debts and taxes, and distributes the balance to the beneficiaries or heirs. I'll talk more about those duties in just a little bit. Then the court terminates probate.

How do creditors know you've died? Well, not very likely by being invited to the funeral! What happens is the court places a notice in your local or regional newspaper, giving that information and asking anyone with a debt to come forward. You might have seen those news items in your local paper. If not, I've reproduced one on the following page to give you an idea what they look like. Incidentally, the fee to run that sort of news brief is paid by the estate.

No Supervision? Whee!

Some states provide for *unsupervised* probate administration, which involves minimal court involvement. It makes the process quicker and less costly than the usual *supervised* administration, which frequently requires court orders and detailed accountings of assets and probate proceedings.

If you foresee battling beneficiaries, then it is probably safer to have supervised administration. The court orders protect the executor from frivolous challenges by disgruntled heirs or beneficiaries.

You might want to check with your attorney to see if unsupervised administration is advisable for your estate, and whether or not you need to request it in your will. In some states you have an automatic unsupervised administration.

Words, Words, Words
Legatee is a word you might occasionally come across in preparing for, and reading about, a will. That is a person to whom money or property is left in a will. However, "beneficiary" is the more common term for that individual.

NOTICE OF ADMINISTRATION

In the _____County Superior Court
Probate Division
In the Matter of the Estate of
Joan Bradford, deceased

Estate Docket
49D08-9702-EU0001

Notice is hereby given that on the 25th day of January, 1997, Matilda Swenson was appointed personal representative of the estate of Joan Bradford, deceased, who died on the 1st day of January, 1997.

All persons having claims against this estate, whether or not now due, must file the claim in the office of the Clerk of this Court within five (5) months from the date of the first publication of this notice or within one (1) year after the decedent's death, whichever is earlier, or the claims will be forever barred.

Dated at _____, this 25th day of January, 1997.

HENRY A. ABERNETHY
Clerk of the _____County Superior Court
Probate Division

Typical legal notice placed by probate court, asking creditors to come forward and file a claim against a deceased's estate.

Duties of Your Executor

Here is what an executor will be required to do, which coincides with what is involved in the probate process:

➤ Petition the court to open probate

➤ Petition the court to admit the will

➤ Notify all beneficiaries to the will, or intestate heirs of the administration of the will

➤ Notify all creditors of the deceased that probate administration is opened (that's the legal notice that will run in the deceased's local paper)

➤ Obtain a performance bond (check back in Chapter 6 for details here)

➤ Collect the deceased's assets and list the assets in an inventory

➤ Seek court approval to sell any assets that might be necessary to pay debts (however, court approval is usually not necessary if a will is properly drafted and includes a power of sale)

➤ Determine and pay claims against the estate

➤ Pay any federal and state income taxes, federal estate, and state death taxes (there's more about these taxes coming up in Part 4 of this book)

➤ Distribute the estate's net assets, according to the court's order, to the will's beneficiaries, or to the heirs if there is no will

➤ Close the estate

Those are the basics. Of course, the estate might have complications that require additional work, such as operating a business for a time and/or selling it; defending a will contest; petitioning the court to interpret a will or determine the appropriate heirs; contesting IRS or state tax determinations and accounting to the court and beneficiaries.

Since state probate laws vary, there may be additional duties, but the ones I have listed are the primary tasks.

Selecting an Executor

Often your first choice will be your spouse. The second may be an adult child. I'll discuss family versus professional executor later, but keep in mind that the more complicated the estate the less likely that your immediate family can or will want to serve as executor.

Here are some questions that might immediately pop into your mind about now regarding an executor. I've added answers.

[1] *Should I ask the executor to serve before I put his or her name in my will?* By all means approach that individual to be sure he or she is willing to take on that responsibility.

[2] *Do I need a back-up executor?* Yes, definitely. The person you name as executor may not be willing or able to serve when the time comes, so always name an alternative executor.

[3] *Does an executor have to know about taxes to do this work?* He or she ought to have a minimal knowledge of paying taxes, although a lot depends on the size of the estate. If it's small, and the executor knows enough to do his or her own taxes, that should constitute sufficient smarts.

[4] *Will the executor be able to do the work required if he or she has a full-time, or even a part-time, job?* Certainly, although that, too, depends on the size of the estate. If the deceased has left a multimillion dollar business, feuding relatives and complicated tax issues, there could be quite a job waiting for the designated person.

[5] *Does the executor have to put up any money to take on this assignment?* No, that performance bond you read about in Chapter 6 is paid out of the estate's assets.

You also need to consider the following when thinking about who might be best suited to handle your estate when you're out of the picture:

➤ **Organizational skills.** If your candidate keeps a good checking account record, he or she should make out fine here. The executor is given a newly set-up estate account, and writes checks and receives money through that account. The deceased's checkbook is rolled into the estate account.

Watch Out
Some of the trickiest parts of an executor's job are tracking down all of the deceased's assets, and putting a dollar value on some of them, like antiques. Keep that in mind when preparing your will.

Quote, Unquote
What's a thousand dollars? Mere chicken feed. A poultry matter.
—Groucho Marx

➤ **Experience in managing assets.** That depends on the size and complexity of the estate. You'll want someone who has at least written a check in his or her life, but the typical estate doesn't present especially tough challenges for anyone you're likely to be considering.

➤ **Investment expertise.** Yes, you might want someone with experience in this area, if the estate is large enough so that money will have to be invested until probate is closed, which could be eight or nine months. Your executor will want to keep a close eye on your other investments, too.

➤ **Ability to get along with your heirs.** This is very important. You want a man or woman who will be contributing to the solution, and not be part of the problem. Choose someone who gets along with everyone involved here, or at least has the kind of temperament that can calm folks down if voices get a little shrill.

➤ **Fees to be charged.** What, if anything, is your candidate likely to charge for performing an executor's duties? Take that into consideration.

Those are some qualities and points to look for in an executor. Sound like anyone you know? Here is a worksheet to help you determine who among your family and friends might fit the bill to handle your estate.

Selecting an Executor

Sometimes choosing an executor is easy: Your spouse wins that slot. Other times the choice can be difficult, as you mentally run down the list of family members and good friends. Here's a worksheet to help you decide whom you might ask—and who would be a good choice for alternate executor.

Name	Organizational Skills?	Experience Managing Assets?	Gets Along with the Family?	Likely to Expect a Fee?	Will Accept the Job?

Best Choice(s) _____

_____

_____

If you think the requirements are a bit heavy for those in your circle, you might want to look to outside assistance.

Help! Bring in the Pros

Many commercial banks have estate departments that provide probate administration services. Instead of appointing a relative as executor, you could select Trustworthy Bank. You might also want to take that route if the assets of your estate are substantial, if there are business interests involved, or tax issues are particularly complex. Probably a bank will only be interested in handling your estate if it has at least $100,000 in assets (not counting your home). They're likely to charge a percentage of the estate, maybe 5 percent, less if the estate is substantially larger, say several million dollars.

Tip
If the trustee you have chosen for a family trust is a bank, then that same institution should be the executor for your will, to ensure continuity of management between the estate and the trust.

If the beneficiaries of your estate are likely to squabble, then you may well want to select an impartial and professional executor. After all, if Johnny and Janey haven't agreed on anything since they were in elementary school, there's no reason to believe they'll get along now handling your estate.

Words, Words, Words
Here are some words you might hear around medium- and large-size law firms. **Associates** are fully qualified lawyers who usually spend several years working for a firm, waiting to be tapped to become a **partner**. **Paralegals** are trained in some legal work, but are not lawyers. They are usually involved in research and rough drafting documents. **Law clerks** might be lawyers, but more often they are law students working for a firm as sort of interns.

Ch-Ching: Probate Costs

Administering a probate estate costs money. Generally speaking, we are talking about these expenses:

➤ **Court filing fee**—That's about $100, it can vary significantly state to state.

➤ **Executor bond premium**—I've already talked about this—maybe $100 or so.

➤ **Executor fee**—Perhaps nothing, otherwise could be as much as 5 percent of the estate.

➤ **Attorney fee**—If your executor chooses a lawyer, an uncomplicated estate should not take a lot of that attorney's time (many use paralegals to do most of the work). Some charge a flat rate, others a percentage of the estate. Again, I'll mention that 5 percent figure. Make sure you understand just exactly what will be included in that fee.

Keeping Those Costs Down

Your estate cannot do much about the filing costs, which are relatively minor anyway. But other fees can be reduced.

➤ Name a family member as executor, if that is appropriate in your situation, because he or she may serve for no fee, or at just a small charge.

➤ If you're dealing with a large estate and opt for a corporate executor, try to negotiate the fee. Many such fees are set, but it's worth shopping around a bit or at least asking the executor you've chosen if she or he will negotiate. As I have mentioned, the larger the estate, the more that fee should come down a bit. The institutional executor usually does not have to pay for a bond, which is a small saving to your estate.

The institutional executor also brings a professional management and investment expertise that may allow the estate to earn more income than would the individual. Too, the corporate executor can use its tax department to make tax decisions which could save the estate considerably in income and death taxes.

➤ If practical, choose unsupervised, rather than supervised, administration. You will recall that earlier in this chapter I touched briefly on the two. Frequently unsupervised administration, or a local, similar version of it, is available and should be used in uncomplicated estates where all beneficiaries or heirs are agreeable toward each other. Unsupervised probate administration, where visits to the probate court only occur to open and close the estate, mean the executor and attorney have less work to do. Their fees should be reduced accordingly.

Tip
If you are concerned that the institutional executor will ignore your personal concerns, like dividing up family mementos, consider appointing a family member as co-executor to the corporate executor. Then you'd have professional management with a personal touch.

How to Avoid Probate

You say you'd like to skip the whole probate process, no matter how much money you can save here and there on expenses?

More than 20 years ago there was a book published called *How To Avoid Probate*. It became an instant best-seller. Probate then was to be avoided or reduced to a minimum. It could be done. It can now, too, and is almost certainly just as good an idea now as it was then.

All you need to do is put your assets in a form of ownership that would not be distributed in your will at your death or go to your heirs, if you die without a will.

Here is a summary of those ownership styles that will avoid probate on your death, if your co-owner or beneficiary survives you:

➤ Joint owners with right of survivorship

➤ Tenants by entirety (spousal real estate)

➤ Surviving spouse's one half of community property

➤ Life estate and remainder

➤ Revocable or irrevocable trust

➤ Life insurance with named beneficiary

➤ Annuities with a successor annuitant

➤ Pension with named beneficiary

Co-ownership only avoids probate if an owner survives. Too often the surviving co-owner doesn't get around to putting another person's name on that document as a new joint owner. Then at the death of that survivor, the property goes into his or her probate estate.

Life insurance policies, many annuities and pension plans permit the owner to name successor beneficiaries.

As long as a beneficiary survives to receive the life insurance proceeds, annuity or pension benefits, those payments will not be included in the deceased's probate estate.

Tip

Review beneficiary designations for life insurance, pension, and annuity benefits periodically to make certain that everyone you currently want to receive those proceeds is named.

Quote, Unquote

A large income is the best recipe for happiness I ever heard of.
—*Jane Austen, Northanger Abbey*

There's another way around probate: the living trust that you read about in Chapter 8. Using a trust avoids probate for all assets put in the trust, assuming that the beneficiaries named are living. Since most trusts go as far down as the second and third generation from the person establishing the trust, this usually isn't a problem.

Of course not all assets are suited for a trust, as you will recall. Too often we become so fearful of probate that we buy a "canned" living trust, fill it out, then forget about it. We assume that our estate is in order. While it just may be, it is more likely we have created chaos for our heirs instead. Determining which property is and is not in the trust (and therefore in and not in the probate estate) can take a great deal of unraveling and be very expensive.

Trusts do have an important role in estate planning. You may certainly be a candidate for one. But avoiding probate shouldn't be your only goal.

Besides, as I have just explained, between having assets in forms of ownership that avoid probate, perhaps having a trust, and taking advantage of the money-saving tips just listed, your heirs' experience with probate shouldn't be that traumatic—or costly.

The Least You Need to Know

➤ All estates, with and without a will, must pass through a state's probate court, for distribution of assets and payment of necessary taxes.

➤ But many of the assets in your estate do not need to go through probate at all.

➤ Choose an executor wisely, according to the demands of your estate.

➤ You *can* shave probate costs—even avoid the process altogether.

Some Unique Probate Situations— Maybe Yours?

In This Chapter

➤ Bigamous marriages

➤ Surrogacy and similar estate puzzlers

➤ Getting an "advance" on an inheritance

➤ Crime *doesn't* pay

Now you know about probate and that court process. It all seems rather clear cut, doesn't it, or at least I hope I've presented it that way.

Ah, but if probate court walls could talk! There is many a twist and turn in estates that have forced a probate judge into the role of present-day Solomon. Sometimes it's a grave Solomon, at other times a judge fighting to hide a smile at a particularly amusing situation or folly of humankind. Here are some variations on simple inheritance issues. Perhaps one applies to you—or might one day.

Love and Marriage(s)

All states recognize solemnized marriages requiring a cleric or a judge, and a few states recognize *common law marriages*. That is when a man and a woman do not have a legal marriage ceremony, but do live together as husband and wife. Some six to eight states recognize common law marriage, but many have abolished it by statute.

Honey, Where Are You?

Throughout this book we have discussed spousal rights in a deceased's probate estate, and assumed, quite understandably, that the spouse was readily identifiable. Well, not every case is that simple.

I had a client I'll call Arnie, who was ready to retire from the military, but had a dilemma that called for legal advice. His pension required him to name his spouse as beneficiary. He had been in the Army, and over the course of his career had been stationed at about nine different bases around the country.

It happened to have been Arnie's habit to select a new wife when he arrived at a new posting. He simply left the previous "spouse" and didn't bother with the formality of a divorce. Sometimes he went through a wedding ceremony with his new bride, but on other occasions the two just began living together as husband and wife.

I reminded Arnie of the law against having more than one wife at a time, and he acknowledged that yes, he had heard something about that. I told him whoever had come first was his legal wife, and the rest were void marriages, which means that no judicial action was necessary to establish that the marriage was invalid.

I thought that might have simplified his problem until I realized his first "marriage" was in a common law marriage state. It would be extremely difficult to determine if he were married or simply cohabiting, since there is no record of a common law marriage, whereas with a legal marriage there is, of course, a marriage certificate that can be produced.

The upshot of Arnie's case? We were never able to determine which "spouse" was which. Actually, Arnie could not even remember the names of some of his blushing brides at those new military assignments!

In the event of his death, could one—or more—of Arnie's wives apply to probate court for spousal rights? Of course, one can *try*. And maybe even win. There is at least one case of a so-called "wife" securing some part of her "husband's" estate, even though there was no marriage. So it isn't a foregone conclusion that, that woman would be left in the cold financially on the death of her common-law husband.

I know *you* will never enter into multiple marriages without making that little side trip to divorce, but keep in mind that bigamy violates civil *and* criminal law. The second "marriage" you enter into without a previous divorce is void. However, children born of a bigamous marriage are entitled to inherit from the father, even though the marriage was invalid. Some states may require alimony be paid to the innocent "spouse," too.

Oooh, That Cold Light of Day

Another client of mine—I'll call her Lydia—was at a party where she met a man who interested her. The feeling apparently was mutual because the two decided to get married that very night. They couldn't do so in Indiana because there was a statutory waiting period, so they drove from Indianapolis straight to Tennessee, and were wed.

The next day, Lydia told me, she woke up with a nasty hangover. There was a man in the room with whom she seemed to have exchanged some serious vows, according to a marriage license on the table. She and her brand-new husband decided to discuss their future, and quickly agreed they had none, at least not together. Since most states require the parties marrying to be sober (or at least not near-coma intoxicated), I suggested that an annulment of that marriage would be possible. Since Tennessee law controlled the marriage, Lydia would have to seek an annulment in that state. She decided upon divorce, but she could have obtained an annulment.

Words, Words, Words
Legally, an **annulment** is a court ruling that says a supposed marriage was never valid. The most common ground for annulment: fraud.

My client's former husband of a few hours will therefore have no claim upon her estate. If she were to die not having married—you'll note I'm not saying "remarried" because their brief union was wiped off the books—he cannot show up in probate court saying he was her spouse just because they were never divorced. An annulled marriage is no marriage at all; there's nothing left to get divorced from.

Pal o' Mine

You may recall that the actor Lee Marvin was engaged several years ago in a noted lawsuit brought by his live-in lover. She sued him to enforce an oral agreement purportedly giving her rights to support and one-half of the property they accumulated during the seven years that they lived together. She argued that for all practical purposes they were living together as common law husband and wife; therefore, she should be entitled to "spousal" property rights. Ultimately the California courts denied her claim. However, some courts *have* awarded recoveries to former lovers on the basis of expressed or implied agreements.

There are two arguments for an award here: 1) palimony is like a marriage and 2) there is some kind of claim for services rendered. Of course, if you define that to include sex, there are laws against that! But it's possible to file a claim perhaps asserting some kind of management of the other person's career.

Marvin's lover's smartest move would have been to have him set up an irrevocable trust for her. Such a trust can never be changed, even if his affection for her someday did. Otherwise, to inherit from him she would have to have been named in Marvin's will.

Birth...

Courts originally disagreed as to whether a child conceived by artificial insemination was legitimate. Fortunately, the statutes in almost all states have clarified that matter.

If artificial insemination is performed under the supervision of a physician, and with the consent of the husband (who is not the donor), the husband is treated as if he were the natural father of the child. The semen donor is not considered the father.

Medical science also makes it possible these days to extract ova from a woman and fertilize them with male sperm, then implant them back into the same woman. Inheritance, child custody and support rights should not be at issue, unless participants other than a husband and wife are involved.

Quote, Unquote
The egg it is the source of it all. Tis everyone's ancestral hall.
The bravest chief that ever fought,
The lowest thief that e'er was caught,
The harlot's lip, the maiden's leg,
They each and all came from an egg.

—*Clarence Day,* "Thoughts on Peculiar Dawns" *(1921)*

Surrogate motherhood for the most part focuses upon the enforceability of the surrogate contract. That usually involves a woman who agrees to be artificially inseminated with the sperm of a man not her husband. The woman would then surrender her rights to the child to the donor and his wife. Often these contracts involve payment to the surrogate mother of money beyond the birth expenses. Since many states have statutes that prohibit selling babies, this arrangement has been challenged. However, the statutes against baby-selling may not apply to the donor-father, since the baby is, after all, his biological child.

Obviously, inheritance, support and custody rights of the child are not easily discerned under these circumstances, particularly as to the donor-father. The wife, for whom the surrogate mother is carrying the child, probably has certain rights. The gist of all this is that the law simply has not yet unraveled this tangled skein to anyone's complete satisfaction.

...and Death

Death used to be defined as the stopping of the heart. That is no longer an adequate definition in a medical era that permits life to be artificially extended by machines.

At the moment of death, the inheritance rights of the heirs or beneficiaries to that individual's will are fixed and determined. A moment sooner or later may make a difference.

I'm not about to discuss the "legal" moment of death—the date and time listed on a death certificate. However, I will examine here the problems involved when related persons die at the same time.

Nearly all states have adopted the Uniform Simulta-neous Death Act. Under this ruling, if there is no evidence that one person survived the other (even for a brief time), then the Act applies as follows:

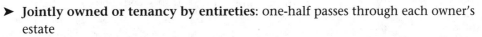

> **Quote, Unquote**
> The art of will-making chiefly consists in baffling the importunity of expectation.
> —*William Hazlitt*, "On Will-Making" *(1821)*

➤ **Wills and intestacy:** the beneficiary or heir is treated as having not survived the deceased

➤ **Life insurance:** the beneficiary is treated as having predeceased the insured

➤ **Jointly owned or tenancy by entireties**: one-half passes through each owner's estate

➤ **Community property:** one-half passes through each spouse's estate

The deceased could have provided in his or her will or life insurance policy that the act will not apply in the event of a simultaneous death with a spouse. The will could state "in a simultaneous death, my spouse is deemed to have survived me."

Let's Not Forget Greed

You might recall the biblical parable of the prodigal son (Luke 15:11). This younger son wanted his share of the family estate before his father died, an event that didn't look like it was going to happen any time soon (Father was in fine health, and seemed nowhere near approaching his final days). The son wheedled his portion from the older man, left home and proceeded to waste the money. Finally, after living in degrading conditions, he came to his senses and returned home. His father welcomed him and forgave him.

> **Quote, Unquote**
> A son can bear with composure the death of his father, but the loss of his inheritance might drive him to despair.
> —*Machiavelli (1517)*

In modern legal terminology, the father of the prodigal son had made a gift to that man against his further inheritance (under intestate law). That is called the law of *advancement.* It does not affect what the prodigal could receive—if his father had, had a will, since advancement only applies in intestate situations. It usually is proven by a written receipt from the individual advancing that money.

Here is an example of how advancement is taken into account in dividing an intestate estate, again using our wayward son.

Assume that the young man received a $10,000 advancement. Then his father dies intestate, leaving a probate estate of $50,000. The prodigal son's advancement would be figuratively added to the probate estate for purposes of division between him and the elder son. That would make the probate estate worth $60,000. It's to be divided equally. Since the prodigal already received $10,000, he would be given only another $20,000 from the estate, with the older brother taking $30,000.

Tip
If there is any inequity in how you leave your children your assets—and there shouldn't be, except for the special-needs child—be sure to spell out your reasons, such as advancing money over the years to one of them. If you do not explain, you'll cause bad feelings among the kids and their resentment toward you.

That should please the older brother. In the parable his nose was quite out of joint at his father's good humor—even celebratory feasting—over his brother's return.

You might want to note here, that if the father had made a will, he might want to follow the same division of his estate. But now that he's setting down his wishes on paper, he could explain a little. To his younger son, after his bequest he might add "I am reducing his share because I have provided for him, etc." The younger brother might have forgotten that gift or gifts over the years. Perhaps the other brother didn't. An explanation is called for.

What Could Be a Problem for You in Probate

Is it real property that could cause you some concern about your estate? Is it a particular relative who might be concerned about an asset of yours? Or maybe there's a gray area in your estate you're just not sure about. Jot down where likely alarms might go off with your will, or later in probate, and what you can do to head them off.

Asset	Possible Problem in Will/Probate	Can I Handle It?	Better Check with an Attorney

Abandoned Spouses and Adultery

This can be a tricky area.

Some state intestate laws deny the spouse who deserts the other, or commits adultery, the right to inherit from that mate. Courts aren't particularly clear on what constitutes desertion, but most require substantial evidence of abandonment before they will impose its forfeiture provisions.

What could that evidence be? Well, if the departing spouse has set up residence elsewhere, especially if he is living with someone else, that could be considered abandonment.

Adultery has a different impact on an estate, or should I say very likely no impact at all. Yes, there is probably in each state some appellate court division that has upheld a ruling in favor of that person's spouse. What you're no doubt looking at here is the adulterer who has set up permanent residence elsewhere. But the ones having, shall we say, a one-time fling? No, that is not likely to impact their estate.

The Missing Spouse

Not to be confused with the mate who has genuinely moved out, or abandoned, his or her spouse, the missing person is, well, just that. There are jokes about the husband who went out for a pack of cigarettes one evening and was never heard from again. On the far more serious side, there is the adult who disappears, perhaps not by choice. Has he or she met with foul play? Years go by with no answers.

The next of kin in those cases would probably ask the court, after the required period of time, to have that person declared legally dead, for inheritance and other purposes.

Murder and Profit? Never!

Most state laws bar anyone who feloniously and intentionally kills from receiving any inheritance from that victim. The statutes bar those found guilty of murder or voluntary manslaughter.

If you watch television news shows and notice a spate of parental killings from time to time, you will be interested to know that those who become orphans by their own hand cannot inherit from the parent-victims.

This bar applies not only to intestate laws, but also to wills and life insurance policies. The killer is treated as if he had predeceased his victim. If the killer and victim had jointly owned property, one-half would go to the deceased's estate and the other half would be owned by the killer. The killer has no further claim to anything solely owned by the victim and his or her half of anything jointly owned.

Words, Words, Words
Corpus delecti, as any mystery fan knows, means the "body of the crime," or proof that a crime has been committed. It does not necessarily mean, as is often assumed, that a body has been found.

Obviously the majority of these cases and examples of problems in probate can be considered pretty rare. The more usual probate estate is quite uncomplicated, causing hardly a flicker of interest in probate court. May your beneficiaries have just such an experience!

The Least You Need to Know

➤ No matter how strange or shady your story, your lawyer must keep it confidential through attorney-client privilege.

➤ Medical marvels in the area of fertility are still presenting puzzles to lawyers and courts when it comes to inheritance.

➤ An advancement to an heir will reduce his or her share of an intestate probate estate. It is usually proven by a written request.

➤ Abandonment and adultery occasionally, more correctly *rarely*, enter into a probate decision; both are difficult to prove.

Part 3
All in the Family—and Just a Little Beyond

What is all this planning for? Or should I say whom is it for? It's for your family, of course, immediate and extended, and perhaps a few very close friends.

So it's important that while you are being so diligent in this work, you anticipate what could call for more attention than usual. Everyone's life is different, of course, with ingredients not quite like the next person's.

In this part of the book you'll learn about some special living situations that might affect you. You will also find out about a few specific, not run-of-the-mill, family circumstances that could have bearing on your will and estate. It certainly pays to anticipate what could go wrong and head off at the pass potential arguments among relatives or—heaven forbid—court decisions one day based on your choices now.

Looking After Your Minor Children

Q: Kids, do we ever stop worrying about them?

A: No, probably no matter how old they—and we—are.

If we are overwhelmed by all that could harm our minor children, what could happen to them if we are not even *here* becomes incomprehensible. What I'll help you with in this chapter is keeping your kids safe, or as safe as it's possible to be with the paperwork anyway, if by some chance you are not around to look after them.

Grim? Sure. But if you grapple with the issue now, you'll feel a lot better knowing your directives are written down and will be followed. Then you can get on with other things relating to the kids that are more fun, like figuring where the money for college is going to come from!

A Minor Issue of Major Importance

You have read in Chapter 6 how important it is to have a will, not just so that your assets will be passed on to whomever you choose, but also for arranging the care of your minor children. (If you have a special needs child of any age, that is certainly a concern to you, too. I'll cover that topic in Chapter 13, although you will still want to read this chapter since there's probably a good deal that will apply to you here as well.)

A *guardian* is a person appointed by law to be responsible for the food, housing, and other needs of a child until he or she reaches legal age. (Of course, guardians are also named for adults who can no longer look after themselves.

Words, Words, Words

A **minor** child is defined by law as one who has not yet reached a majority age. Okay, what's a **majority**? Well, that can vary in different states for different purposes. For example, it might be 18 for voting, 21 for drinking. Some states consider 18 a majority in wills and estates, while others say 21. Throughout these pages we'll use 18 as a majority.

Quote, Unquote
Rigid justice is the greatest injustice.
—*Thomas Fuller, MD, "Gnomologia" (1732)*

Usually your will names a guardian and the court appoints that person or couple, unless the court determines it is not in the child's best interest for the named guardian to serve.

As you saw in Chapter 6, if you are a single parent and have no will, the state decides who'll get to raise your kids. That could be the other biological parent if he or she is living, or your parents or a sibling. If you're starting to hyperventilate about now just reading some of those choices, then you can see how important it is that your wishes are set down in a will. I'm sure you don't want your children handed about like so many parcels.

If a guardian does need to be appointed for your child, state law will specify a preference list for the judge to follow. While laws do vary, it is common to follow this order:

➤ Any request in a will or other written instrument (if you have no will, then of course legally you've got no preference)

➤ Any request by a child at least 14 years of age

➤ A relative of a child (grandparents, aunts, uncles, etc.)

The court's overriding concern is the appointment of a guardian who will serve the best interests of the child. The court will do the best it can, but how much better it would be for your kids if the judge had your directives to consider.

If you are married, your spouse is likely to assume the legal and actual role of guardian if your children inherit money from you. But there are exceptions. If a surviving parent hasn't taken an active interest in the child or has outright abandoned parenthood, then he or she may not be the court's choice. A child with serious health disabilities calls for a guardian who will undertake extra duties.

The Guardian's Duties

A guardian has two primary responsibilities:

➤ Rear the child

➤ Manage the child's assets

The guardian appointed by the court performs one or both of these functions until discharged of them. More specifically, the guardian is responsible for:

➤ Petitioning the court for appointment as guardian

➤ Securing a performance bond for him- or herself

➤ Preparing an inventory of the child's assets, that could include property from your probate estate (through a will or intestacy), life insurance proceeds and pension benefits, as well as Social Security payments due the child

➤ Investing and managing the child's assets

➤ Providing for the child's support, care, education, and training

➤ Encouraging the child to be self-reliant and independent so that he or she becomes an adult capable of handling the money that will be inherited

➤ Periodically accounting to the court about income, expenses, etc.

➤ Filing necessary federal and state tax returns on the child's income

➤ Closing the guardianship when it is no longer needed

The guardian is responsible for reporting all income and expenses both to the court and to the child. That accounting may be on an annual or biennial basis, depending on state law. The guardian is to use the funds for the child's livelihood, which includes necessities and perhaps amenities, like a first car for the youngster when he or she reaches driving age.

In many instances the guardian is not paid a fee—usually it is a family member who takes on that role and does not expect payment.

Words, Words, Words
A **ward** is a person of any age who is under the care of a court-appointed guardian. This is an archaic term, rarely heard these days outside of old—very old— movies, where the ward is usually a child or teenager.

Tip
If a home or any other asset is to be kept in the family for the use of the child, you need to specify that in your will. Most state laws require the guardian to sell assets that will not earn income.

When the child reaches age 18, the guardianship is terminated. The guardian files his or her final accounting and distributes the assets to the child.

At this point you may want to pause and contemplate your child receiving your estate at age 18. Is it likely to be large? Do you think he or she could handle the money? Is the child too young right now for you to be able even to guess?

A trust is likely to be the answer to any dilemma that issue might pose. It can delay distribution of assets until the child becomes more mature. I'll explain how this works in a few pages.

How to Select a Guardian

Tip
It's wise to name an alternate guardian in your will, just in case the primary guardian is later unable or unwilling to serve.

Let me tell you, this is *hard*. My wife and I have four sons, two of whom have now reached adulthood. Over the course of the years in our various wills we have had five different guardians, and almost as many different alternates. While a family member or friend might be willing to be guardian for one child, maybe even two, taking on four calls for a real martyr.

You want to select someone who will rear your kids the way you would, and manage their assets wisely. There are several factors to think about in selecting a guardian or guardians.

Age

This is especially true if you are considering your parents. They aren't as young as they once were (but, hey, who is?). You probably drove them nuts on more than one occasion, but they had the resiliency of youth then, and the energy to meet those demands.

As grandparents, they are wonderful. But they know that when the grandchildren start acting like kids they can be sent home. That can't happen if you appoint them guardians.

Quote, Unquote
If men do not keep on speaking terms with children, they cease to be men, and become merely machines for eating and for earning money.
— *John Updike, "Assorted Prose" (1965)*

Your parents love your kids, but may want them around only part of the time. One generation gap is wide enough. Two could be a chasm.

On the other hand, grandparents *could* work if they have asked for the job of guardian (and you agree they would do a good job of it), and in some cases if the children are old enough so that your parents won't be raising small tykes. Taking in a 14- and 16-year-old brings its own, shall we say, challenges. On the other hand it will be only a few years until those kids are grown. This is a decision that, as you can see, calls for serious thought.

You might prefer to consider a couple closer to your age. Their parenting skills, which you will have observed, are well honed by daily use and not, for the most part, out of practice by grandparenthood.

Marital Status

Your child needs to fit comfortably into a family environment. A husband and wife who have a solid marriage and children close to your child's age may be ideal.

We all know perfectly excellent single parents who rear their children to be what you would hope for yours. By all means if you know someone who fits that bill, don't exclude that individual from consideration. Or the single person with no children, perhaps a sibling of yours or your spouse's, who is particularly close to your child. However, two parents do make it easier on the child—and the guardians.

Here is something you will want to keep in mind though. If you are naming a married couple as guardians, consider the possibility of their divorce one day. Indicate who should be the guardian in that event, no matter how unlikely it seems to you now.

Lifestyle and Child Rearing Skills

Your child is used to you and your family life. If you want continuity, or as close as you're likely to find it in a guardianship situation, then you'll look for someone who is likely to fit within that pattern. That's not to say that the child can't succeed in a family that doesn't emphasize what matters to you in rearing kids. It's just that it's harder to do. For example, if religion is important to you and your family, you won't want the guardian to be an atheist.

Child rearing attitudes vary, of course. There is no one right way. But you have your own style, and probably want your guardian to follow that sort of system. If firm-but-fair is yours, you're not likely to look for a guardian who believes that children should be "free to do their own thing." Taking a child from a fairly structured family life to a guardian who plans only for the next few minutes could spell disaster for a kid.

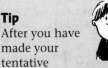

Tip
After you have made your tentative choice of guardian, observe the individual with your children, and discuss with the person(s) you've chosen as guardian how comfortable everyone would be likely to feel in that household.

Compatibility

As I mentioned, most courts will listen to a child's wishes if the youngster is at least 14 years of age. If your male teenager detests the very perfume that Aunt Maude wears when she gives him a big smooch at family reunions, and she gave him socks when he entered high school, for which he's never quite forgiven her, then you may want to rethink Aunt Maude.

Talk with your kids and find out whom they feel comfortable with. That may not decide it for you, particularly if your son likes oft-married bachelor Uncle Dave because he has plenty of "babes" around, but at least their input can move you toward a decision, as it would a judge.

Family Relationships

Your brother or sister may be your best choice. But if there are likely to be squabbles over which brother or sister, that's all the more reason to put your choice in your will.

Favoritism

Some folks do play favorites. If you have three children, and your proposed guardian dotes on one child, giving him more attention, consideration, and gifts than she gives to the other two, you might want to give second thought to your choice. At least have a candid discussion with the kids who aren't the favorite. They probably have noticed the different treatment and won't be inclined to give that person the benefit of the doubt if she becomes the guardian, especially when discipline is administered or money spent.

Managing Money

Some guardians make superb substitute parents and can manage money wisely. Others can fulfill one of those obligations, but not both. If your guardian choice will be a great parent, but always seems to be just one step ahead of the bill collectors, then take the tradeoff and go with him or her. Parenting should be your first consideration. You can turn to someone else to manage your child's assets. Which brings us now to your other choice: the trust.

First, though, is your head spinning about now with all the "perfect" traits you're supposed to look for in a guardian? Here is a worksheet to help you sift it all out. Perhaps your choice is an obvious one. If it isn't, putting your thoughts on paper should help you select an individual or a couple who could do a good job of caring for your child, should anything happen to you.

Choosing a Guardian

You've probably given some thought to your kids and a likely guardian, perhaps even before reading this chapter. Still, it helps to see on paper the pros and cons of various family members and friends who might be candidates for guardianship. Take a few moments—no, take as long as you need, this shouldn't be rushed—to set down your thoughts. Your work may lead you to answers that will be satisfying all around.

Name(s)	Good points	Any negatives?	Will they accept the job?	Can they manage money?	The kids like them?
_____	_____	_____	_____	_____	_____
_____	_____	_____	_____	_____	_____
_____	_____	_____	_____	_____	_____
_____	_____	_____	_____	_____	_____
_____	_____	_____	_____	_____	_____
_____	_____	_____	_____	_____	_____
_____	_____	_____	_____	_____	_____

Best guardian(s):_____

Best alternate(s):_____

The Trust Alternative

If your proposed guardian is a poor money manager, you may want to establish a trust to manage your child's assets.

You might want a trust anyway. It certainly should be considered by anyone who has significant assets to leave to a minor or special-needs child. That could be $50,000 or more in cash, life insurance, stocks, bonds, and other savings, not including the value of your house.

A trust can accomplish the following for you:

➤ Manage the child's property (stocks, certificate of deposit rollovers, and the like)

➤ Distribute the property later than age 18, if that is your wish

➤ Get around a spendthrift child's problems

Chapter 8 has a complete discussion of trusts. What I'll talk about in this chapter is trusts as they specifically apply to minors.

The trustee you choose can be an individual or a corporate institution, usually a bank. If you choose a corporate trustee, then you will have the professional management and protection from risk that comes with that choice. Most trustees report to the guardian at least quarterly, and many will assist in filing the child's income tax returns.

You can establish a *revocable living trust* now, which would receive all your probate assets, life insurance, and retirement plan proceeds, or you can include a trust in your will—a *testamentary trust*—and accomplish the same thing.

Let's look at Carrie and Steve, who have two small children. The couple established a revocable living trust in planning for their kids, funded only by a life insurance policy on Steve's life, with the trust as the secondary beneficiary (Carrie is first beneficiary). Steve's and Carrie's wills provide for each other first, then the probate estate goes to the children's trust.

The kids' trust could be structured like this:

➤ Trustworthy Bank as its trustee

➤ The children are the primary beneficiaries of the trust, and will receive the income and as much of the principal as is necessary for their support

➤ When the younger child becomes age 22, the trust assets will be equally divided and each child will get one-third of those assets (upon written request). The balance of each child's share will be distributed when each child turns 25.

➤ If a child dies before final distribution to him or her, then the other child receives that share

Quote, Unquote
I'm still not sure what is meant by good fortune and success. I know fame and power are for the birds. But then life suddenly comes into focus for me. And, ah, there stand my kids.
—*Lee Iacocca, Talking Straight (1988)*

You can establish similar distribution ages, or any ages you choose.

That reminds me of a friend whose son was the beneficiary of the father's trust. The son graduated from college and wandered around trying to "find" himself. He insisted the income from the trust keep flowing. The trustee called the young man in and told him when he got a job the spigot would be opened, but until then it was shut off. He found a job.

There are no tax breaks with a minor's support trust as above; it simply delays distribution of the inheritance until the children are more mature and can make better choices with your hard-earned money.

Special Requests

You can create trust terms that best fit your child, or make for differences between your kids.

The heroic woman who consented to be guardian for my four boys was a little concerned about housing the additional brood in her home. I told her we could provide in the trust that the trustee could allow some funds for home improvement.

She then asked about family vacations. We said the trust could specify that money could be used for her children, as well as for our kids, to get away. Indeed, the trust could provide for vacation money for the guardians to go off on their own without the children, a sort of reward for their efforts.

Like ours were, your particular concerns can be addressed in a trust.

> **Watch Out**
> A creditor might lend your child money, expecting to be repaid from income or principal distribution of that child's trust. The wise person preparing the trust includes a clause that orders the trustee not to distribute funds where the chief beneficiary is the child's creditor. No trust should be without that clause.

Giving Your Kids Cash Gifts Now

You may have some spare cash that you want to give to your minor children, but don't want them to spend it now. You have some options:

➤ A gift to a custodial account

➤ Three forms of minor's trusts

In Custody

Most states have a gifts-to-minors statute. The parent establishes a custodial account at a savings institution or transfers stock in the custodian's name (that'd be your name or that of any adult you choose) for the benefit of the child. When the child becomes of legal age, as defined by the statute, she receives the property outright. The child reports the income during the custodial period.

Federal law may require the income received from custodial accounts be taxed to the child at the parent's highest rate until the child becomes 14.

The parent's gift is excluded from federal *gift* tax because of the $10,000 annual exclusion (one can give

> **Tip**
> If you establish a custodial account or minor's trust, do not use the assets to support the child because you will be taxed on its income. Remember, the child is the owner, not you, the transferor, so if you cannot afford to relinquish ownership of the property, do not establish a custodial or minor's trust.

any person $10,000 or any married couple $20,000 each year without any tax repercussions). The custodial account will not be in the parent's estate and therefore will not be subject to federal estate tax if another person is selected as custodian.

To avoid inclusion in your estate for federal tax, choose a close relative or friend to serve as custodian. (That individual can choose to do nothing except make minor investment decisions, such as rolling over a certificate of deposit.)

A Trusty Trio

The tax code and several court decisions have provided a few types of minor's trusts known as Section 2503(b), Section 2503(c), and Crummey trusts. There are minute differences among the three that would numb your mind if I were to explain them, but the gist of the three is:

➤ They establish a trust

➤ They make a gift for the minor to the trust, which receives the maximum annual gift tax exclusion for the transferor (there's that annual $10,000 again)

➤ They delay distribution to the minor until age 21 or later

Each has variations on those themes that you may want to explore with your attorney.

Your Child and Your Estate: Entitlements

You read in Chapter 6 about a child's rights to inherit under state intestate laws when you have no will. In Chapter 7 you saw how to include your kids in that will.

Quote, Unquote
A father is a banker provided by nature.
—*French proverb*

If you are a divorced mom or dad providing child support, you may want to ask your attorney about your support obligations as they pertain to your estate. In some states the divorced parent's requirement to support a child is not terminated by that parent's death, but the amount of the support may be modified, revoked, or commuted to a lump sum by the court.

Most states have a family support statute that requires a specified amount—it can vary, but let's say, oh, $8,500—to be distributed to a surviving spouse and/or children, whether you had a will or not.

Also, divorce decrees may require the support-paying parent to maintain life insurance on his or her life, which may be the exclusive claim the child would then have against the deceased parent's estate. The child, of course, is the beneficiary.

The Least You Need to Know

➤ You ought to name a guardian, and also an alternate, in your will for minor children.

➤ The guardian is responsible for rearing the children and managing their assets.

➤ Consider a trust to manage your children's assets, should you die, because of its flexibility.

➤ Child support might be collected from a deceased parent's estate upon death, whether there is a will or not.

Chapter 12

Holy Wedlock: Sometimes a Deadlock

It's bliss. It's a battlefield. It's both—and occasionally at the same time. That's marriage, all right, or so it would seem from all one hears and reads on the subject.

The law has many occasions to intrude into the lives of married couples, from good times to bad moments. All the legal paper shuffling that goes along with marriage, and then perhaps separation and divorce, can also affect an estate plan. Here's what can happen— and what you can do if distressing times hit you.

Spousal Rights

Before we get into the *sturm und drang* of much of this chapter, may I ask if you're planning to be married soon or even just eventually? Good for you. My wish is that none of what follows in this chapter will apply to you. Do me a favor, though. Here is a listing for you to refer to in order to make sure the estate paperwork for both of you is in order when you march down that aisle. It affects spousal rights. Keep it in mind and read it again just before you marry.

GETTING MARRIED? CHECK THIS OUT

Congratulations! This isn't a very romantic suggestion, but before you make that trip down the aisle, you and your spouse-to-be need to review some estate papers, to get your house, figuratively speaking, in order. The marriage license is proof that you will soon become a new legal entity. It's time to look at some other documents that could or should be changed before you trade vows.

➤ **Your wills**. If you do not each have one, it's smart to have them drawn up so that you can provide for each other. Please, no joint wills.

➤ **Employee benefits, life insurance policy, Individual Retirement Account, and qualified retirement plan**. You will probably want to change the beneficiary for those investments to your spouse, or at least review the documents to be certain that you still want the beneficiary you have named.

➤ **Forms of property ownership**. Will you be buying a home? Do you already have one in your name? You might want to review Chapters 2 and 3, about ownership styles. Perhaps you'll want to hold real and personal property as "joint tenants with right of survivorship," the most common ownership style for spouses.

➤ **Prenuptial agreement**. Will you be having one? There's a discussion of prenups in Chapter 3 (with a sample agreement you can read over), and another one in this chapter. Remember to use separate attorneys for drawing up an agreement.

Now let's get back to the time after some marriages, when problems can crop up.

Tip
Did you recently marry and move to another state? Don't forget to update your estate plan to take into account requirements in your new state for a will and other documents.

After the marriage ceremony, each spouse has certain legal rights. In states like California and Texas, the husband and wife have community property rights. In non-community property states—New York and Illinois, to take two examples—the law also specifies certain marital rights upon divorce or death.

Marriage is a fragile institution in our modern life, for a number of reasons. To ignore that fact is to proceed at your own risk—and possibly to the risk of your financial future. Read on and you'll see what I mean.

A Different Kind of Election

It's your will. You can completely cut your spouse out, or leave only a small portion of the probate estate to him or her.

Of course if you intend to make either of those moves, I would suggest not letting your husband or wife view your handiwork unless a divorce is already inevitable, or you have a prenuptial agreement. I once had a client who was the wife of a friend. In the will I drew up for her she left one-half of her estate to her parents, one-quarter to her parochial high school, and one-quarter to her husband. As far as I know, her husband was unaware of his relatively unimportant position in his wife's testamentary scheme. And of course I could not tell him. The couple eventually got divorced.

A spouse who is left out of his or her deceased spouse's will or given a small share of the estate has the right to challenge the terms of that will. This is known as *elect against the will*. It is a strategy for married couples only, and permits the party left out to go to court for a fairer shake. He or she is saying in effect, "Whatever he left me, it's not enough. I'm electing against that will." This isn't the same as a *challenge* to the will, which is open to any heir or beneficiary. An election is just for spouses, and already assumes some rights for the survivor.

Quote, Unquote
Marriage isn't a tram. It doesn't have to go anywhere.
—*Iris Murdoch, A Severed Head (1961)*

The spouse who elects against a will must file that election within the statutory period of time. That time can vary, but might be perhaps five months after the estate is opened.

Most state laws allow a surviving spouse who elects against the deceased spouse's will to receive from one-third to one-half of his or her probate estate. Usually that is the same share that he or she would receive under intestate law.

If the election is untimely (presented beyond the accepted deadline), or improperly made, then the surviving spouse receives only what the will provides. However, any property jointly owned by both spouses, and any life insurance or pension with the survivor as beneficiary, would go to the surviving spouse, since those assets are not part of the probate estate.

"Bumping Up" an Estate

Several states have laws that increase the probate estate for purposes of the spousal election, when certain transfers would otherwise diminish the part of the estate that the surviving spouse would receive. This increase is often referred to as the *augmented estate*.

Let me give you an example. Say that, for whatever reason, you don't want your spouse to inherit the bulk of your estate, or maybe not even a penny of it. So you set up a trust and place all of your property in that trust, thinking your spouse will have no access to that money, even if she or he decides to elect against the will.

Not so, at least in certain states. The court will take that trust property and deposit it right back into your probate estate, for spousal election purposes just where you didn't want it to be.

Let's look at another example. Meet Ray, who lives in a non-community property state and has several assets in his own name:

➤ Three expensive cars

➤ A condominium in Florida

➤ A substantial savings account

➤ A significant investment portfolio

➤ A large life insurance policy

All except the life insurance proceeds would be part of Ray's probate estate.

But Ray intensely dislikes his wife Michelle, and the idea of her enjoying his property and money after he's gone drives him nuts. So he creates a trust and transfers all his solely owned assets, except the cars, into the trust. The trust provides nothing for Michelle. Ray changes the life insurance beneficiary to his daughter Eden. Shortly thereafter, Ray dies. His will leaves not a scrap to Michelle.

Watch Out

Consult an attorney before making any property transfers with the intent to thwart your spouse's election against your will. State laws vary as to what is considered part of the augmented estate.

Quote, Unquote

In the multitude of counsellors there is safety.

—*Proverbs 11:14*

Michelle can elect against the will and receive her share of the probate assets, which now consist only of the automobiles. This is a fine kettle of fish, the fuming widow thinks. But wait. State law may allow her to elect against an augmented estate, which includes the property in trust. Whether the life insurance proceeds are considered part of the augmented estate varies with each state. Most pensions are subject to federal law, which prevents a spouse from being cut out of benefits.

The laws in her state give Michelle the green light to elect against an augmented estate. She *runs* to a lawyer.

Actually, the election could bring a most satisfactory ending to this for Michelle. She could get one-third of everything. As for Ray...well, we'll never know his response to Michelle's good fortune, will we?

It's important to note here that a surviving spouse may waive his or her rights to elect against a will by signing a prenuptial agreement. That's our next topic for discussion.

The Prenup as Love Flies out the Window

They're called prenuptial, premarital and antenuptial agreements, but they all mean the same things: a document where prospective spouses settle certain property rights before the marriage, in the event of divorce or death of one party. I discussed prenups in Chapter 3 as they apply to property ownership. Now I'll tell you what happens when problems arise in a marriage.

They're for "Just Folks," Too

Prenups are not used only by millionaires and movie stars. Older couples, or indeed couples of any age, remarrying after the death of or divorce from a spouse, often are concerned about keeping for their children the assets they bring into that new marriage.

A prenuptial agreement will specify that each spouse waives his or her right to any intestate share (if there is no will) and waives any right to elect against the other's will.

The provisions of the prenup attempt to keep as separately owned any property brought into the marriage. But spouses frequently will convert each's solely owned property into jointly owned property with right of survivorship. That results in the surviving spouse receiving the property, thus reducing the assets going to the deceased spouse's children and perhaps negating an important part of the prenuptial agreement.

Spouses can agree to modify or revoke their prenuptial agreement. But those wishes must be in writing, and signed by each partner.

If a married couple does not have a *pre*nup, they can, if they choose, make a *post*nuptial agreement, which could contain the same terms as a document drawn up before the wedding.

A prenuptial agreement can also get into questions of alimony, into wills and trusts and, as you saw in Chapter 3 and in the sample prenup agreement there, just about any area the couple wants.

Tip
If you have a prenuptial agreement that provides for the bulk of your assets to go to your children, then make sure the title to those assets remains solely in your name.

Avoiding a Challenge to a Prenup

Joe is about to marry Angelina. It's his second marriage, the first having ended in divorce. Joe's concerned about a possible second divorce and its financial impact. He also wants to make sure that when he dies the bulk of his estate goes to the children from his first marriage. Angelina understands, and she agrees to the pact.

Joe should take the following steps to be sure there are no loopholes in his agreement with Angelina:

➤ Hire an attorney to draft the agreement.

➤ Completely disclose all his assets and liabilities to Angelina. Courts will more readily enforce a prenuptial agreement if it is clear that the spouses knew what rights each would give up in the event of a divorce or a death. Hiding assets will almost always guarantee a challenge to the agreement, perhaps a successful one.

Watch Out
The person who initiates the prenuptial agreement might be tempted to offer his or her lawyer's services to the other partner. Bad move. That would be a conflict of interest that the courts will probably not look kindly on when deciding whether to enforce the prenuptial agreement. Two parties call for two separate lawyers.

➤ Recommend to Angelina that she hire her own lawyer to review the proposed agreement. If she does not want independent legal advice, then the prenuptial agreement should clearly state that she was told to engage a lawyer but chose not to.

Finally when considering upsetting a prenuptial agreement, courts do retain the right to alter the effect of a prenup if it would result in extreme hardship for either spouse. For example, if both parties assumed that each would be self-supporting upon divorce or the death of the other, and injury or illness precluded that, then the court could specify support payments to the disabled spouse.

The American Way of Divorce

We are the marrying kind in America, yet about half of us later end up in divorce court. Take a look at this table to see how we rank when compared with some other countries.

Country	Divorce rate per 1,000 Population
DIVORCE AROUND THE WORLD: LOOK WHO'S AHEAD	
U.S.	21%
Denmark	13%
Sweden	13%
United Kingdom (England and Wales only)	13%
Canada	11%
Netherlands	9%
Germany	7%
Japan	6%

Source: U.S. Department of Commerce, 1993
Note: In 1990 figures, France stood at 8%, Italy at 2%.

Almost all states have a no-fault divorce (or dissolution of marriage) law. State laws usually have a residency requirement and a waiting period between the petition and the order granting the divorce. Several states require mandatory counseling before the decree is granted. But the marriage *will* be dissolved if one party desires it.

For detailed advice on divorce and child custody, I recommend Brent W. Terry's *The Complete Idiot's Guide to Protecting Yourself From Everyday Legal Hassles;* it's got several excellent chapters on these issues. But let me go into financial and tax consequences of divorce, and how divorce can affect your estate here.

Those areas can include:

➤ Property settlement

➤ Child custody and support

➤ Alimony or separate maintenance

➤ The tax consequences of all of the above

Remember that a prenuptial agreement may determine the terms of any property settlement, alimony or separate maintenance for one party. Child custody and support will be set by the divorce court. What follows assumes there is no enforceable prenuptial agreement.

Watch Out

You don't see much of legal separation anymore. Folks seem to proceed straight to divorce. However, if you do seek a legal separation, that is certainly a move that calls for a review of your estate plan. Remember, though, no matter how separated you are, and how far away your estranged spouse, you are still married in the eyes of the law.

Property Division

Mark and Millie are splitting up. The couple have the following assets, with noted market values:

House	co-owned	$100,000 [net, or less mortgage(s)]
Household goods	co-owned	$30,000
Cars	co-owned	$30,000 [net, or less auto loan(s)]
Savings	co-owned	$10,000
His pension		$200,000
Her pension		$50,000

Most divorce courts would add up the assets and divide by two. Perhaps you've gone through a divorce and are saying "That didn't happen to me! I got the shaft and he(she) got the mine." Be that as it may, most laws require an equitable distribution of the marital assets.

Courts certainly can consider factors that could affect a distribution, such as:

➤ Who acquired the assets and how (gifts or inheritance)

➤ Income and property of spouses before marriage and at present

➤ Duration of marriage and health of each spouse

➤ Need of custodial parent to occupy the home

➤ Spousal maintenance or alimony

➤ Liquidity of assets

➤ Financial future of each spouse

➤ Spousal fault in wasting assets

➤ Tax effects

Quote, Unquote
Love commingled with hate is more powerful than love. Or hate.
—*Joyce Carol Oates, "On Boxing" (1987)*

Tip
If you think there might be a problem with your children having regular access to your parents after your divorce, you can make grandparental visits an issue in your divorce decree.

This list is illustrative and not exhaustive. Certainly each divorce is unique, and state laws vary.

Remember, too, that community property states generally treat all assets acquired during marriage from either spouse's income as community property. This means that each spouse has a one-half ownership in those marital assets, no matter how the property is titled. This form of property ownership will affect the divorce. (You might want to review Chapter 3, which also talks about community property.)

Child Custody and Support

Courts award custody of minor children based on what they determine is in the best interests of the child. Naturally, parents should try to work together to establish an amicable custody arrangement that benefits all concerned.

Usually the non-custodial parent provides child support through minority, and often through age 21 if the child is attending post-secondary school (i.e., college or trade school). Many states have established child support guidelines to determine the amount of support to be paid.

Income and Some Other Tax Consequences

Let's return to Mark and Millie's divorce. Mark is an accountant making approximately $75,000 a year; Millie is a public school teacher earning $30,000. They have one child, Manny, age 5.

If one spouse pays the other alimony, then the paying spouse gets a tax deduction and the recipient spouse reports the payment as gross income.

Mark, who is in the higher tax bracket, might be willing to pay alimony, perhaps as a form of property settlement, to get a welcome tax deduction. Millie, therefore, may receive more from the divorce financially because of the tax saving for Mark.

If the spouses split the property, they can determine which property each is to choose because there are tax consequences that result from disposition of selected property. For example, if Millie keeps the house and eventually sells it when she is age 55 or older, under the present tax law, the first $125,000 of profit from the sale (i.e., capital gains) is excluded from taxation. (Note: At this writing, Congress is considering a bill that will exclude from capital gains tax home sales up to $500,000. That's for a principal residence owned by taxpayers of any age.)

If Mark relinquishes his share of the house in return for all of his pension (half of which his former wife would otherwise be entitled to), it is likely he will be taxed on all of the benefits when he receives the pension payments.

Words, Words, Words
We all know (and a few of us have experienced) **alimony** as a court-ordered payment from one spouse to another after a divorce. However, these days it is more common for money to be paid to an ex-spouse for property settlement; in other words, for a former spouse to buy out, in periodic payments, the other's share in real estate, investments, and so forth.

If Millie is awarded custody of Manny, Mark will pay child support. Tax law gives the custodial parent the right to the dependency exemption unless the parent waives that right. Since Mark is in a higher tax bracket, Manny's dependency exemption is worth more to him, and he may be willing to pay for that exemption with higher child support payments. Also, while Manny is living with Millie, she can file in the more advantageous tax status—head of household—while Mark will be relegated to filing as a single person.

Complicated, huh? Divorce isn't as simple as marriage. You ignore the tax implications at your own financial peril!

Watch Out
Thoroughly discuss the tax consequences of your divorce with your attorney and with your accountant, or you could wind up paying more to the IRS than you need to.

Gift Taxes

If Mark and Millie divide their assets during the process of divorce, the division will not result in any gift taxes as long as they are still married at the time they make the transfers.

Similarly, if a married couple had a postnuptial agreement that transferred assets from one spouse to another while married, there would be no gift tax. However, there might be a gift tax on any transfer made under a prenuptial agreement if the transfer occurs before the marriage.

There is a more comprehensive discussion of gift taxes in Chapter 16.

The Least You Need to Know

➤ If a surviving spouse has been left little or nothing in the deceased spouse's will, he or she can elect against that will and receive from one-third to one-half of the estate.

➤ A prenuptial agreement can limit the rights a spouse has against the other's assets in the event of divorce or death.

➤ Tax planning is an important part of the divorce process.

➤ A divorce calls for another look at your estate plan, specifically your will.

Chapter 13

Special Planning for Special Situations

In This Chapter

➤ Disability: special tactics

➤ "Living together"

➤ Big wins, and major financial losses

➤ Parenting your grandchildren

➤ Professionals and farmers

Not everyone fits neatly easily into any of the categories and circumstances that I've described so far in this book. Maybe after reading previous chapters you've said to yourself "Well, that's true for everybody else, but with me..."

If you feel you're often the exception rather than the rule, then this chapter may be for you. In it I address special situations, and you may well find yourself—and the answers you seek—here.

Planning for the Disabled Child—of Any Age

Statutes define an incapacitated person as one who has a severe and chronic mental or physical impairment that is likely to continue indefinitely. Needs certainly vary among the handicapped. Some require a guardian, others certainly do not and manage quite well on their own, although they will have certain medical needs throughout their lives.

The range of potential disabilities as they affect the young person's work is so significant that no more than general advice can be offered here. Some kids will be able to earn enough to support themselves, others may be able to work at a minimal level, and still others will never be able to be gainfully employed. Clearly any planning must account for your child's potential economic success.

If you have a child who is physically or mentally disabled, then you know most of such kids' needs are financial as well as personal. Parents provide a great deal of both, but sometimes the financial part becomes too great, and Mom and Dad must seek government assistance.

To preserve your estate for your other children, and enable the disabled child to receive needed support, it's often necessary to keep family assets from that child, especially as he or she grows to legal adult age. This is because government aid is often withdrawn or reduced when a child becomes an adult and has assets that can be used for his or her support.

> **Words, Words, Words**
>
> **Medicaid** is a state-run health plan, with federal government contributions, to help lower-income residents, which, in the context we're talking about here, would include your disabled child of any age, who has little or no income.

For children, there are a number of programs that can help. For example, federal law mandates special education programs to serve those with physical or mental disabilities. They begin at the pre-kindergarten level and continue through age 21. These entitlements are available at no cost to the family. Also, for those who are capable of post-secondary education, educational grants and special services may be available.

There are several federal programs for financial support. The specifics are beyond the scope of this book, but you'll want to know, if you aren't already hooked up to them, there's Supplemental Security Income and Medicaid, plus Social Security disability payments, that could be available for your child.

Your Child's Assets

Since many entitlements have requirements that limit the income or asset resources of the disabled person, you need to take those limits into account in your financial planning. Consider doing the following:

➤ Review beneficiary designations in your will, life insurance policies, retirement plans and IRAs, trusts, and savings bonds to be sure your child isn't named in them

➤ Avoid joint tenancy ownership of property with the disabled child, which creates more assets for him or her

➤ Create a special trust for the child

➤ Name a guardian in your will who is sensitive to the child's special needs

Watch Out
Grandparents should consider *not* providing for the disabled child in their will if this would raise the child's assets to a level high enough to disqualify the child for public assistance.

A Trust May Be the Answer

Instead of giving your child money outright through a will or a life insurance policy, you might establish a trust. You would certainly need to consider the gift, estate, and income tax consequences. On the other hand, a well-planned practice of giving (see Chapter 17) and an independent trustee for a trust can avoid most tax problems.

Sara was a widow with several adult children. One of them, Alan, had medical problems that held him to a part-time, minimum-wage job, and would do so for the remainder of his life. Alan lived at home with Sara, and she was concerned that, when she died, Alan would need a house to live in and someone to handle his finances, even though he probably did not need a guardianship.

She established a revocable living trust and placed her house and investments in the trust for her life, and thereafter for Alan's life. Her grandchildren would receive the remainder of any assets left after Alan died. Sara consulted her other children before doing this so that they would understand why they would receive very little from her estate, although their kids would eventually benefit.

A trust is established to provide the amenities that government assistance cannot or will not. The goal is to provide a lifestyle for the child that best fits his or her needs. (The needs of Alan will of course, differ from those of others with disabilities.) The trust must be drafted so that it keeps the assets for your child and does not reimburse the government for its basic expenditures.

Quote, Unquote
The joys of parents are secret, and so are their griefs and fears: they cannot utter the one, nor they will not utter the other.
—*Francis Bacon, "Of Parents and Children" (1625)*

Medicaid places severe limits on its aid for special-needs children who are reaching adulthood and have significant assets. To avoid this from happening in your situation, try to obtain a court order appointing a guardian of your choice, naming that individual in your will. He or she might be able to make certain gifts from the child's assets, or establish a support trust like the one Sara set up for Alan. If the child is institutionalized, and you are paying for that care, the guardian and trust can handle payments from your estate.

When consulting an attorney about caring for your child with special needs, be sure the one you select fully understands the various federal and state entitlement laws.

Living Together/Planning Together

It's also legally called cohabitation, but we seldom see that expression anywhere these days. What we're talking about in these pages is a little more than living together. It's about life partners with a serious commitment on both sides, but where there is no marriage. With such long-term relationships there is often, maybe usually, the desire to share assets and, of course, incorporate the other person into one's estate plan.

There are few laws that apply to the legal rights of partners outside of marriage. Those with such living arrangements have no legal status. Contract law may apply to some arrangements, and the so-called "palimony" suits have been used as a means of trying to enforce support agreements. But the "significant other" has no inheritance rights under state intestate laws.

Some 13 states, however, recognize common law marriages, where a man and woman cohabit for a statutory period and publicly acknowledge themselves as husband and wife. And at this writing, several states are determining the legality of gay marriages. Certainly any couple, even if unmarried, can provide for each other in their wills if they choose. But remember, if you are not legally married, you do not have the right to elect against a will (you read about such an election in the previous chapter). Electing against a will is limited to a spouse.

Challenging your partner's will won't be a victory for you because if you are successful in having the will declared invalid, the deceased is considered to have died intestate (without a valid will). Then the state will decide who the heirs are—and none of them will be you.

Keeping Some Assets Out of Your Will

Joint ownership is a possibility here, and it would provide the surviving half of the couple with the property immediately at his or her partner's death. Keep in mind, though, that creating joint ownership in real estate gives both parties an interest in that property that is not easy to alter if the relationship changes.

You might also want to consider life insurance, with the partner named beneficiary. Do the same with other investments, and they, too, will go directly to him or her at your death, avoiding probate and possible family squabbles.

Only a spouse has a right to the other spouse's qualified pension plan, but that plan could have any beneficiary you name. Consult a professional about any tax or other consequences.

Perhaps the wisest choice here would be a revocable living trust. You could establish the trust, fund it currently or in the future with life insurance and the assets from a pour-over will (those are assets that go through a will and then into a trust). The partner could be the current income beneficiary of the trust, or the future beneficiary, upon your death.

Any income from the trust would be taxed to the creator or grantor (that's you), and would be subject to gift tax to the extent the partner received income. (But the annual exclusion should be available. There is more about gift tax in Chapter 16.) The advantage to the revocable aspect is that you can change the arrangement of the trust if your life changes.

Tip
Check with your employer. A growing number of companies are providing benefits for same- or opposite-sex life partners.

Finally, the tax laws aren't much help to partners outside of marriage. The couple cannot file a joint return, nor can one take the other as a dependent. There is no gift or estate tax deduction for a non-married partner.

By all means, it's smart to have a written agreement regarding any financial or property ownership arrangement you have with your partner. That's for the protection of you both, to forestall litigation between the two of you, as well as between a survivor and the deceased's heirs.

The Role of Custodial Grandparent

According to 1995 U.S. Census Bureau figures, there are nearly 4 million children now living in a household headed by a grandparent (although a parent might live in the house also). And in 1.5 million U.S. households there is no parent present.

These arrangements can vary. Some grandparents are legally in charge of their grandchildren through adoption or guardianship. Others have taken on that responsibility informally, with their son's or daughter's consent.

Are you raising, whether for the moment or until adulthood, your grandchildren? If you think you must have legal custody of your grandkids in order to be eligible for services and benefits for the child, that's not true. Many of them are available without you taking that step.

You'll want to do two things here if you find yourself responsible for children—at this stage of your life:

➤ Get as much information as you can about help available, both in the government and private sector, and through an appropriate support group in your area. The American Association of Retired Persons (AARP) sponsors an information clearing-house called Grandparent Information Center (202-434-2296) that can direct you to specific local and national agencies.

➤ Review your estate plan. You might want to move beneficiaries around, even if just for a time. Or set up a trust for your grandchildren. If you are raising your grandkids because their parent(s) have problems with drugs or alcohol, those conditions might be different one day, and you may want to check your estate plan again. This could be a continually changing situation for you.

Eureka! We're Rich: Handling Sudden Wealth

I don't know your family, so I have no clue if you're likely to come into an eye-popping inheritance from your Uncle Forsyth. I don't know if someone's likely to ring your doorbell and declare you the latest $250,000 winner in the Publishers Clearing House Sweepstakes either.

Winning your state lottery is a long shot, but obviously there are winners every week. One could be you. (Take a look at some trivia about those lotteries around which we build our dreams, one dollar at a time.)

LOTTERY NUMBERS

➤ The first state to have a lottery was New Hampshire, which began selling lottery tickets in March, 1964.

➤ In North America there are currently 37 states, the District of Columbia, and six Canadian provinces that offer lottery games.

➤ The entire North American lottery industry had gross sales of more than $37 billion in fiscal year l996. Sales contributed more than $12 billion to such programs and services as education; natural resources; parks and recreation; police, fire, and teacher retirement funds; senior citizens support, health care, and more.

➤ New York state wins! The Empire State had gross sales of more than $3.6 billion in fiscal year 1996, making it the highest lottery organization in North America. That same year the lottery contributed more than $1.4 billion in revenues to the state's education fund.

➤ More than $19 billion was paid in prizes to winners in North America in fiscal year 1996. Another way of putting it: that's an average of $52 million paid every day.

➤ More than 250,000 retailers sell lottery products throughout North America.

➤ Retailers were paid more than $2 billion in commissions for selling lottery products in fiscal year 1996.

Source: North American Association of State and Provincial Lotteries

In any event, you could wake up one morning to find yourself in the money. By all means allow yourself some champagne and toast to your new fortune, while visions of sugarplums with all kinds of fancy price tags dance through your head.

Quote, Unquote
Wealth is known to be a great comforter.
—*Plato, The Republic (4th c. BC)*

More Money, More Taxes

Then stop. Before you make another move, and after the champagne high wears off, think. Estate taxes, which were of marginal concern to you before, now loom ominously. You probably will be in a higher tax bracket, so "deductions" and "tax-exempt" become significant words. Yes, you have left behind your middle class tax concerns, and good riddance, you say. But now you have inherited the rich person's tax worries, which call for a whole new set of strategies.

What you need to do after absorbing your good news is run, don't walk, to your estate planning team (remember those men and women you engaged in Chapter 1?). Do not make any major expenditures or investments without their advice. More than one lottery winner, or inheritor of a small fortune, went from wealth to bankruptcy through unwise spending and investment.

You need immediately to do the following:

➤ Analyze all your assets and project your new income

➤ Review your life insurance and casualty/liability insurance, now that you have more to protect

➤ Revise your estate plan

If you won the lottery, you have instant cash, but the pay-out is spread over as many as 20 years. If you receive a gift or inheritance, it may be in the form of assets that could be difficult to convert to cash, such as stock in a close corporation, real estate, or valuable collectibles. Illiquid assets require special planning. Obviously, cash can be invested in numerous ways to create high-yield, tax-exempt income, or growth in the investment. If you receive non-cash assets, then the income flexibility is greatly reduced.

You may need to add more life insurance, particularly if estate taxes will bite into a cash-poor estate. Since you might buy and own more real property, visit your insurance agent and increase your casualty coverage. If you're involved in an accident with your expensive new car, a lawsuit will surely follow, so increase your automobile liability coverage.

Revising your estate plan may require rethinking your goals and the documents executed to further them. That includes who will benefit and by what means. Leaving everything to your spouse may have made sense before when the "everything" was relatively modest, but does it now? Or what about the children? You want to rear loving and responsible kids, not sponges. Perhaps giving something to charity is also possible now.

Often a well-drafted revocable trust can be used to manage assets for you and your spouse, then continue to manage those assets for your children.

Tax planning becomes crucial at this time. A QTIP trust for the spouse and a credit shelter trust to take advantage of the estate unified credit are important considerations. Making gifts that qualify for the annual exclusion and reduce your estate require proper training. All of these are explained in the next part of this book, about taxes. Transferring ownership of life insurance policies might be another option.

Finally, don't forget your will. All your planning may be for naught if your will is not an integral part of your estate file. Remember, everything you own solely is distributed by your will.

The most the federal estate tax can take is 55 percent of your assets. Don't overplan to the extent that the tax tail wags the planning dog. First and foremost must be your goals for yourself and your family.

About Bankruptcy

Bankruptcy is growing in this country. In 1996 the jump in the number of personal bankruptcies was greater than it has been since the mid 1980s, when we were in the midst of a serious recession. Take at look at the statistics in the table on the following page.

Financial distress has a myriad of causes. Some are self-inflicted, like running up credit card balances. With other folks, the problem is corporate downsizing that might have led to a job loss. Or perhaps there have been enormous medical bills. Or a divorce.

Obviously the concerns of wealth transfer and high taxes don't apply here, but financial and estate planning are still important.

Budgeting, debt consolidation, cashing in assets, and reducing one's lifestyle expenses could be sufficient to turn things around without your turning to bankruptcy. Remember, bankruptcy does clear most of your debts, but it remains on your credit report for 10 years and can keep you from obtaining new credit for major purchases you may need down the road.

ANNUAL U.S. PERSONAL BANKRUPTCY FILINGS

Year	Total Non-Business Filings	Annual Percent Change
1980	287,570	
1981	315,818	9.82%
1982	310,951	–1.54%
1983	286,444	–8.56%
1984	284,517	–0.68%
1985	341,233	19.93%
1986	449,203	31.64%
1987	495,553	10.32%
1988	549,612	10.91%
1989	616,226	12.12%
1990	718,107	16.53%
1991	872,438	21.49%
1992	900,874	3.26%
1993	812,898	–10.82%
1994	780,455	–4.16%
1995	874,642	12.07%
1996	1,125,006	28.62%

Source: American Bankruptcy Institute

Help! And Perhaps Some Relief

Before taking that first step to filing for bankruptcy, by all means first contact the National Foundation for Consumer Credit. This is a nationwide, nonprofit group that, through local Consumer Credit Counseling Service offices, has helped millions of Americans in serious debt to restructure those debts with their creditors. The service continues to assist them during the time it takes them to pay back the money owed. That help is either free or at a token charge.

To find the address of the CCCS office nearest you, call the foundation's referral line at (800) 338-2227. A recording will give you the address you need in your locale.

Tip
Review your assets to determine how to maximize your bankruptcy exemptions, such as making a larger contribution to a qualified retirement plan. You will probably be able to afford that as you will no doubt continue working, and will have the income to make that contribution.

If bankruptcy does seem to be the only answer for you, consult an attorney who specializes in that area of the law. You can find one by calling your local bar association, and asking for the names of attorneys who handle such matters. Do that as soon as you have decided on filing. Serious debt can threaten your health, marriage, and family, and needs to be quickly addressed.

While bankruptcy exemptions can vary from state to state, the debtor who resides in a state that uses federal exemptions can keep from his or her bankruptcy creditors up to:

➤ $15,000 equity (fair market value) in his or her residence

➤ $2,400 interest in a motor vehicle

➤ $8,000 in household goods

➤ $1,000 in personal jewelry

➤ $8,000 in the cash value of a life insurance policy

In addition, qualified retirement plans and life insurance policies are exempt from bankruptcy creditors.

Better times *will* come. Keep moving forward with your estate plan, and don't for a moment think you do not need a will because you don't have that many assets. You still have some, and you might also need to provide guardianship for minor children.

The Professional: Different Planning Needs

Physicians, dentists, attorneys, accountants, and other professionals licensed by the state to practice have some unique estate planning needs. For example, they cannot sell their practice in the same way other businesses can be sold because, among other restrictions, the purchaser must also be licensed in that profession.

Usually the estate planning necessary for those with high incomes and substantial investments applies to professionals. If this means you, here are a few matters you'll want to note.

Choice of Business Form

At one time the larger qualified retirement plan benefits made operating as a C corporation the logical choice. However, all forms of business organizations offer essentially the same retirement opportunities.

There are still some employment fringe benefits in C corporation status, but these often can be obtained by other means, such as through the other spouse's employer. The choice of business entity can limit a professional's liability for an associate's negligence, but not for his or her own malpractice.

Disability, Retirement, Divorce, and Death

Since your income in this area stops when you are no longer working, it's certainly smart to purchase disability insurance.

The limited marketability of your practice means that you should have a buy-sell agreement if you are practicing with others in a partnership or corporation. The agreement can cover both retirement and untimely death, and be a source of retirement income for you or an estate for your family.

If you're a sole practitioner when you opt to retire, you may have to hire a business broker to find a buyer for your practice. The major asset of your business—the client or patient list—may be of limited value to the purchaser. Adequate life insurance is vital to create an estate when the practice doesn't.

In several states, the value of a professional license is considered marital property for divorce purposes. I hope you'll have other assets to trade off; if not, divorce can seriously impact your estate planning here.

Down on the Farm: Also Special Needs

Are you a farmer? Then you may or may not know you have a unique position under the IRS Code and under some other government programs. I don't have the space in this book to go into all of them, but here are some planning opportunities.

➤ **Choice of business entity.** Many family farms have incorporated to take advantage of tax laws and more limited liability. For example, the farm home not only serves as your residence, but also as a deductible business office.

➤ **Accounting choices.** Cash and accrual basis accounting methods are permitted, and you can also use the crop method, which permits the deduction of crop expenses when the income is received. In addition, some capital improvements can be considered farming expenses, rather than depreciations, which must be spread over several years.

➤ **Federal and state programs.** Government loan programs are often available at attractive rates. Conservation and forestry incentives can provide cash for land that is not needed for crops. Certain crop reduction or diversion assistance can bring additional revenue. A number of states provide a lower property tax assessment for farmland.

➤ **Estate tax valuation and payment**. Under certain conditions, a family farm may be valued for federal estate tax purposes at its value as a farm, rather than at the *highest and best use* for that property. This is a term used by government and planning officials to mean the optimum use for a particular parcel of land, as they see it. For example, specific acreage might be seen as a shopping mall or a housing development. In addition, the estate may be eligible for the installment payment of the federal estate tax, which has interest-only payments for the first five installments, then the balance payable in 10 years.

Quote, Unquote
When tillage begins, other arts follow. The farmers therefore are the founders of human civilization.
—*Daniel Webster, "Remarks on Agriculture" (1840)*

You have seen in this chapter how special health/living/work situations can bring concerns and problems not always easily answered. Still, if one of these situations applies to you, by going to the right sources you *can* find solutions—and the way to a valuable estate plan.

The Least You Need to Know

➤ Proper planning for the disabled child can protect him or her, as well as ensure assets for your other children.

➤ Having everything in written contracts can best protect the property rights of unmarried couples living together.

➤ There is help for the custodial grandparent, in both private and government sectors.

➤ Sudden wealth or financial reverses require immediate planning adjustments.

➤ Professionals and farmers have special tax penalties and tax benefits unique to them.

Chapter 14

Family Feuds: Avoiding One over Your Estate

In This Chapter

➤ Wills can be contested

➤ Grounds are diverse

➤ Toughest challenges

➤ Making your will challenge-proof

It is the stuff of drama—challenging a will. "Then, Lieutenant, just as Great Uncle Simon was planning to change his will..." or words to that effect have turned up in dialogue in motion pictures and television dramas since both appeared on the scene.

Challenging a will isn't quite that dramatic in real life. It's families squabbling, threatening, seeing lawyers, not speaking—and continuing all of this sometimes for years. Naturally you don't want to see your loved ones carrying on like that about *your* will. Here's how to prevent it.

Challenging a Will: What'll Do It

Your will *can* be contested. Any beneficiary or heir can challenge it. What you need to know is the "why" and the "how" of will contests, so that you can prepare a nearly lawsuit-proof last will and testament. Read on.

The person contesting the will has the burden of proof. He or she must convince the court that the will should not be admitted to probate by proving one or more of the grounds (reasons) for finding that will invalid.

If a will is successfully contested, the deceased's estate is distributed, according to state intestate laws, to his or her heirs. Or a contest may revive an earlier will of the deceased's.

I'll tell you first about the usual grounds for a will contest.

Plain Incompetence

The testator (that's the person who's writing his or her will) must be at least 18 years old and mentally competent. Courts look to several factors in determining mental competence. That's whether a person:

Quote, Unquote
Discord gives a relish to concord.
—*Publilius Syrus,* "Moral Sayings" *(1st c. BC)*

➤ Knows that he or she is making a will

➤ Knows the extent and value of his or her property

➤ Knows the persons who would *ordinarily* be the beneficiaries of the will

➤ Understands the disposition as to the beneficiaries in his or her will

If there is a contest based on competency, expert witnesses, such as the deceased's doctor, and friends and acquaintances who knew the deceased *toward the end of his life* (having last seen him five years ago won't count) will testify as to their observations.

Tip
When signing a will, you may want to select credible witnesses who can readily attest to your mental competence. For example, if you are in a hospital, rehabilitation center or nursing home, consider first using your doctor or a nurse as a witness.

Someone in the early stages of Alzheimer's disease, who fulfills the above-mentioned requirements can have a will drawn that will stand up in court. So will a man or woman mildly retarded who, again, can satisfy those requirements. It's not the illness per se that's in question, but rather the testator's degree of understanding while suffering from it.

If you, as testator, have a history of medical problems that can affect your judgment, then that would be relevant evidence for a challenge. But quirky behavior, or cutting a child out of the will, in itself is not enough to mount a successful challenge.

Undue Influence: A Toughie to Prove

Except in the most obvious of cases, this is hard for a challenger to prove. The beneficiaries who receive more than others will be suspected of unduly influencing the deceased to make a will in their favor. The usual suspects include second spouses and favored children.

Anyone attempting to protest that will must prove:

➤ Undue influence was exerted on the testator

➤ The effect of the undue influence was to overpower his or her mind and will

➤ It produced a will (or a provision on the will) that expresses the intent of the one exerting the influence, and not that of the testator, and the will (or provision) would not have been made if it weren't for that influence

What is evidence of undue influence? Well, there are a few things one can look for here:

➤ Testator was in a weakened physical or mental condition, making him or her more susceptible to undue influence or domination

➤ Arranging for the will isolated the testator

➤ The person alleged to have exerted the undue influence had the opportunity to exercise it

➤ The disposition unduly favored the person exerting the influence on his or her family

Often the person contesting produces evidence that the deceased's wishes were overridden by another, usually someone who is trusted by the testator. This trusted person, in essence, told the deceased who was to benefit from his or her will.

The easiest cases for the courts involve a confidential relationship that is perverted to divert the deceased's natural wishes away from his or her relatives, to another person or persons. Here's a good example. Lawyers, unfortunately, sometimes draft wills for clients that provide substantial devises to the lawyer or his or her family. Not only is that unethical conduct on the part of any attorney, but it also will probably result in a successful will contest by anyone who decides to take up that challenge.

Quote, Unquote
Go first class—your heirs will.
—*Handstitching on a throw pillow*

What's harder to prove? That would be a situation involving some child or children receiving more than the others. You might not know there is no law requiring a parent to treat each child equally in a will. Still, some children deserve more, such as a special-needs child who will require long-term care (but it may actually be in the child's best interest to leave him *less*; see Chapter 13). Some children have more financial resources than others. Some children become alienated from their parents; others have had the burden of caring for them. There are many reasons why parents give preference to one child over another. Is that fair? In the case of the disabled child, yes, and the other children probably understand that. In the other instances, well....

If you are going to show some preference in your will, you should consider a letter or videotape stating your reasons for that choice. If Roberta is a doctor married to a multi-millionaire and Clarissa is single and a sculptor with a fairly low income, you may get away with a discrepancy in what you leave. The letter or video may help Roberta understand why you left the bulk of your assets to Clarissa. That *could* help those who would otherwise feel shortchanged to understand and accept your decision. But don't bet on it. Not dividing equally among the kids is very likely to cause resentment among them—and toward you long after you're gone.

Tip
Few wills are contested on the grounds that the deceased was forced into making one (duress) or induced to sign something that later turned out to be a will (fraud). Those illegalities do make for a good mystery plot, though. I highly recommend you read Agatha Christie's *Why Didn't They Ask Evans?*

I once drafted a will for a woman who left half of her estate to her daughter; the other half was divided among her grandchildren. At the funeral the daughter's tears were freely flowing. But once the will was read, there was a dramatic change, and the daughter probably would have kicked the coffin if it had been there. A will contest was narrowly averted, but animosities lingered in that family for a long time.

Poor Execution

You know that your will must be signed by you, and your signature witnessed. Most states require two adult witnesses. Attorneys usually go through a little ceremony here.

Attorney: Do you declare this to be your Last Will and Testament?

You: I do.

Attorney: Do you wish that we two serve as witnesses to your will? (the lawyer and someone from his or her office)

You: I do.

You sign the will first, then the witnesses do. If you are physically unable to sign, you can request that another person do so for you in your presence and in sight of the witnesses. Your will states that another person has signed for you. You must tell your witnesses that they are signing your will, but you don't have to allow them to read it.

Slip-ups do occur, often when a person writes and executes his or her own will. Common mistakes include:

➤ No witnesses or poorly selected witnesses

➤ Witnesses signing outside each other's presence

➤ Failure to use a self-proving clause (there's a sample of that statement in Chapter 7)

Many states allow the person making a will to attach to it this brief document, where essentially the witnesses swear to having been present at the signing of the will and note that the testator was of sound mind and was signing freely.

Most will forms you can buy at a local stationery store, or those on a computer disk, will have a line for witness signatures, so if you do it yourself you probably won't miss that aspect of execution.

Your two witnesses (some states require three) must be at least 18 years of age and otherwise competent. If there is any question about the proper execution, or your competence, then those persons will surely be called to testify in any will contest.

> **Briefs**
>
> FILE 132
>
> In the Line-Forms-on-the-Right-at-Probate Department: If you're a Grateful Dead fan, you certainly remember when Jerry Garcia, the group's leader, died in August 1995. In March 1997 the final tally on his estate came in: $9 million.
>
> Immediately after the rock musician's death there was a scurrying for parts of those assets, a battle that continues. It was also reported in March 1997 that lawyers for his third and last wife asked a judge to reverse his decision awarding a $4.6 million divorce settlement to wife No. 2. An assortment of business partners, former lovers and acquaintances also filed more than $38 million in claims against the estate.

Witnesses, but Not Beneficiaries, Too

One other point: You shouldn't have anyone who's a beneficiary witness your will. Many state laws deny the witness his or her bequest in a will, or limit what he or she can receive to an amount that is no greater than what he or she would come into as an heir if the deceased died intestate. If the beneficiary is an unnecessary witness (a third witness when only two are required), then that rule does not apply.

Here's an example. Let's say Jacob leaves one-half of his residuary probate estate to his son, Joseph, and divides the other one-half among his other eleven children, saving a little for his loyal servant Jim. Joseph was one of two witnesses to Jacob's will. Poor Joseph. Assuming that Jacob's wife does not survive him, but the other children do, Joseph's intestate share would be one-twelfth, not one-half, as stated in the will. And servant Jim, who happened to be the other witness, would be much worse off. He was left $10,000 in the will, but in fact he would receive nothing, since he was not one of the sons and was a witness. Jacob's will would be valid, but the witnesses much sadder for the experience.

"Messing Up" a Will

What looks to be a revoked will can also cause a court challenge. Mutilated or marked-on wills will cause a contestant to argue that the testator intended to revoke that document and the evidence is the torn will, or the one with handwritten notes on it. So be careful never to make handwritten changes on a will.

The "Don'ts" We Often "Do"

A simple will, which is all that most of us need, isn't that expensive. Save yourself worries and your family from a possible will contest: see an attorney; shop around for the best fee.

Now that my bias has been clearly expressed, let's consider some ways you could get into trouble, legally and otherwise, with a will. And I'll tell you how to avoid such trouble.

Making Abusive Remarks

The probated will is a public document, open to anyone who cares to see it. One of my clients wanted to vent her frustrations about her daughter, whose life, in the woman's eyes, had been less than exemplary. The phrases she proposed to put in her will were expressive and colorful, and derogatory in the extreme. She had every right to cut the daughter out of the will, but not to abuse her in public. Family disputes are tragic enough without that. I reminded her that she might reconcile with the daughter, but not get around to changing the will. In the end, she toned down her language.

Making an Omission Without Explanation

You can choose whomever you want to receive your probate estate (remember, however, a spouse may have a right to elect against the will). If you want to delete one of your four children as a beneficiary, that is your privilege. I mentioned earlier in this chapter that a letter or videotape explaining why you have chosen to do so may be a satisfactory way to allow the child to understand your motives. The same advice applies if the child doesn't get an "equal" share, and there is no special needs child involved. In any event, explaining your reasoning can head off a will contest.

Making Promises: Don't

Court decisions abound involving a deceased who allegedly promised someone that he would be left something in the will for services rendered.

For example, Ivan promises a neighbor, Sam, that if Sam handles the upkeep of Ivan's house and yard, then Ivan will leave him something in his will. Ivan dies, and—what do you know—leaves everything to his third cousin.

Sam is incensed. Is he going to see an attorney? Is the attorney going to take his case? Is he going to get anything from the estate? Answer: yes, yes and maybe.

A better system for both Ivan and Sam would have been a written contract that specified Sam's duties and compensation, rather than a devise in Ivan's will. Sam can file a claim against Ivan's estate if the executor won't honor the contract.

Tip
If you do want to reduce a particular child's "expected" inheritance, consider giving the child some memento that he will treasure, and then indicate that other considerations result in that child receiving nothing else from the will. That could soften the blow a bit. It might also give the child no grounds to contest the will if you clearly indicate why his interest is not what he might have expected.

Making Codicils That Change Beneficiaries

A codicil (a separate paper amending a will) changing an executor or a guardian probably won't overly concern anyone and hardly ever results in a will contest.

Here is a sample codicil changing executors. As you can see, it is quite a simple form. Still, before you consider adapting it for yourself, be certain to check with your attorney or your state to make sure it meets requirements where you are.

Watch Out
Never use a codicil to reduce the amount a beneficiary is to receive from your will. You are almost guaranteed a will contest from that disappointed individual. Make a new will instead.

CODICIL TO THE LAST WILL AND TESTAMENT
OF

_____

I, _____, domiciled in _____, do make, publish and declare this to be the First Codicil to my Last Will and Testament executed by me on the 31st day of July, 1987, in the presence of _____ and _____ as witnesses.

I hereby remove _____ as personal representative and substitute _____ under Article V of my Last Will and Testament.

In all other respects, I hereby ratify all of the provisions of my Last Will and Testament dated July 31, 1987.

IN TESTIMONY WHEREOF, I have subscribed my name to this my First Codicil to my Last Will and Testament consisting of one typewritten page, all in the presence of the persons witnessing it at my request on this _____ day of _____, 199___, at.

_____
Testator

The foregoing instrument, consisting of this page, was signed, published and declared by _____ to be his First Codicil to his Last Will and Testament, in our presence. We then at his request and in his presence, and in the presence of each other, signed our names as witnesses to the Codicil this _____ day of _____, 199___.

_____   residing at _____

_____

_____   residing at _____

_____

(Note: A self-proving clause should be used with the Codicil, just as with a Will.)

A Joint Will? No!

Togetherness is fine, but there are some things we just gotta do on our own, you know? And making your own will is one of them. You and your spouse should have separate documents. The provisions can be reciprocal: everything to each other, then to the children. Or you can make different provisions.

Just don't have a joint will. When one of you dies, the joint will may not be changed by the surviving spouse without running the risk of a will contest. Those who were beneficiaries in the joint will, but are no longer in a subsequent will, may claim that the surviving spouse was legally bound to the provisions in the joint will.

Two wills really don't cost much more than one, and you can avoid that potential problem.

Making a Separate List of "Gifts"

Frequently we have several items we'd like to leave to a particular family member or friend, but we don't want to list them in a will. Most state laws allow you to prepare a list of that property, and the names of persons you want to receive those items. Many states require that, that list must exist at the time the will is executed and not subsequently be changed, and that the list be in the testator's handwriting or signed by him or her.

It's easier to decide what property to give a person and put that devise in the will. As to other items, consider making gifts now, or leave a letter to your beneficiaries asking them to distribute those mementos among your family and friends. The letter will not be legally binding, but your beneficiaries probably will honor your wishes.

Making Changes on the Will

That's right, *on,* not *in,* the will. As I have said, if you want to change your will, execute a codicil or prepare a new will. Don't line out cousin Calvin's name and replace it with niece Nancy's. Any changes on the will after it is executed will not be valid. You run the additional risk of the court treating substantial changes as reflecting your intent to revoke the will. A disgruntled heir may be tempted to contest the will on that basis; if he or she is successful, your estate would be distributed to the intestate heirs.

Families squabbling over an estate can be intriguing in mystery books, and funny in television sit-coms. But in real life, such feuds are not terribly attractive. You can easily avoid one by making sure your will is as challenge-proof as it can be. It's really not that difficult.

The Least You Need to Know

➤ A will can be challenged, but the burden of proof is on the challenger.

➤ To avoid a contest over your estate, take every step you can to make your will challenge-proof.

➤ Be careful, if you use a do-it-yourself will, to make no mistakes that a disappointed beneficiary can latch onto.

➤ Spouses should not execute a joint will.

Part 4
Taxes You Must Pay, and Those Maybe You Don't

Now we come to what you might not have been looking forward to reading about—taxes. You'll certainly find a variety of them here, from the federal estate tax to a tax levied by some states on what they call "intangibles," such as stocks and bonds.

Tax matters are important to your estate, of course, because the more you can legitimately hold back from the grabby IRS, the more there will be for you and your family. So while unfortunately I do have to tell you about all these taxes, I'll also have the pleasure of helping you keep them down to a minimum, and sometimes avoid them altogether.

That's about as good as the news gets in a tax chapter, and since we're talking about your hard-earned money, you should find that darned nice to hear. Let's get on with the savings.

Chapter 15

The Wonderful World of Federal Estate Taxes

In This Chapter

➤ Taxing estates over $600,000

➤ Basics of computing the tax

➤ Marital and other deductions

➤ Transfers that skip a generation

Ah, so many taxes. Here is the first of them: the federal tax levied on your estate.

"Isn't dying bad enough," you're probably thinking, "without being hit with a new slew of taxes—in absentia, of course." I couldn't agree with you more. But for now that's the law of the land, and so here they are—estate taxes spelled out.

The Magic Number is $600,001

First you should know that officially the *federal estate tax* is a levy placed by the federal government on the transfer of property from the deceased to those who inherit. If $600,000 or less is transferred, there is no estate tax, unless there have been prior taxable gifts, which I'll go into. Also, if you leave all your property outright to your spouse, there is no federal estate tax at all (that's the marital deduction, which I'll also talk about).

The tax begins at $1 over $600,000.

If you're reading this and saying "Hah, I should only have an estate worth $600,000," then I urge you to stop feeling impoverished and do some fast math. Do you remember the assets form you filled out in Chapter 1? If you have, for example, a $300,000 life insurance policy and a home valued at $150,000 (although any mortgage would be a deduction from the gross estate), you're already at $450,000, and we haven't even touched on your other assets. So do read on. All of this could apply to you.

I must say, though, that in actuality only 1.6 percent of all estates will be affected in 1997 by this tax. It's a small figure, but because of inflation, the increase in value of stocks and bonds and other factors, the number of taxable estates *is* expected to double by the year 2007—from 37,000 in 1997 to 73,000 then. That's according to the Congressional tax staff studying estate tax reform. Some are hoping to abolish the tax, or increase the amount excluded from the tax. But that tax will raise some $100 billion in the next five years, so it's not an easy sum of money to dispense with quickly.

Spreading the Wealth to Avoid the Tax

There are ways of handling your "wealth" if you fall into the estate tax asset figure. Take Ted, as an example. When he died, his wife inherited one half of his property ($500,000), and the other half ($500,000) went to their children. Ted had made no substantial gifts in any one year. While his estate for federal estate tax purposes is $1 million, none of it is taxed, since $500,000 goes tax-free to his wife (remember, she's got that marital deduction) and the other $500,000 does not exceed the threshold figure of $600,000. Perhaps Ted did a bit of estate planning?

The federal estate tax, incidentally, is paid from the estate before any disbursements are made to beneficiaries or heirs.

What's in the Pot? Just About Everything

The federal estate tax includes the probate estate and property owned by the deceased where ownership transfers to another individual upon the deceased's death. (The spouse gets a marital deduction.)

Let's use Audrey as an example. She owned the following: her home (worth $200,000) and corporate stock, which she jointly owned with right of survivorship with her daughter, Paula (worth $200,000). She also had a life insurance policy ($300,000) with the proceeds payable to her other daughter, Diana. The house is in her probate estate; the stock and life insurance proceeds are transferred to the daughters at Audrey's death. All of the estate is subject to the federal estate tax, because it totals $700,000.

Another Important Figure: $10,000

This number will be mentioned frequently throughout all of Part 4. It's a common tax break and a good one. Essentially it is a *gift tax*. (Chapter 16 goes into much more detail about this gift tax.)

The first $10,000 of any gift you make to any person during any calendar year is excluded from taxation.

If you are married and have a child, you and your spouse can give that child a total of $20,000. Married couples can use those two annual exclusions (worth $20,000 per recipient), even if only one spouse owns the property. That is called *gift splitting*.

Take Mary for example. She gives her stock in ABC, Inc. to her son. The stock is worth $20,000. If Mary's husband joins in the gift (and files the appropriate gift tax return), there will be no tax because both are using their annual exclusions ($10,000 + $10,000). You'll see the words "*annual exclusion*" often in the next four chapters too. They refer to this $10,000 gift.

Tip
You can reduce your estate by using this exclusion. For instance, you could give your child $10,000 each year for 10 years. By then you would have transferred $100,000 free of any gift tax, and there would be no reduction in your lifetime $600,000 exclusion.

The Gross Estate

This is where we'll begin calculating the federal estate tax. Basically, you take the gross estate, subtract expenses and other allowed deductions, and then add certain taxable gifts.

At the end of the specific explanations that follow, you'll see a worksheet. It will show you in numbers the explanations that follow.

Let's start with our base item, the gross estate.

The value of the property on the date of the deceased's death—the *gross estate*—generally determines the amount that is subject to federal estate tax. Here is a list of property that would be included in the gross estate:

➤ Property solely owned by the deceased

➤ Certain gifts transferred within three years before death (for example, a life insurance policy ownership transferred to another owner)

➤ Transfers where the deceased retains a life estate (see Chapter 2) or has the power to revoke the transfer, such as a revocable living trust (see Chapter 8)

➤ Survivor annuity and survivor pension (when the owner was the first to die)

➤ Jointly owned property

—half included if jointly with spouse

—all included if owned with another person

➤ Property over which deceased had *General Power of Appointment.* What's that? Look at it this way. I die and I own some property. I give my wife not the ownership, but the power to give that to another individual whom she wants to have it. This is a rarely used transfer, confined for the most part to pretty sophisticated estate planning in the millions of dollars.

➤ Life insurance proceeds paid to the estate or where the policy was owned by the deceased (most of us own our policies, but someone else could also own an insurance policy on our life)

So essentially any property that someone else receives because of your death will be included in your gross estate.

Briefs

Artist Georgia O'Keeffe died in 1986 at the age of 98. Her estate included approximately 400 works of art. The executor and the IRS agreed that the total art valued individually amounted to $72,759,000. Since that was the value if all of the works were sold at once, both parties agreed that there should be a discount for federal estate taxes. The executor contended that the value should be discounted 75 percent, while IRS experts argued for a range of 10 to 37 percent. The Tax Court compromised: For tax purposes the art would be valued at $36,400,000.

I'll illustrate all of this with Anita's estate. She is married and has two adult children. According to a prenuptial agreement, Anita's husband waived any right to her probate estate, so her will leaves the stocks/bonds to her church, and the farm to her children. She lives in a non-community property state (see Chapter 3). Anita owns the following:

Property	Ownership	Value
house	with husband	$200,000
household goods	with husband	20,000
savings/checking	with husband	20,000
stocks and bonds	Anita	200,000
farm	Anita	800,000
pension	(husband survivor)	200,000
life insurance	(children beneficiary)	200,000
	Total value of the property	1,640,000

The gross estate for federal estate tax includes:

➤ Half each of the house, household goods, and savings/checking (the husband is considered to have owned the other half of each asset). That's a total of $120,000.

➤ The stocks/bonds, pension, farm, and life insurance proceeds. That's a total of $1,520,000.

Anita had not made any taxable gifts within the last three years, which would be included in the gross estate, nor had she established a revocable trust. (Most gifts made within three years prior to death are not in the gross estate.)

She had not received from anyone a general power of appointment either.

If Anita had lived in a community property state, all the marital property would be community property (again, Chapter 3), so the surviving spouse's half interest in the marital assets would not be part of Anita's gross estate.

Great! Tax Deductions Allowed

The gross estate is, fortunately, reduced by certain allowed deductions. The most frequently used are the charitable deduction, the marital deduction, expenses of administering the estate, and the deceased's debts and certain of her taxes.

Let's examine them.

Tip
Charities that qualify for federal *income* tax deductions will almost always qualify for the federal *estate* tax deduction. Chapter 17 contains several suggestions for charitable arrangements that could qualify for income tax deductions when made, as well as estate tax deductions.

Charitable Deductions

As you have seen, Anita left her stocks and bonds to her church, which is, of course, a charity. That entitles Anita's estate to a charitable deduction. Gifts through a will, or through life arrangements that are paid by an estate, qualify for this deduction.

Hooray for the Marital Deduction!

Here is a very popular deduction that includes all property that the surviving spouse receives outright or through certain qualified marital trusts.

Returning to Anita, we see that her husband received the following:

➤ Half of their house, half of their household goods, and half of their savings/checking account, because they owned each asset jointly with right of survivorship, and he survived her; altogether this property totaled $120,000. (He already owned the other half of each asset as co-owner.)

➤ $200,000 as survivor on her pension plan.

The total amount of the marital deduction here is $320,000.

Quote, Unquote
Wealth: any income that is at least $100 more a year than the income of one's wife's sister's husband.
—*H. L. Mencken*

The QTIP and Credit Shelter Trust

Let me explain something else to you here briefly. Sometimes a spouse receives property in trust, where he or she is the only income beneficiary. If upon the surviving spouse's death the amount is included in his or her estate for federal estate tax purposes, then the marital deduction is available for the deceased spouse's estate tax. The surviving spouse would be beneficiary of the trust income, then the principal would go to others (e.g., children) at his or her death. This is an exception to the general rule that the spouse might receive the property outright to qualify for the marital deduction.

This qualified trust is often referred to as a QTIP (Qualified Terminal Interest Property). There must be an election (choice) to treat a QTIP trust as a marital deduction in the deceased's estate.

The spouse who has significant assets may want to establish two trusts:

➤ One trust involves a QTIP (for the marital deduction).

Tip
Here's another IRS phone number; this one puts you in contact with its Forms Distribution Center. You can call (800) 829-3676 to request free publications. You might also want to ask about the agency's tapes and films.

➤ Another trust, funded with $600,000, called a "credit shelter trust," for using the unified credit equivalent amount. I'll explain that in the next few pages.

Combining the QTIP trust with the credit shelter trust could mean that the deceased's estate will not have to pay any estate tax.

The property transferred to the spouse's QTIP trust provides a marital deduction *and* the $600,000 that is exempt from the tax, which goes to the credit shelter trust, may equal the gross estate. Both trusts could be used to support the spouse during his or her life.

Deductible Expenses

The estate might have quite a few costs. There could be probate administration expenses (filing, executor, and attorney fees). There could be debts on the estate property, such as a mortgage on the home, and bills that were unpaid at Anita's death. Likewise, there may be taxes that Anita would have had to pay, such as income tax on earnings in the year before she died, or property taxes on her real estate.

Anita's estate actually had the following deductions:

Probate expenses	$50,000
Mortgage on farm	50,000
Income taxes due	5,000
Property tax on farm	5,000
That comes to	$110,000.

Tallying It Up

All of Anita's estate's deductible expenses include:

Charitable	$200,000
Marital	320,000
Other (above-mentioned)	110,000
Total	$630,000

> **Quote, Unquote**
> The wisdom of man never yet contrived a system of taxation that would operate with perfect equality.
> —*Andrew Jackson*, "Proclamation to the People of South Carolina" *(December 10, 1823)*

Her whole tax computation looks like this so far:

Gross estate	$1,520,000
(less) deductions	630,000
Taxable estate	$890,000

That's quite a reduction from the original figure, isn't it?

Anita did not make any post-1976 taxable gifts (gifts that are in excess of the annual exclusion of $10,000 per recipient, or $20,000 if the spouse joins in making the gift). Therefore her tax base is the same as her taxable estate.

If there are gifts in excess of the annual exclusion, then they would be added to the tax base. For example, if Anita had given $50,000 to one of her children in 1996 (and her husband joined in the gift), the taxable portion of the gift would be $30,000 ($50,000 gift less $20,000 annual gift exclusion for both of them).

How Does 37 Percent Sound?

Now we're getting to the important numbers.

The federal estate tax rate begins at 37% and goes up to 55% (Anita's highest marginal rate, on the last $140,000 of her taxable estate is 39%).

Since Anita's taxable estate is $890,000, the computation looks like this:

$248,300 (on the first $750,000)

$54,600 (on the next $140,000)

$302,900 (on the taxable estate $890,000)

This tentative tax of $302,900 is computed using the IRS estate tax table you can see on the following page.

But wait a minute. Anita has several tax credits available to reduce her tentative tax.

To Anita's Credit

First there is what is known as the *unified tax credit*. That's a lifetime tax credit of $192,800 on gifts or your estate. Over the years, if you make gifts, that credit is reduced according to the size of those gifts. Indeed at your death you may have used up the credit, so that it is not there to benefit your estate.

If the Amount with Respect to Which the Tentative Tax to Be Computed Is:	The Tentative Tax Is:
Not over $10,000	18 percent of such amount
Over $10,000 but not over $20,000	$1,800, plus 20 percent of the excess of such amount over $10,000.
Over $20,000 but not over $40,000	$3,800, plus 22 percent of the excess of such amount over $20,000.
Over $40,000 but not over $60,000	$8,200, plus 24 percent of the excess of such amount over $40,000.
Over $60,000 but not over $80,000	$13,000, plus 26 percent of the excess of such amount over $60,000.
Over $80,000 but not over $100,000	$18,200, plus 28 percent of the excess of such amount over $80,000.
Over $100,000 but not over $150,000	$23,800, plus 30 percent of the excess of such amount over $100,000.
Over $150,000 but not over $250,000	$38,800, plus 32 percent of the excess of such amount over $150,000.
Over $250,000 but not over $500,000	$70,800, plus 34 percent of the excess of such amount over $250,000.
Over $500,000 but not over $750,000	$155,800, plus 37 percent of the excess of such amount over $500,000.
Over $750,000 but not over $1,000,000	$248,300, plus 39 percent of the excess of such amount over $750,000.
Over $1,000,000 but not over $1,250,000	$345,800, plus 41 percent of the excess of such amount over $1,250,000.
Over $1,250,000 but not over $1,500,000	$448,300, plus 43 percent of the excess of such amount over $1,250,000.
Over $1,500,000 but not over $2,000,000	$555,800, plus 45 percent of the excess of such amount over $1,500,000.
Over $2,000,000 but not over $2,500,000	$780,800, plus 49 percent of the excess of such amount over $2,000,000.
Over $2,500,000 but not over $3,000,000	$1,025,800, plus 53 percent of the excess of such amount over $2,500,000.
Over $3,000,000*	$1,290,800, plus 55 percent of the excess of such amount over $3,000,000.

*For large taxable transfers (generally in excess of $10 million) there is a phase-out of the graduated rates and the unified tax credits.
Source: Internal Revenue Service

Tax Rates for Federal Gift Tax and Federal Estate Tax (1996)

In addition to the unified credit, the federal tax allows a *state death tax credit* based upon IRS tables (you can see the figure here that spells that out).

State Death Tax Credit for Federal Income Tax

(A) Adjusted Taxable Estate* Equal to or More Than	(B) Adjusted Taxable Estate* Less Than	(C) Credit on Amount in Column (A)	(D) Rate of Credit on Excess Over Amount in Column (A) (Percentage)
0	$40,000	0	None
$40,000	90,000	0	0.8
90,000	140,000	$400	1.6
140,000	240,000	1,200	2.4
240,000	440,000	3,600	3.2
440,000	640,000	10,000	4.0
640,000	840,000	18,000	4.8
840,000	1,040,000	27,600	5.6
1,040,000	1,540,000	38,800	6.4
1,540,000	2,040,000	70,800	7.2
2,040,000	2,540,000	106,800	8.0
2,540,000	3,040,000	146,800	8.8
3,040,000	3,540,000	190,800	9.6
3,540,000	4,040,000	238,800	10.4
4,040,000	5,040,000	290,800	11.2
5,040,000	6,040,000	402,800	12.0
6,040,000	7,040,000	522,800	12.8
7,040,000	8,040,000	650,800	13.6
8,040,000	9,040,000	786,800	14.4
9,040,000	10,040,000	930,800	15.2
10,040,000		1,082,800	16.0

Adjusted Taxable Estate = Taxable Estate—$60,000

Source: Internal Revenue Service, 1996

Since Anita's taxable estate is $890,000, her state death tax credit is $27,120, using the IRS tables.

So Anita's final tax is as follows:

Tentative tax		$302,900
less credits of		
Unified	$192,800	
State death tax	$27,120	= $219,920
Federal estate tax		$82,980

Watch Out
There is a deadline for paying the estate tax. Usually it's nine months from the date of death. However, there are special installment payment provisions for certain family farms and small corporations.

That's the absolute bottom line. You think that's a lot to owe? Keep in mind the original amount of Anita's estate—over $1.5 million.

Now here is that worksheet I promised you earlier, that will show you in one place how these figures added up.

Gross estate (transferred property)			$1,520,000
Subtract:			
	Expenses, debts, certain taxes	$110,000	
	Losses during probate*	$-0-	
	Charitable devises	$200,000	
	Marital deduction	$320,000	= $630,000
	Taxable estate		$890,000
	Add post-1976 taxable gifts	$-0-	
	Tax base	$890,000	
	Tentative tax (tax base × tax rate)		$302,900
Subtract:			
	Unified tax credit	$192,800	
	Other tax credits**	27,120	= $219,920
	Estate tax due		$82,980

*For example, casualty loss, such as fire destroying house
**Includes state death tax credit (see chart in this chapter)

Taxing Each Generation

Watch Out
Obviously it's wise to turn to the accountant who is part of your estate planning team before attempting to work around the GSTT. (No doubt you've been consulting the appropriate professional member of that team through major steps you've been taking with your estate plan anyway, haven't you?)

The government will track you down, and your children, and your children's children and...

Congress wants to tax each generation of yours if it can.

If you don't plan to make a gift in your will of over $1,000,000 to your grandchildren, then skip this section.

Suppose a taxpayer wants to skip the next generation (his child) and leave all of his money to the second generation (his grandchildren). He figures his daughter's estate is large enough already to be taxed when the time comes, so why leave his daughter money that will only be added to her estate tax?

Unfortunately for taxpayers, Congress has thought about that too. The generation-skipping transfer tax (GSTT) is imposed when the next generation (children) is bypassed in favor of a later generation (grandkids). The tax applies to gifts and transfers by death. The current tax rate is 55 percent.

Now, each person has a $1 million *exemption* from the GSTT. A husband and wife could transfer $2 million through gifts and devises in their wills to their grandchildren free of the GSTT. However, an estate or gift tax may still apply there.

The Least You Need to Know

➤ Estates of over $600,000 may be subject to the federal estate tax.

➤ A gross estate for tax purposes includes all property transferred to someone else because of death.

➤ Thanks to the marital deduction, property going outright to a spouse is not taxed.

➤ The federal estate tax begins at 37 percent and rises to 55 percent.

Chapter 16

Gifts—and Gift Taxes

A gift is a thoughtful, sometimes simple, gesture.

The IRS may see it differently, though, and can slap you or your estate with quite a tax. You might have done things differently if you had known the tax and estate ramifications of your generosity. Let's see how you can make someone else happy, while keeping a smile on your own face.

How to Present a Gift

Legally, there are certain elements of giving that make a gift a gift, as far as your estate plan goes, and also with the IRS, when it comes to taxpaying.

Instead of my simply spelling them out, let's imagine this little scenario, which contains those necessary elements. I'll explain them later.

Aunt Agatha has promised you her antique oak chest, certainly a handsome piece of furniture, when she dies. Your aunt means well, but there are several "ifs" that could be impediments to your receiving that chest. You will receive that gift:

➤ If she owns the chest when she dies

➤ If she has a will specifically devising the chest to you

➤ If her estate has enough assets to pay its debts (the chest might have to be sold to pay outstanding bills)

In this instance I would suggest you follow my advice and have Aunt Agatha make a gift of that chest to you now. Here, briefly, is why.

To have a valid gift three things are required:

1. The donor (in this case your aunt) has to have the intent at that moment to make the gift

Words, Words, Words

Merriam Webster's Collegiate Dictionary defines a **gift** as "something voluntarily transferred by one person to another without compensation." In other words, no strings, ever.

2. The donee (you) has to accept the gift

3. The gift property has to be transferred from the donor to the donee

Okay, now let's continue. You persuade Aunt Agatha to go along with this script.

Scene: The room in Aunt Agatha's house where the oak chest is situated.

Prop: Video camera, held by a third party.

Aunt Agatha: Joanie, I give you my oak chest *[points to chest as camera goes from aunt to chest].*

You: Aunt Agatha McCleary, thank you so very much for this lovely oak chest. I accept your gift.

[camera shows you patting the chest as Aunt Agatha moves—or appears to move—it toward you]

Words, Words, Words

A **bailee** is one who temporarily possesses, but does not own, a property. An example might be a parking garage near your office that has a copy of the key to your car. (This isn't a commonly used expression, as you have probably surmised since you no doubt have never heard of it. Most haven't.)

But Aunt Agatha, this chest looks so right in this house. Please keep it for me as bailee until later.

Aunt Agatha: I will keep it for you as bailee.

End of script.

What you now have is a gift presented to you. When Aunt Agatha dies, you'll send a copy of the videotape to the executor of her estate to prove the oak chest is yours.

That's one way to handle a gift. As you have seen, it fulfills the three elements of gift giving, and there can be no mistaking the intentions of the donor, or the one accepting the gift. It's neat and clean.

We don't have our camcorders always handy, of course. In this chapter we'll discuss some other giving styles, their benefits, and tax consequences.

The Federal Tax Nobody Knows

The *federal gift tax* is a levy on a transfer of property by gift. You must tell the IRS if you make any gifts over $10,000 in cash or property.

Let's say you feel very generous today. Life has been good, so you want to spread the wealth (yours) around a little. Your spouse deserves something special, so you give her 100 shares of Huge Consolidated, Inc. (value $20,000). Junior and your little princess have matured more quickly than you'd expected, so you give each of them 50 shares of good old Consolidated for the holidays, with each gift worth $15,000. Shucks, it's just a little something.

When tax time comes around you ask your accountant if those gifts are deductible on your 1040 form.

Your accountant smiles. Deductible? In your dreams. You must file a gift tax return for both by April 15, which she will, of course, be happy to prepare for you at her usual fee. Your gift to your wife calls for no tax because of the marital deduction. But the stock to your kids? If your wife has gone in on the two $15,000 presents with you, then there is no tax because of the $10,000 annual exclusion, or $20,000 per recipient from both of you, even if the spouse does not own the gifted property. If she has not, then you must pay tax on each of the $5,000 amounts above that figure.

A gift tax. What a wonderful country to come up with so many ways to be taxed!

Have you heard of this charge? Take an informal survey of your friends to see if they are familiar with it. Not many will be. When I was taking a graduate law class about 15 years ago, the lecturer, who worked for the gift tax section of the IRS, commented, not entirely facetiously, that they held a celebration every time a gift tax return was filed, there were so few of them.

So why do we have this tax? Well, for revenue of course, but mostly to protect the federal *estate* tax.

Quote, Unquote
To give and then not feel that one has given is the very best of all ways of giving.
—*Max Beerbohm*, "Hosts and Guests" *(1920)*

Quote, Unquote
What with your friend you nobly share
At least a rescue from your heir
—*Horace*, "Odes" *(c. 23–15 BC)*

If you could make a deathbed gift of all your property, without any tax, then the Treasury coffers would not get much in the way of estate tax revenue. So your gifts must be taxed.

Don't unduly worry. There are many exclusions to this tax. It's important, though, for you to understand the tax if it should be money you need to pay one day, and for you to know enough about it to be able perhaps to avoid it when estate planning.

When You Aren't Taxed

You might be thinking about now of all your gifts over the last several years. Were they *taxable*, for pete's sake?

No, no, relax. Not every gift is subject to the federal gift tax. There is, of course, that $10,000 exclusion, and most of us give presents to family and friends that fall well below that figure. Gifts to a spouse (more about that coming up) or a charity can be made free of any tax. Since the gift tax is based on yearly gifts, the annual $10,000 exclusion and spousal gifts eliminate most gifts from taxation.

There is no tax levied on gifts of educational tuition, either, or paying another's medical expenses. Also, joint savings accounts, joint stock brokerage accounts, and joint U.S. savings bonds are not considered gifts and are not subject to the tax when they're established.

So if Mom opens a savings account with Trustworthy Bank, and puts her daughter, Fran, on the account as joint owner with right of survivorship, there is no gift to her daughter unless Fran withdraws funds for herself. If she does, Mom has made a gift.

Tax-Free Gifts to a Spouse

Outright gifts between husband and wife are technically subject to the federal gift tax, but the marital deduction reduces each gift to zero taxation. Therefore, spouses can shower each other with presents without any concern for the gift tax.

However—and isn't there always a however?—if a spouse is given only a life estate interest in property, (meaning that it is hers only for her lifetime; see Chapter 2) or an irrevocable trust is created in which he or she is the life income beneficiary (see Chapter 8), then the tax law is a bit more complicated. Using a QTIP (Qualified Terminal Interest Property; see Chapter 15) avoids the gift tax. The election must be made, and then property would be included in the recipient spouse's estate for federal estate tax purposes.

Tip

Gifts of services are not subject to the gift tax. For example, your receiving free advice from another, such as investment counseling, would not be taxable (but could, of course, be quite valuable to you).

For example, Jennie creates an irrevocable trust for her husband, who receives an income interest in the trust. If the QTIP is made, and his interest will be subject to federal estate tax upon his death (it wouldn't otherwise), then the marital gift deduction applies. That's because the QTIP is treated the same for gift tax purposes as an outright gift to a spouse—available for the marital deduction.

The QTIP is fairly sophisticated tax planning and may not be useful for most couples, particularly those whose combined estate would not exceed $1.2 million.

A Variety of Gifts

The gift tax is imposed on taxable gifts made each year, accumulating those gifts and imposing a progressive levy. No tax is due until taxable gifts of over $600,000 are made.

If you have made gifts in excess of $10,000 to someone other than your spouse, then you must file a gift tax return by April 15 of the next year. Since the gift tax applies to all gratuitous transfers, you must carefully record all those over the $10,000 exclusion. Gifts may include:

➤ Outright transfers

➤ Below-market interest rate loans or forgiven loans

➤ Transfers to an irrevocable trust

➤ Creation of co-ownerships in property or a remainder interest in property

Let's consider these in a little more detail.

Outright Transfers—What's That?

It means that the person getting the gift has all legal rights to it, whether cash or property. There are no restrictions to ownership.

Let's say you give your child corporate stock worth $20,000, or $20,000 in cash. That is an outright gift, or transfer, and subject to the gift tax (unless your spouse is going in with you on the gift, with his or her $10,000 exclusion).

Below Market Rate Loans

If you lend your son money interest-free, or below an established interest rate, then the amount of interest you *should have received* if the loan had the appropriate interest is treated as a gift of that interest by you to your son.

For example, let's say the loan was in the amount of $50,000, and had no interest attached. Assuming the federally prescribed interest rate to be 10 percent, then the first year's forgiven interest is $5,000.

Words, Words, Words
To **forgive** a loan, or interest on a loan, is to grant the one borrowing that money relief from payment of the debt. This should be in writing, of course, and dated.

If you have made no more than $5,000 in additional gifts to your son in that year, the annual exclusion will apply and there will be no gift tax due. You will have come in under your $10,000 figure.

However, the IRS may not be finished with you yet. It could require you to report the forgiven interest *as if it were* paid to you by your son, which means additional income to the donor.

Watch Out
Be careful when lending large sums of money to a child and, if the child is married, his or her spouse. Be sure that both know whether that money is a gift, or a loan that you expect to be repaid. Serious misunderstandings, and sometimes a family rift, can arise over the years when it is not spelled out clearly.

Loans to children may be structured to minimize taxes. Interest might be low enough to use the annual gift tax exclusion, and a family member loan of $100,000 or less that isn't used to generate investment income may not be taxable to the lender.

Let's say you want to lend your child money to help him or her buy a home. The loan is $100,000, and you charge no interest. You could:

➤ Avoid the gift tax, assuming that it's determined that the interest, if charged, would have amounted to no more than $10,000

➤ Avoid the income tax, if your child had no more than $1,000 in net investment income for the year

If you later completely forgive your child's loan, then that will also be a gift and will be subject to gift tax, minus your annual exemption in the year the loan is forgiven.

When the Revocable Trust Works Best

You learned about trusts in Chapter 8. Here's how they can work in a gift situation.

Hannah established an *irrevocable* trust for her daughter, Shirley, and contributed $100,000 to that trust. It was to accumulate income until Shirley was 25 years old.

Hannah's gift to the trust is indirectly given to Shirley; therefore, the transfer is subject to the gift tax.

However, if Hannah had established a *revocable* trust, where she retained the power to revoke, then the gift would not be complete and not subject to the gift tax. See what that slight difference in wording between "revocable" and "*ir*revocable" can do to a tax picture?

Co-ownership: Togetherness and Taxes

Maria owns her home. She executes a new deed to the place with her son Yuri as tenant-in-common for one-half of the property. Maria has made a gift to Yuri that is subject to the gift tax. The value of that gift is one-half of the fair market value of the home at the time of the gift.

If Maria had made Yuri a joint tenant with right of survivorship, or had deeded the property to him and kept a life estate (you read about that in Chapter 2), the value of the gift would be the fair market value of the home at the time of the gift *less* an actuarially determined amount based on Maria's life expectancy.

Using IRS tables, Maria would compute the value of her interest, which then would be subtracted from the total value of the property, to determine the amount Yuri received subject to the gift tax.

Prior Gifts and the Unified Credit

Any prior year's taxable gifts are added to the current year's gifts to determine the total taxable gifts. Therefore you should keep copies of all your previous gift tax returns so that that cumulative figure is available, as well as any gift taxes paid.

Remember that your gift tax unified credit is $192,800 (equivalent to $600,000 in taxable gifts). If you make any taxable gifts, then the unified credit is accordingly reduced.

Missy gave her son $610,000 in 1996. She had not made any prior taxable gifts. Applying her annual exclusion ($10,000) and her unified credit, she will pay no gift tax. However, upon her death, there will be no unified credit left, so that all of her property may be subject to the federal estate tax.

Taxable gifts that reduce the unified credit may be good estate planning if the gift is of appreciating property (in other words, if it's likely to increase in value). Without a gift, the property would be included in the estate at a much higher value, if kept until death. Be careful to consider the income tax law when you give appreciating property. See the accountant member of your estate planning team.

Briefs

FILE 132

There are gifts, and then, of course there are gifts. There was a merchant named Guyot, who lived and died in Marseilles, France. He amassed a large fortune by working hard and saving most of his money. His neighbors jeered at him, considering him a miser, and avaricious. Local boys threw stones at him.

Eventually, M. Guyot died, and in his will was found the following: "Having observed from my infancy that the poor of Marseilles are badly supplied with water which they can only purchase at a high price, I have cheerfully labored the whole of my life to procure for them this great blessing, and I direct that the whole of my property be laid out in building an aqueduct for their use."

Estate and Gift Taxes Go Hand in Hand

Each of them has that one unified credit ($192,800), which, again, is the equivalent of making $600,000 in taxable gifts, having a taxable estate over $600,000, or a combination of the two—taxable gifts and estate—that exceeds $600,001.

Jim, who is divorced, gave his daughter, Kelly, $260,000 in 1996. He had made no other taxable gifts to date. His taxable gift was $250,000, because of the $10,000 annual exclusion. Applying the tentative tax rate of 34 percent to that $250,000 means a gift tax of $70,800. Jim has a unified credit of $192,800, so there is no gift tax due. However, he has reduced his unified credit to $122,000 ($192,800 less $70,800). If his federal taxable estate exceeds $350,000 ($600,000 less $250,00), then the estate will begin paying an estate tax at a 37 percent rate (see the federal tax chart in Chapter 15).

Take a look at the calculations here to see how the numbers applied to Jim.

Gifts during the year (at fair market value)	$260,000
Subtract	
Deductions:	
Marital	$-0-
Charitable	$-0-
Annual exclusion (per donee)	$10,000
Taxable gifts for year	$250,000
Add: Taxable gifts from all prior years	$-0-
Total of current and past taxable gifts	$250,000
Compute gift tax (use tax rates for gift and estate tax)	$70,800
Subtract:	
Prior gift taxes	$-0-
Unified credit	$192,800
Gift tax due	$-0-

That takes care of Jim's 1996 gift. If in 1997 Jim makes a taxable gift to his daughter of $450,000, the unified credit will be exhausted and he will have a tax on the excess of $100,000 at 37 percent. When he dies all those taxable gifts and any subsequent ones will be added to his taxable estate to determine his federal estate tax.

Did you get all of that? Here is a box that will sort of personalize gifts, to help you separate one from another, tax-wise.

Gift Giving from the IRS Perspective

Here are some situations where you might be handed a present, perhaps quite a handsome one. What are the tax implications? That won't matter to you because the donor is responsible for paying gift tax. But these examples will give you some idea of how you will be taxed when you feel the urge to give someone close to you a little something.

Gift	Donor's Tax Situation
On your birthday Aunt Maude gives you her diamond earrings and brooch, valued at $4,500	No tax due—gift falls under $10,000 allowed exclusion
Your Dad gives you $15,000 toward the down payment on a condo	If Mom doesn't go in with him on the gift, using her $10,000 exemption, Dad will be subject to pay gift tax on $5,000
Your godfather gives you his $12,000 stamp collection	Subject to gift tax on $2,000
Your spouse gives you a $20,000 automobile for your birthday	No tax due—an outright transfer, marital deduction
Your significant other gives you a $20,000 automobile for your birthday	$10,000 of that is subject to federal gift tax

Deferring Gifts for Minor Children

What if your child is a minor and you don't want him or her to have the money right away?

To take advantage of the annual exclusion, you recall that you must give a current ownership in cash or property. Putting the gift in the typical irrevocable trust won't do. However, the tax code does provide three possibilities I introduced you to in Chapter 11, on minor children, that can help you obtain the annual $10,000 exclusion for your gifts:

Words, Words, Words

A **Crummey trust** takes its name from the court case involving a gift to a minor child and whether it would qualify for an annual tax exclusion. Crummey is the name of the taxpayer who brought suit. He won his case.

➤ A trust with Crummey powers (an irrevocable living trust that allows the beneficiary or his or her guardian to withdraw the contribution within a specified period of time)

➤ An Internal Revenue Code 2503(c) trust

➤ A custodial account

To give you an example, let's look at May. She creates an irrevocable living trust that provides that her minor child, Tim, cannot receive any income or principal from the trust until he becomes 25 years of age. The trust allows her son's guardian (his father) to withdraw the annual contribution of $10,000 if done so within 30 days of the gift. The father wisely chooses not to exercise that right. This transaction qualifies for the annual exclusion.

Instead, May could have established a similar trust, with Tim as the sole beneficiary if the principal and income would be distributed to him outright upon becoming 21. This is a Section 2503(c) trust and likewise qualifies for the annual exclusion.

Or May could have established a custodial account for her son under the Uniform Gift to Minors Act (or Uniform Transfer to Minors Act) and make an annual contribution that would qualify for the exclusion. Tim would be entitled to the account when he became of legal age to receive it under state law (either age 18 or 21, depending on the state).

Watch Out
Use a custodian for your minor child's account that is neither you nor your spouse, since the custodial funds could be included in your or your spouse's estate at death. Choose instead a trusted relative or friend.

The Least You Need to Know

➤ The federal gift tax applies to taxable gifts over $600,000.

➤ Gifts of $10,000 or less per year may be made to anyone free of gift tax.

➤ Husband and wife can add each of their annual exclusions together so that they can give a combined nontaxable gift of $20,000 per year per recipient.

➤ A loan given tax free or at a reduced rate may be subject to tax because the interest *not* paid is considered a gift to the loan recipient.

➤ Giving away appreciating property will reduce the estate tax.

Chapter 17

How Charitable Donations Can Save You Money

In This Chapter

➤ The benefits of giving

➤ Many varieties of gifts

➤ Good, and better, tax implications

➤ Gifts after retirement

If you are generous to family and friends, and can afford the money, you are probably also generous to your favorite charities.

Can you save money while giving to a worthwhile cause? Yes indeed. Planning allows you to arrange charitable contributions in a way that will maximize your personal objectives with appropriate tax incentives. Read on.

Tax Savings and Philanthropy

Americans have always been a generous people. Our religious institutions, universities, local United Way agencies and civic organizations, among other groups, have all prospered with our gifts.

Take a look at the table here, showing how generous we have been to national charities. Have you contributed to some, perhaps many, of them?

10 Largest U.S. Charities Evaluated by NCIB*

Support/Revenue	Charity
$1,781,406,000	American Red Cross
$700,200,000	Memorial Sloan-Kettering Cancer Center
$630,310,147	ARC of the United States (Association for Retarded Citizens)
$472,800,000	Planned Parenthood Federation of America
$391,750,000	American Cancer Society
$379,509,649	National Easter Seal Society
$317,737,000	American Heart Association
$231,755,000	City of Hope
$218,595,000	CARE
$193,508,000	Nature Conservancy

National Charities Information Bureau, 19 Union Square West, New York, NY 10003—1997

Tip
Not all charities qualify for income, estate, and gift tax deductions. Public charities such as churches, educational institutions, hospitals, and government offices (any of them—U.S. Treasury Department, State of Nevada, etc.) *do*. To see which others qualify for such deductions, check with the IRS; it has a list of qualified charities.

Here are some of the benefits of planned giving:

➤ Fulfilling your charitable goals

➤ Providing income tax deductions for the value of the charitable gift

➤ Avoiding the capital gains tax when giving appreciated property

➤ Retaining income rights to the property donated to the charity

➤ Increasing lifetime income by converting low-yielding assets

➤ Supplementing retirement income

➤ Obtaining professional asset management

➤ Reducing federal estate and state inheritance taxes

Clearly, charitable donations should be considered part of your estate planning. The following pages point out several different methods to make them fulfill your goals, from outright gifts to charitable trusts and pooled income funds.

Briefs

Lilly Endowment, Inc. is an Indianapolis, Indiana–based, private philanthropic foundation with assets of over $5.2 billion in 1995. It was established in 1937 by three members of the Lilly family through gifts of 17,500 shares of stock worth $280,000 in their pharmaceutical business. In 1995 the endowment paid $110.9 million in grants for community development, religion and education, mainly in Indiana, but also throughout the United States.

Which Assets to Give

Just what you choose to give to charity has important tax implications. After all, doing good does not preclude doing well for oneself.

The tax deduction for charitable gifts is usually the fair market value of the property given. But the law requires that certain types of property to be deducted at what it cost the donor to purchase, not its current market value.

To explain the difference, consider Willie. He bought ABC, Inc. stock in 1980 for $40,000. It is now worth $60,000. He gives the stock to State University. He wants to deduct from his income tax the full value of the stock contribution, rather than just the amount he paid for it.

The tax code permits individual taxpayers to deduct charitable contributions if they itemize their deductions (Schedule B, form 1040). However, there are some limitations regarding the deduction.

> ➤ No deduction can exceed 50 percent of the taxpayer's Adjusted Gross Income (AGI).

> ➤ If you are giving appreciated property, then you may be limited to 30 percent of your adjusted income.

> ➤ Ordinary income assets (inventory, for example) are deductible at the inventory cost.

Confused? Here's an example that should help.

Assume that Willie had an Adjusted Gross Income (AGI) of $100,000. If he wanted to take the full value of his contribution of $60,000, he would have to spread the deduction over two years since he would be limited to 5 percent of his AGI ($50,000) in the year he made the gift in all events, and 30 percent of his AGI ($30,000) since that is the yearly maximum for capital gains assets like stock.

Or he could take the gift's cost (or tax basis) of $40,000 as a deduction in the year he gives it because the 50 percent of AGI rule applies when he limits his deduction to what

Quote, Unquote
Posthumous charities are the very essence of selfishness when bequeathed by those who, when alive, would part with nothing.
—*Charles Caleb Colton*
"Lacon" (1825)

the stock cost him. The amount of deduction that Willie cannot take in the year of contribution because of the maximum percentage rules will be available for him to take in the next tax year.

Back to Willie, who is certainly generous to his alma mater. He is a professional landscape artist, and now donates several of his own paintings to the university. Since the sale of his works would create ordinary income to him, he can only deduct his cost in producing the works, up to 50 percent of his AGI.

Here is another consideration. Willie purchased XYZ, Inc. stock in 1990 for $20,000. The stock is now selling for $10,000. If he gives the stock to the university he will get only a $10,000 deduction. However, if he sells the stock, and then gives the proceeds to the university, he will receive a tax loss deduction of $10,000 *and* the charitable deduction of $10,000.

Like Willie, you might consider selling property you own that has depreciated and taking a tax loss (if available). Then make a charitable contribution of the proceeds.

This is an estate-planning area where you will certainly want professional help. In this case, of course, that will be the accountant who is a member of your planning team.

Getting Donations in Order

Timing is everything, even here. A charitable donation saves you more in taxes when your tax rate is at its highest.

Tip
Do you like a particular charity, but are not certain you want to give them a sizable sum? If you have the time, do some volunteer work for that group first, to make certain you agree with its policies and programs, and how it spends its money.

Olive gave $10,000 to Healthy Hospital in 1995, her last year of employment, when she made $100,000 (her tax rate was 31 percent for that part of her income over $56,500). In 1996 she gave another $10,000, but her only income then was earned from investments of $20,000 (her tax rate was 15 percent).

Her contribution in 1995 saved her $3,100 in taxes ($10,000 gift *times* 31 percent tax rate), while her 1996 contribution saved her $1,500 in taxes ($10,000 gift *times* 15 percent tax rate) for a total tax savings of $4,600 in two years.

If Olive had made a $20,000 gift in 1995, she would have saved $6,200 in taxes ($20,000 gift *times* 31 percent tax rate). By making the gift in the year she had her highest earning she could have saved $1,600 in taxes.

Some Years You Give, Some You Don't

Alternating years when you make charitable donations could also save you in taxes, particularly if you don't have many other itemized deductions (e.g. mortgage interest, state taxes). You *can* choose between a standard deduction or itemizing each year.

For instance, one year you would not itemize but take the standard deduction, which was $6,700 in 1996 for married persons filing jointly. Then the next year you could make the bulk of your charitable contributions and itemize deductions.

That's what Art and Susan did. They regularly give $4,000 a year to their synagogue. Each year they have approximately $2,000 in other itemized deductions. In 1995 they gave nothing to the synagogue, but in January 1996, gave $4,000, then an additional $4,000 later in the year.

The couple did not itemize in 1995 (and wouldn't have anyway, even with a charitable donation because the standard deduction was $6,550), but did so in 1996 because their charitable contributions plus other itemized deductions ($10,000) exceeded their standard deduction ($6,700). Thus they saved taxes by alternating years for charitable contributions.

Lots More Ways to Donate

The tax law provides for a myriad of ways to make charitable gifts and take income, gift and estate tax deductions. Here are some:

➤ Outright gifts

➤ Charitable annuity

➤ Charitable remainder trusts

➤ Charitable lead trusts

➤ Pooled income funds

➤ Charitable remainder in residence or farm

➤ Charitable bargain sale

The first way to make a charitable contribution has been amply illustrated in previous pages. Most of us simply give our money to a charity, but perhaps we should consider some of the preceding alternatives.

Tip
Keep in mind the charitable deduction is only available for the net value of property transferred to the qualified charity. If the donor retains some interest in the property, the amount of the deduction will be reduced by the value retained by the donor, or given to another non-charity, such as a relative.

The Charitable Annuity

Maureen decides to give some land she owns to a favored charity. In turn the charity agrees to pay her an *annuity* for her life. In essence Maureen has made a transfer, or sale, of one asset (her land) for another asset (the charity's annuity). Using IRS tables (see

Chapter 15), you can compute how much of the value of the gifted property will be returned to her in the form of the annuity (non-deductible) and how much of its value the charity will keep (deductible). Maureen can only deduct the net value of what the charity gets.

Charitable Remainder Trusts

The tax deduction for a *charitable remainder trust* operates on the same basic principles as the charitable annuity.

Charitable remainder trusts have a non-charity as an income beneficiary, with the remainder (the principal) going to a charity when the income interest terminates.

The person creating the trust (the grantor) often will be the income beneficiary. Frequently the spouse is included as a joint/survivor income beneficiary. There is no tax for the gift to the spouse because of the marital deduction. However, if anyone other than a spouse is an income beneficiary, then there is a gift (but the annual exclusion of $10,000 per donee may be available).

There are two types of these remainder trusts: *annuity* and *unitrust.*

The annuity trust is required to pay a set percentage of the *initial value* of the assets to the non-charitable beneficiary. The unitrust must pay a set percentage of the trust assets *valued annually.*

The minimum percentage of payout for each is 5 percent. Additional assets can be contributed to the unitrust, but not to the annuity trust. The income tax deduction will be based on actuarial and income tables prescribed by the IRS.

Let's say Carl establishes a charitable remainder trust with $1 million. He and his wife, Jennifer, are income beneficiaries. When they die, the trust will terminate and the charity will receive the remainder of the trust assets.

If this is an annuity trust, then the amount Carl and Jennifer will receive as income will be fixed, based upon the payout percentage and the initial contribution to the trust.

Quote, Unquote
A small gift is better than a great promise.
—*German proverb*

But if this is a unitrust, then the amount Carl and Jennifer will receive as income will vary each year, based upon the payout percentage and the annual valuation of the assets.

The unitrust can be structured more flexibly than the annuity trust because later contributions and contributions of appreciating assets will increase the income available, and could be timed to increase the payout when the donor has retired and is in a lower tax bracket.

Charitable Lead Trust

This is essentially the flip side of the remainder trust. In the *lead trust*, the charity gets the income for a set time period, and the donor or some non-charity receives the principal after that time period. The longer the term for the income payments to the charity, and the higher the payout, the greater the income tax deduction.

Beth establishes a charitable lead trust and contributes $500,000. Her church is to be the income beneficiary for 10 years. Then the remainder will go to her daughter.

The income from the trust will be taxed to Beth only if it exceeds the amount of income paid to the charity. Since the daughter receives the remainder interest there is a gift to her that is subject to the gift tax (but there is no annual exclusion since she does not have a present right to the property).

Words, Words, Words
To endow a hospital, college, or similar public or charitable facility is to make a grant of money providing for the continuing support or maintenance of that institution.

Pooled Income Funds

Many charities have established *pooled income funds*. Here the donor gives cash or property to the fund, which is made up of contributions from other donors, and in return receives income for life (or lives, if a spouse is included). This is similar to the gift annuity you read about earlier.

A pooled income fund may provide several advantages to the donor in addition to the tax deduction. The charity provides professional management, and there is now a diversified investment portfolio, which could mean a higher return if the donor contributed a low-income yielding asset.

Other Charitable Gifts

The list goes on. Tax law permits you to deed your personal residence or farm to a charity, while you retain a life estate in that property and receive an income tax deduction for the actuarial value of the charity's remainder interest. The personal residence doesn't have to be the home in which you are currently residing either.

Tony, for example, lives most of the year in Ohio, but spends a good part of each winter in Florida. He may deed either or both homes to a charity, while retaining a life estate so he can use that residence and receive a tax deduction.

Here's another way to give: If you have an asset that you would like to convert to cash, keep some proceeds, and give the rest to charity, then you might enter into a *bargain sale* with a charity.

Watch Out

There's a way to learn as much as possible about your favorite charity— its history; programs; use of funds; tax exempt status, if any; percentage of fundraising that goes toward programs and percentage used for administrative costs; and more. The National Charities Information Bureau's "Wise Giving Guide" is published quarterly. A single copy is free. Call (212) 929-6300.

Quote, Unquote

Lend before witnesses, but give without them.
—*Anonymous*

A bargain sale is a sale of property to a charity or another person for less than its fair market value so that the difference is a gift to the purchaser.

If Tony, for example, sells some land he purchased several years ago to his college for less than its appraised fair market value, he will be taxed on a portion of the gain (the difference between what he paid for it and what it's worth now) and also receive an income tax deduction on the "gift" portion of the sales price.

Any mortgage on the sold/gifted property will increase the bargain seller's gain. It's treated as if the debt is released when the seller transfers it to the charity.

Retirement and Beyond

Most of us buy life insurance to protect our families while the children are growing up. After that the life insurance becomes more expensive and less important, particularly if our estate will be ample for the rest of our lives.

If you like, you can change the primary or contingent beneficiary of the policy and name a qualified charity.

If the charity is the primary beneficiary you can receive a charitable deduction for the premiums you pay. Upon death the charity will receive the proceeds. So for a relatively modest premiums payment, you can leave a substantial amount of money to charity. (The charity must be the owner of the policy for you to receive the tax deduction.)

Perhaps you can't spare anything now to give to a charity, but after your death your estate could part with some money. You can leave a specified amount or a percentage of your probate estate to one or several charities.

The Least You Need to Know

➤ Gifts to charities may qualify for an immediate income tax deduction.

➤ Charitable gifts are usually valued at their fair market value at the time of the gift.

➤ Gifts in a charitable trust or pooled income fund can create income *and* a tax deduction for the donor.

➤ Life insurance policies and devises in a will allow the donor to make a substantial gift at little or no expense.

Chapter 18

State Taxes: When and How You Can Be Hit

Too often we focus on the big dog (the IRS) and forget about the little puppies (state taxes). In estate planning it's important to consider all taxes as obstacles to building wealth. That goes for real estate taxes, sales tax and a number of other "pups."

Here's what your beautiful, much-loved state can do to you, tax-wise (although in all honesty there are some states that can do something *for* you as well).

Inheriting? The State Has Its Hand Out

There's good and bad news here. Every state has some form of death tax (inheritance or estate). On the other hand, those rates are considerably lower than the federal estate tax rate (37–55 percent), although many begin the tax at a much lower estate value than the federal estate tax, which starts at over $600,000.

Tip
Who pays the inheritance tax? Well, technically it is the beneficiary whose interest is reduced by the amount of the tax. However, you could provide in your will that your estate pick up any death tax for your beneficiaries. Consult your lawyer about the wording for handling those taxes the way you want in your will.

Watch Out
The time allowed for payment varies here. Most state laws make the executor personally liable if the tax is not paid. There also may be a tax lien imposed on estate property transferred to a beneficiary if the tax is not paid.

First, a few definitions so we'll all know what we're talking about here.

An *inheritance tax* is a state levy on what each beneficiary receives from the estate.

A state's *estate tax* is similar to the federal estate tax because it is a tax upon the *net* estate of the deceased, based on the right to transmit property from the deceased's estate to its beneficiaries.

Transfers (assets distributed through a will) that are subject to state death taxes typically include those that are subject to the federal estate tax. That would be a will, intestacy, life insurance, retirement plans, jointly held property and the like.

The inheritance tax usually has *graduated rates* that vary in amount for different classes of beneficiaries, with those of a close relationship to the deceased subject to lower rates than those of more distant relationships. For example, the tax rate on an inheritance by the deceased's child would be lower than the rate on an inheritance by a cousin.

Frequently a *state inheritance tax* will have several exemptions, such as transfers to a spouse or to a charity, and varying exemption amounts for transfers to estate beneficiaries (again, often based on their relationship to the deceased).

The state estate taxes are imposed in a method similar to the federal estate tax, or by using the state death tax credit on the federal estate tax return. State death taxes usually allow certain deductions, such as debts, funeral expenses and estate administrative expenses.

Where Did You Say You Live?

I asked you that question once before, a few chapters ago, when I suggested that you decide what state to consider your permanent residence for any number of purposes. In this chapter that purpose is state death tax.

Legal residence, or *domicile*, of the deceased determines which state can impose its death tax. Real estate and tangible personal property are usually taxable in the state where they are located, while all other property is typically taxed by the state in which the deceased had legal residence.

I am an Indiana resident, and I co-own a house, cars, savings accounts, etc. in Indiana. Therefore my property will be subject to Indiana inheritance tax upon my death. If I also owned a farm in Nebraska it would be subject to Nebraska death taxes.

I'll mention the subject of permanent residence again at the end of the chapter, in another context.

One, Two, Three—Ways of Taxing You

Here is a brief summary of the three different types of state death taxes:

➤ Estate tax based only upon federal state death tax credit

➤ Estate tax and tax based upon federal state death tax credit (a *pick-up tax*, which is a levy that is the difference between the estate tax and the state death tax credit)

➤ Inheritance tax and tax based upon federal state death tax credit (pick-up tax)

Let's look at them in more detail. The following table will help you with state death taxes, although you will have to look at the size of your estate to determine which state's tax is best for you.

Where Not to Die:
State Estate and Inheritance Taxes

States with an estate tax and additional tax based upon federal tax's estate tax credit	States with inheritance tax based upon the federal estate tax's state death tax credit	States with a state death tax and additional tax based upon federal estate tax's state death tax credit
Alabama	Connecticut	New York
Alaska	Delaware	Ohio
Arizona	Indiana	Oklahoma
Arkansas	Iowa	
California	Kansas	
Colorado	Kentucky	
District of Columbia	Louisiana	
Florida	Maryland	
Georgia	Montana	
Hawaii	Nebraska	
Idaho	New Hampshire	
Illinois	New Jersey	

continues

continued

States with an estate tax and additional tax based upon federal tax's estate tax credit	States with inheritance tax based upon the federal estate tax's state death tax credit	States with a state death tax and additional tax based upon federal estate tax's state death tax credit
Maine	North Carolina	
Massachusetts	Pennsylvania	
Michigan	South Dakota	
Minnesota	Tennessee	
Mississippi		
Missouri		
Nevada		
New Mexico		
North Dakota		
Oregon		
Rhode Island		
South Carolina		
Texas		
Utah		
Vermont		
Virginia		
Washington		
West Virginia		
Wisconsin		
Wyoming		

Note: Puerto Rico has its own estate tax.

Estate Tax Based on Federal State Death Tax Credit

California, Florida, and Illinois are three of the larger states that have a death tax based upon the federal state death tax credit. Whenever a federal estate tax is payable, these states have an estate tax that equals the amount of state death tax credit. For example, using the IRS tables (Chapter 15) for a taxable estate of $890,000, the state death tax credit would be $27,120.

Estate Tax and Additional Tax Based upon Federal State Death Tax Credit

New York, as you can see in the chart, is one state that has its own estate tax, as well as a tax based upon the federal state death tax credit. For New York residents, the minimum New York estate tax is equal to the amount of the maximum federal credit for state death taxes.

The estate computes the New York estate tax; if that tax is less than the federal state death tax credit, then the latter is the tax imposed (a pick-up tax).

Briefs

John Dorrance, once the sole owner of Campbell Soup Company stock, died in 1930, leaving a $115 million estate. He had a residence in New Jersey, but lived most of the year in Pennsylvania. Upon his death his estate was probated in New Jersey, and that state taxed the estate. Pennsylvania claimed his legal residence (domicile) was there, and also taxed his estate. Whoa, said the estate. They appealed to the United States Supreme Court, which refused to accept the appeal. The estate was taxed in both states.

Inheritance Tax and Additional Tax Based upon Federal State Death Tax Credit

Whew, these headings are getting long. What this one means can be explained quite briefly, though. Indiana is one of 16 states (see the chart) that are blessed with an inheritance tax, and a tax based on the federal estate death tax credit. Unlike the estate tax, the inheritance tax is computed on who receives the estate. Again, it's the closer relatives who have more sizable exemptions and are taxed at a lower rate than distant family.

If the inheritance tax is less than the federal estate state death tax credit, then an additional tax is imposed to "pick-up" the difference.

For estates of $600,000 or less, the most advantageous tax is the one solely based upon the federal estate tax's state death tax credit, since it is determined by the taxable estate, which is zero.

Some States Even Tax Your Gifts

Really. The guilty ones here are Connecticut, Delaware, Louisiana, New York, North Carolina and Tennessee. They must feel compelled to do so to "protect the integrity of the estate tax," which is the same reasoning the feds use.

In many instances, state gift taxable transfers are similar to the federal gift tax, which you read about in Chapter 16. Connecticut and New York, for example, allow an annual exclusion of the first $10,000 to any donee each year. However, the Connecticut gift tax rate is different from its inheritance tax rate, while New York's rate is the same as its estate tax rate.

Quote, Unquote
Taxes, after all, are the dues we pay for the privileges of membership in an organized society.
—*Franklin D. Roosevelt, in a speech, Worcester, MA, October 21, 1936*

If a state has a gift tax that has a lower rate than its estate or inheritance tax, then gifts can reduce death taxes later.

In states that do not impose a gift tax, gifts certainly can reduce the state death tax.

Not to be outdone by the IRS, 25 states impose a generation-skipping transfer tax, so if you plan to give your grandchildren more than $1 million, beware of this state tax. The tax is usually the maximum state tax credit allowable under the Internal Revenue Code. My advice is not to try this without benefit of counsel.

Pesky State Income Taxes

Still more taxes, folks.

Here are those fine states that do not have a personal income tax: Florida, Nevada, South Dakota, Texas, Washington and Wyoming. The rest of our states tax our income at various rates.

Many state income taxes begin with the Adjusted Gross Income figure on the federal tax return, and also have deductions similar to those on your federal return. Federal and state income tax planning can provide a double reduction in your taxes.

Quote, Unquote
The state is never so efficient as when it wants money.
—*Anthony Burgess, "You've Had Your Time" (1990)*

State income tax is imposed on any legal resident of the state, and often upon income earned in the state by those who live elsewhere. Some states also tax income if you have resided in the state for several months during the tax year. What is taxable income for one state is not necessarily the same for another, although many states use the federal income tax definition (usually by taking the federal Adjusted Gross Income amount).

But that's not all: Many states allow cities and counties to impose a local income tax. Does it ever end? It doesn't seem to!

A Retirement Residence

Estate planning tip for the day: Be sure to die a resident of a low-tax state.

Your work may dictate where you earn your income, but retirement is another matter. Consider the entire tax burden when selecting a state for retirement. The state income tax you pay should be less as your income decreases, of course, but the property tax on your home may be onerous.

States just love to collect taxes, as you have seen. Many are delighted if you decide to live within their borders—income taxes now, death taxes later. As I noted earlier, legal residence is important. For one thing, it matters in determining your heirs (some states have intestate distribution that is different from others), the validity of your will and state taxes.

You should have only one legal residence (domicile), but often the evidence about which is your permanent home is mixed, particularly if you are retired and living in different states in different seasons of the year.

Briefs

Edward Green's estate was more fortunate than that of John Dorrance, described a few pages ago. Green was a wealthy resident of Maine who died in the mid-1930s. Four states claimed his legal residency and the right to tax his estate. Their cumulative taxes and the federal estate tax exceeded his estate of $42 million! The Supreme Court took the case because the states were suing one another. The court awarded the inheritance tax to only one of the states, claiming a person can have only one legal residence.

Florida has a Declaration of Domicile form. If you want the Sunshine State to be your legal residence, then execute that document. Even if your state has no provision for a similar declaration, you may want to execute such a form for your state and keep it among your important documents. Your lawyer can help here.

If you have not clearly established one state as your legal residence, then your estate could be taxed by any state in which you have residency at the time of death.

Make sure that the following are evidence of your legal residence:

➤ Driver's license and license plates

➤ Income tax return

➤ Mailing address

➤ Proof of membership in local organizations

➤ Will, trust and other estate planning documents mentioning that address

Ideally, upon retirement you should give up any former residence and transfer all your assets to what you want to be considered your domicile.

Some Other State Taxes to Consider

If you are planning a move to another state upon retirement, you will want to consider what's waiting for you there in the way of state taxes. It can make quite a difference in your retirement lifestyle and budgeting.

Some of those taxes include state sales tax, which the overwhelming majority of states do charge. Sales tax ranges from 3 to 7 percent, but sometimes the effective rate is higher because it is combined with local sales taxes. In many states, prescription drugs and food are exempt from sales tax.

All states have property taxes, or real estate taxes. However, there are several programs nationwide that can help seniors with a property tax burden. The three most common are:

➤ *The circuitbreaker*, a property tax credit where benefits are determined by both your income and by property tax payment guidelines. There are two types of circuit-breakers: the *sliding scale* and the *threshold*. Sliding scale programs rebate a percentage of property tax liability. Threshold programs rebate the amount of property tax that exceeds a certain percentage of your income.

➤ *The homestead exemption* or *credit*, which reduces the property taxes on a home-owner's primary residence

Quote, Unquote
His money was twice tainted: 'tain't yours and 'tain't mine.
—*Mark Twain*

➤ *The deferral program*, which allows older or disabled Americans to put off paying property taxes until after death or upon sale of their property. This is not entirely free, however. Usually a somewhat below-market interest rate is charged on the taxes that are being deferred. The tax deferral and all accumulated interest usually are represented by a lien on the property.

Chipping Away at Your Pension

A few states charge income tax on pensions earned within the state, even though the taxpayer no longer resides in that state. These states are California, Connecticut, Kansas, Louisiana, Massachusetts, Minnesota, New York, Oregon, Vermont and Wisconsin. Let's say you've earned your living in Kansas and then retire to Arizona. You'll pay taxes on your pension to Kansas.

And...

Some states also levy a tax on what is known as intangibles, such as stocks, bonds, cash and bank deposits, accounts receivable, patents and licenses.

You can see how important it is to give careful thought to where you'll live after you retire. All of those taxes, small and not-so-small, can eat away not only at your estate, but also on the money you've got to live on—don't call the moving van until you've worked out all the numbers!

Tip
In deciding where to move, you might call the Department of Revenue of the state that interests you to learn about taxation there. Other sources of information: the local tax collector's office in the community you're considering; your real estate agent there, and the reference department of the local library.

The Least You Need to Know

➤ Most states have an inheritance or estate tax and a "pick-up" tax equal to the federal state death tax credit.

➤ Six states—Connecticut, Delaware, Louisiana, New York, North Carolina and Tennessee—have their own gift tax, which is similar to the federal gift tax.

➤ State income tax planning should be coordinated with federal income tax planning.

➤ Legal residence determines which state imposes its death tax on everything except real and tangible personal property.

Keeping Your Wealth Within the Family

In This Chapter

➤ Partial gifts

➤ Selling to the family

➤ Gifts to youngsters

➤ The family business

Let's assume that you want a family member, or perhaps the whole clan, to inherit from your estate.

That can be done—to everyone's benefit. Here are some suggestions, a few you may have read about briefly in other chapters, plus some new strategies. All are designed to keep your assets in the bosom of your family. Match them up one against the other to see which would work best for you. Just as important as keeping wealth in the family, of course, is how to make that transfer at the least cost to you (or them). I'll tell you how right now.

Quote, Unquote
An ounce of blood is worth more than a pound of friendship.
—*Spanish proverb*

Chapter 19

Charity Begins at Home

Probate and taxes take time and toll, so our goal is to minimize both.

The transfer laws are fairly simple and you've read about them earlier in these pages. For example, making a gift requires only that the donor intend to make that gift, the donee accept, and a physical transfer occur. Likewise, upon death the will distributes probate assets to the named beneficiaries, or the living trust continues to provide principal and interest for its beneficiaries.

The rub in all of this, of course, is taxes. Let's see what we can do about that.

The Next Generation

Most couples with children quite naturally want to pass on their assets to those kids, either now or through their estate. There are a number of ways to do this:

➤ Outright gifts

➤ Trusts with split income and remainder interests

➤ Rearranging business assets

➤ Purchasing life insurance, annuities, or other easily transferable assets

➤ Creating joint interests

➤ Gifting property but retaining a life estate in it for the donor

➤ Below-market rate loans or gift loans (the latter might be a loan to a child that is then forgiven)

➤ Bargain sales of property or installment sales with annual forgiveness of payment

➤ Employing children in the family business

➤ Wills

Tip
All transfers during your life require you to determine how much less money you can afford to live on. You don't want to give away too much; one day you may need some of that money for your own purposes.

All of these require planning and thorough consideration of the tax consequences. You can read about some of them in earlier chapters of this book and can, of course, discuss them with your accountant.

Certainly transfers to your spouse are considered within the purview of this chapter, because they are most easily made, with little tax consequences, and are likely to result in your property ultimately going to the children after your spouse's death. (Of course that assumption may not be true if the spouse is not the parent of your children.)

Giving Something—and Keeping It

Perhaps you'd like to make a gift—but only sort of. How about a partial transfer of property to someone else?

Bonnie owns a condominium in Florida. She wants to keep ownership and use it during her lifetime, then wants the title to go to her daughter. Bonnie could deed the condo to her daughter and retain a life estate that would accomplish her goal. (There's more about a life estate in Chapter 2 and Chapter 17.)

Retained interest in property is subject to federal estate tax, and may be liable for state death taxes. The interest given up (for example, the remainder after a life estate) is subject to federal gift tax (but with no allowance for the annual exclusion since it is a future interest).

Trust Them

You can establish a trust for yourself (and your spouse), reserving the right to the income and withdrawing the principal, with the remainder going to your child upon your (and your spouse's) death.

Ken created a *revocable* living trust for himself and his spouse, deposited assets in the trust, and lived off the income. Upon the death of Ken's wife, and then Ken, the assets went to his adult children outright.

Income from revocable trusts is taxed to the grantor, or creator, who established the trust. There is no gift tax to the children because they receive nothing until the parent's death. But the children will have to pay federal estate tax when their parent dies and they get the trust's assets.

If you create an *irrevocable* living trust, then there is a gift to beneficiaries of the trust. The annual gift tax exclusion is available for a gift to income beneficiaries.

The value of the grandchildren's remainder interest, which could be small if their parents are young, may be subject to the generation-skipping transfer tax (remember that has a $1 million exclusion).

Dina transferred $200,000 into an irrevocable living trust for the life of her four children, then the remainder to her grandchildren. If Dina's spouse joins in the gift, then their annual exclusions will amount to $80,000, assuming the actuarial value of the income interest is at least $80,000 (4 [one for each of the four children] times $20,000 [$10,000 exemption for each of the two parents]), and the balance would be subject to gift tax (but a unified credit, the equivalent of which is $600,000, would first apply).

Watch Out
Be sure you talk over with your children any gifts or investing you want to make for your grandkids now rather than later. What you have in mind might conflict with your children's ideas and plans.

An irrevocable trust, with the grantor retaining no rights, will not be included in the grantor's estate, and income from the trust will be taxed to the trust and its beneficiaries.

The value of the grandchildren's remainder interest, which may be small if their parents are young, might be subject to the generation-skipping transfer tax, but only if it exceeds $1 million (which is the exclusion limit), and the exclusion is applied on the gift return.

Considering Co-ownership

You might want to own property, such as bank accounts or stock, with another person. When you create jointly owned property that transfers an undivided interest at the time it is created, the survivor receives the entire interest at the other's death.

In case that isn't completely clear to you, I'll give you an example. Grant adds his son to his savings account as joint owner with right of survivorship. He also owns a house, and executes a deed in which his daughter is joint owner with right of survivorship.

No gift tax occurs in creating a joint ownership in a savings account (withdrawal by the non-depositor is a gift). A gift is considered complete only upon withdrawal from the bank account. But the creation of a joint ownership in other property is an immediate gift. The annual exclusion (that $10,000 you've been reading so much about) is available. All this means that Grant owes no tax for the savings account with his son, when established, but he might owe on the property he now owns jointly with his daughter if its value at the time the new deed is drawn exceeds $10,000.

Quote, Unquote
If wisdom were offered to me with the proviso that I should keep it shut up and refrain from declaring it, I should refuse. There's no delight in owning anything unshared.
—*Seneca*, "Letters to Lucilius" *(1st c.)*

The gift tax does not apply to the creation of the savings account because the son only has a "right" to withdraw the money, while the daughter owns the house, just like her father.

Jointly held property is subject to the federal estate tax. Income is taxed to the income recipient.

Life Insurance

You might want to purchase life insurance, particularly group term, and then transfer policy ownership to a child. That could provide a substantial benefit to the child at little expense to you, and may be appropriate when you don't need the coverage to protect your family in the event of your untimely death.

A life insurance policy transferred more than three years before the owner-insured's death is not subject to estate tax, and gift tax applies only to the value of the policy (e.g. term is its cost to purchase a policy on the insured's life, and whole life is a variant of its cash surrender value). Because of special IRS rules, the transfer is a gift, but the value of the gift is limited to its cash value at the time of transfer, which may be for less than the face value proceeds collected later.

Loans Within the Family

They aren't that unusual (naturally we're not talking about the can-you-let-me-have-twenty-until-payday variety), and can be an excellent means of shifting wealth to a child.

Casey lends his son $100,000 at 0 percent interest per year, with installment payments of $10,000 each year. There is a promissory note evidencing the debt and a mortgage on the home his son purchased with the funds. While Casey has never indicated any plan to do so at the time of making the loan, he has for several years completely forgiven those annual $10,000 debt payments.

Gift tax applies to below-market interest loans to the extent of a federal funds rate because the borrower doesn't pay the same interest he would on a commercial loan. Thus, he is, in effect, "given" the interest by the lender. However, the annual exclusion is available. The federal income tax treats income as if the lender has received the interest, but only to the extent of the borrower's net investment income (interest and dividends received by the borrower from the invested money) if they exceed $1,000 and if the loan is for $100,000 or less. An annual exclusion is available for the installment forgiven. Please also see a related discussion in Chapter 16.

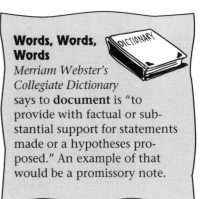

Words, Words, Words
Merriam Webster's Collegiate Dictionary says to **document** is "to provide with factual or substantial support for statements made or a hypotheses proposed." An example of that would be a promissory note.

Don't forget to document this loan, and enforce its provisions the way you would any other. The IRS is not particularly happy with this type of arrangement, so you'll want to cover yourself.

Your Family as Buyers

Selling an asset to a family member keeps it in the family. You can structure the sale on an installment basis or as part gift and part sale, which is what is called a *bargain sale*.

Alex sold some land to his son for $100,000, payable in ten equal installments, with a 10 percent per annum interest rate. The property had cost him $10,000 when he first purchased it. He also sold another parcel to his daughter for $50,000 (it was worth $100,000 at the time of this sale). That property originally cost Alex $10,000 as well.

Tip
You might want to consider the sale of appreciating property to a family member, since the appreciation occurring after the sale will not be included in the seller's estate. Only the proceeds from the sale when the property had a lesser value will be included.

Alex's installment receipts and interest will result in taxable income. Each installment of $10,000 from his son involves $9,000 of gain and $1,000 of non-taxable return of his original cost. Alex may want to forgive some of the installment payments, which would be a gift (but the annual exclusion is available). He must be careful to do so in a manner that would not allow the IRS to claim a pre-arrangement.

Alex's bargain sale to his daughter is one-half taxable gift, the other half a taxable sale, with the income tax amount reduced by one half of Alex's original cost of the land. He may want to structure the bargain sale with installment payments to take advantage of the annual gift tax exclusion.

Gifts to Minors

Outright presents to minor children are all right for birthdays and holidays, but only when they come in gift-wrapped packages or are relatively small amounts of cash.

For any sizable amount (over $10,000), consider one of the following:

- ➤ A custodial bank account
- ➤ Custodial property (stocks, bonds)
- ➤ A minor's trust
- ➤ A living trust

You don't want your child to waste your hard-earned cash, so it's important to keep his or her hands off the money while still young.

Nan establishes a custodial account at her local bank for her daughter and deposits $10,000 in the account each year. She purchases stock for her son for the same amount, and names a custodian. Her choice of custodian for both is her brother, Bob.

Custodial accounts and property are in custodianship until the donee reaches the age of majority as indicated by that state's gift to minors law. Gift tax law applies, with the annual exclusion. Custodial accounts are not included in the donor's estate if he or she is not the custodian. Income is taxed to the minor.

Quote, Unquote
Put not your trust in money, put your money in trust.
—*Oliver Wendell Holmes Sr.*, "The Autocrat of the Breakfast Table" *(1858)*

An alternative to custodial accounts that have basically the same income, gift, and estate tax advantages is a *minor's trust*.

Ben creates just such a trust for his daughter, age 2. The trustee is the Trustworthy Bank. The trust will distribute all income and principal to the daughter when she becomes 21; if she dies before then, all the trust property will be in her estate. (A minor's trust can also be extended beyond 21.)

The gift to a properly designed minor's trust qualifies for the annual exclusion. The trust assets are not subject to the donor's estate tax if he or she maintains no control over the trust, and the income is taxed to the trust and beneficiary.

Another example of a trust that allows the annual gift tax exemption is the so-called *Crummey trust*, which gives the child or his or her guardian a brief period to accept an outright gift before it goes into the trust. That is useful if the grantor wants to continue the trust beyond the beneficiary's 21st birthday.

A irrevocable living trust, which is not specifically designed to qualify for the annual gift tax exclusion, would reduce the donor's unified credit for each gift. While its terms may be very flexible (as contrasted with the prior custodial accounts and minor's trusts), it can be expensive because of the reduction in the credit. If a long-term trust is considered necessary because of a child's disability, you might want to refer to Chapter 13, which discusses that particular situation.

Splitting It with Your Spouse

If you're looking to save on taxes (and who isn't!), mind the annual gift tax exclusion. As I've explained more than once already in this book, you can give $10,000 to anyone outright and not pay a single penny in taxes on that money. And if your spouse joins in the gift, then your exclusion automatically doubles. Your spouse need not have an ownership interest in the property given (that is, the money for the gift can come from the other partner).

Sherry gave her son $100,000 from her own funds in 1996. Her husband joined her for gift tax purposes. The two annual exclusions reduce the taxable gift to $80,000, and each spouse can use his or her unified credit to apply to his or her taxable gift of $40,000.

The split-gift election is particularly helpful to transfer the maximum property at minimum gift tax when one spouse owns very few assets.

Your Business for Your Benefit

You own a business, whether it is a sole proprietorship, partnership or corporation. If you control the company, you may want to pass it on to your children. You want to leave behind your little niche of capitalism to those who can most appreciate it—your family.

Often the parent/owner wants to retain control while gradually transferring ownership to the next generation. Usually that is easier to structure with a corporation than with a partnership or limited liability company, but it is certainly available for the latter two business entities as well.

Watch Out
Be realistic in determining whether your children are interested in owning your business, or are indeed capable of running it. Also be prepared to compensate those who *don't* want the business, especially in ways that will not interfere with those who do.

Transferring Company Stock

Jay owns all the outstanding stock in House Calls, Inc., a repair service. He could give 40 percent of the stock to his two children and still control the corporation. Or he could restructure the stock and create voting and non-voting common stock, retaining all or a majority of the voting stock so that he stays in control of the business.

Gifts of stock are subject to the gift tax, but the annual exclusion and wise use of the unified credit may significantly reduce that tax. This is especially true if you can justify a

Watch Out
Corporation stock restructuring may have adverse income tax effects. Consult a tax expert before making any move.

substantial discount in the value of the gift because it involves owning only a minority interest in that stock. Periodically giving stock to your children as it becomes clearer that they will be responsible can significantly reduce the parent's estate and income taxes.

S corporation (a corporation where the income is taxed to the shareholders) tax laws changed in 1996 to permit a variety of trusts to own S corporation stock. This can provide additional planning opportunities for S corporation owners.

Buy-Sell Agreements

Another way to transfer your family business to a member or members of your family is through a buy-sell agreement. In such an agreement family members would purchase your interest in the business at your retirement or upon your demise. This would provide cash during retirement years or for your estate survivors and would keep the business within the family.

Tip
Children-shareholders could purchase life insurance on the life of the parent-shareholder and use that money to fund an estate stock buyout upon the death of that parent.

Employing Your Kids

Wealth can also be transferred through the employment of your children. Many family businesses have done this. Children, even when still in their teens, can earn spending money from the business. Full-time jobs there allow parents to share the wealth (and responsibilities). And reasonable wages are deductible business expenses. Income can be shifted from the higher tax bracket parent to the lower-bracket children.

Rich, and Staying That Way

The very wealthy are probably not spending a lot of time reading this book. They probably have droves of tax lawyers doing their estate planning for them. On the outside chance that one or more of you who are reading this do fall into that category, I offer this brief section of tips.

GRATs, GRITs, GRUTs, CRATs, and CRUTs, are the heady stuff that excite tax planners who have clients able to pay hundreds of dollars per hour in fees. The first three GRs are trusts that have forms of annuity payments. The trust grantor, or creator, transfers assets into an irrevocable living trust, which pays him or her income. Upon death the trust principal goes to the remainderman (the person designated to receive the trust fund when it ends). The transfer is subject to gift tax and the trust asset will be partially included in the grantor's estate for federal estate taxes.

GRs can be used to transfer appreciating property to the next generation, who will benefit from the appreciation, while the grantor receives some income from the assets. The same or better results may be achieved by other means discussed in this chapter.

The CRs involve charitable trusts, which have been discussed in Chapter 17. The advantage is a charitable deduction, but the disadvantage for the children is that they won't see a penny—the charity gets it.

Likewise, you could sell your children property in exchange for an annuity, which would have much the same effect as the GRs without the complications. The parent receives income, and the property is kept in the family. The income tax impact is reduced since the gain is spread over the term of the annuity.

My personal favorite involves gifts in trust to grandchildren (thus skipping one estate-taxable generation and saving those taxes). Properly structured, the gifts may qualify for the annual gift tax exclusion and minimize the reduction of the unified credit. The generation-skipping transfer tax (GSTT) can be avoided for transfers of $1 million or less.

Jack gave his wife $1 million because she doesn't have much money in her own name and any gift to a spouse, as you know by now, is not subject to gift taxes. Since the couple's children are well provided for, Jack and his wife have now established a well-crafted plan to transfer $2 million to the grandkids without incurring the dreaded GSTT (her brand-new $1 million, plus $1 million from Jack).

If you like the idea of skipping your children because they do not need the money, and want to pass everything, or nearly everything, on to your grandchildren, following is a diagram that will show you at a glance some of your options.

> **Quote, Unquote**
> Nothing is more admirable than the fortitude with which millionaires tolerate the disadvantages of their wealth.
> —*Rex Stout*

> **Words, Words, Words**
> A **tontine** is a sort of annuity gimmick. It's named after Lorenzo Tonti, an Italian banker who died in the mid-18th century. Basically, it's a joint financial arrangement whereby the participants contribute usually equal amounts of money to a prize that is awarded entirely to the participant who outlives all the others.

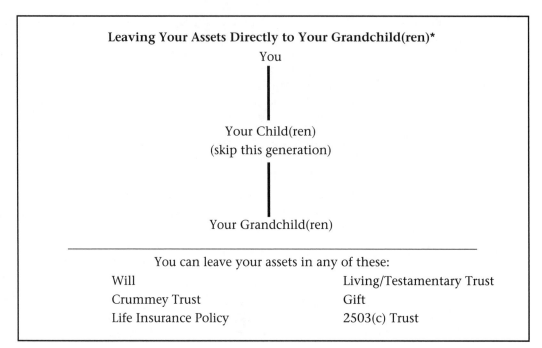

Leaving Your Assets Directly to Your Grandchild(ren)*

You

Your Child(ren)
(skip this generation)

Your Grandchild(ren)

You can leave your assets in any of these:

Will	Living/Testamentary Trust
Crummey Trust	Gift
Life Insurance Policy	2503(c) Trust

* *Be careful of the generation-skipping transfer tax (GSTT) if you are transferring more than $1 million.*

The Least You Need to Know

➤ Gifts in the form of a trust can create income for the grantor and keep assets in the family.

➤ Gift loans can shift income and assets to children.

➤ A parent can purchase a life insurance policy and give it to a child, providing significant death benefits at little expense.

➤ Family businesses can be restructured to form an orderly transfer to the next generation, and to reduce taxes.

Words for the Wise—Key Terms You'll Want to Remember

401(k) plan: A qualified retirement plan, usually involving contributions made by both employer and employee.

actuarial value: Value of a property interest, or a right that you own, based on life expectancy tables; for example, a life estate is valued based on the life expectancy of that person.

administrator: Person appointed by a court to represent an estate when no will was provided or the will does not name an executor. May also be called a personal representative.

alternate valuation date: A date no more than six months after a person's death that may be used for evaluating assets in an estate for federal estate taxes.

annuity: Investment that pays a fixed amount for a specified number of years or for life.

annuity trust: One form of charitable remainder trust that pays a fixed amount regularly according to the value of a gift at the time it is set up, age of donor, and interest rates.

appreciated or appreciating asset: An asset whose value has increased or continues to increase in value due to a variety of factors, including inflation.

beneficiary: A person designated to receive income or assets in a will or trust.

buy-sell agreement: Contract between partners or co-owners of a business that determines the conditions and price for a buyout by one or more of the owners at the death or retirement of one.

cafeteria plan: Employee fringe benefit plan permitting the employee to select among a variety of tax-free and taxed benefits.

cash surrender value insurance: Life insurance that contains a savings account along with coverage for the life of the insured.

charitable lead trust: Gift made in trust to a recognized charity that includes income payable to the charity for a set time, with the remainder returned to the donor or another non-charity.

charitable remainder trust: Gift made in trust to a recognized charity that includes income payable to the donor during that person's lifetime. At the death of the donor, the remaining value of the gift belongs to the charity.

codicil: A written and properly witnessed legal change or amendment to a will.

community property: Assets and property acquired after marriage and owned equally by marriage partners (such property is recognized in nine states).

community property agreement: A document that legally transfers title of property owned by both the marriage partners to one of the surviving spouses.

condominium: Several persons owning their own apartments in a building or complex, with an undivided interest in the common areas.

cooperative: Housing style where buyers purchase shares in the corporation that owns the building. Tenant shareholders hold a proprietary lease that gives them the right to their units.

custodian: Trustee of Uniform Gift to Minors Act accounts or property set up for minors.

devise: A gift by will.

domicile: A person's fixed place of residence that he or she considers the permanent address.

donee: Person who receives a gift.

donor: Person who gives a gift.

durable power of attorney: A power of attorney is a legal document that gives another person full legal authority to act on that person's behalf, including signing checks and similar means of handling money. A durable power of attorney continues to be in effect when the person giving the power is incapacitated or disabled.

estate planning: Orderly arrangement of assets and a plan for conveying them to heirs and others in a manner calculated to minimize taxes, expenses, and delays.

estate tax: Federal and state tax that taxes the transfer of wealth upon death.

executor: Person or institution named in a will to carry out its provisions and instructions. The female term is executrix.

fair market value: A price agreed to by a willing buyer and a willing seller in a free negotiation.

fiduciary: A person acting primarily for another's benefit in confidence, good faith, prudence, and fair dealing, such as a trustee or executor.

future interest: A property interest that gives right to future possession or use; a remainder interest in a trust is a future interest.

grantor: The person who establishes or creates a trust. Also called a settlor.

gross estate: Total dollar value of all one's property for estate tax purposes.

group life insurance: Term life insurance provided at group rates, usually by an employer.

guardian: A person who is legally responsible for managing the affairs and the care of a minor or incompetent person. A guardian is appointed by the court.

health care power of attorney: A document that gives another person the authority to make medical decisions for the person executing it.

heir: A person legally entitled to receive another person's property through inheritance.

imputed interest: Rate of interest assigned by Internal Revenue Service to a less-than-market rate loan or a no-interest-rate loan. Lender must pay taxes on imputed interest even if no money is actually received from borrower, who usually is a family member.

incidents of ownership: Usually associated with insurance. Includes any control, such as being able to change a beneficiary, encumber a cash balance for loan collateral, or cancel a policy.

individual retirement account (IRA): A retirement account established by an individual and not an employer, where the contributions may be tax deductible.

inheritance tax: A tax levied in some states on inherited property. Tax rates typically depend on the relationship of the heir to the deceased.

intestate: Dying without a will.

irrevocable: When applied to a trust indicates, it cannot be changed or cancelled.

joint tenancy: Owning property jointly in some form, with the right of survivorship.

kiddie tax: Slang for federal income tax on minors up to age 14.

life estate: An interest, such as income from a trust, that continues for the life of the person holding that interest. Can also refer to real estate, where ownership is divided in half: one half is the length of the homeowner's life, the remainder willed to the heir and becoming his or hers when the property owner dies.

living trust: A revocable or irrevocable written agreement into which a person (called settlor or grantor) transfers assets and property along with instructions to the trustee for the management and future distribution of assets.

marital deduction: A federal estate tax deduction for property received by the deceased's spouse.

medicare: A federal government program to assist elders in the payment of medical expenses. Medicaid is a state-run program, with federal government contributions, to pay for the health care of needy persons of any age.

pay-on-death: An account or bond where a person is named to receive property upon the death of the owner.

personal property: Movable property (tangible), such as furniture and motor vehicles, and property that represents an interest in other property (intangible), such as stock certificates and bank accounts.

personal representative: Another name for a person who is charged with managing an estate; same as executor or administrator.

pick-up tax: An estate tax levied by some states equivalent to the federal state death tax credit.

pooled income trust: Charitable remainder trust where cash or readily marketable securities are combined with similar contributions from others and managed like a mutual fund.

pour-over will: A will designed to cover property that has not been transferred to a living trust. Assets are "poured over" into the trust for management.

prenuptial agreement: A contract agreed to by a couple prior to marriage that defines rights upon death or divorce.

probate court: A specialized court in each state set up to handle the management of wills, estates of persons dying without a will, and other functions, such as guardianships.

probate estate: Property and assets of the deceased, distributed under direction of the probate court.

QTIP trust: A marital trust that permits the estate to receive a marital deduction even though the surviving spouse has only an income interest in the trust.

Qualified retirement plan: A plan that is entitled to special tax treatment upon contributions to that plan and income earned during its existence. Defined benefit, defined contribution, and 401(k) plans are examples.

remainder interest: Property usually left in trust to another after the death of one or more who have an income interest.

separate property: Property owned only by one marriage partner that is kept segregated from the couple's community property.

settlor: Another term for the person who establishes and funds a trust. Also called grantor.

spendthrift trust: Trust established for a beneficiary who lacks money management skills to prevent the beneficiary from spending a legacy unwisely.

supervised procedure: Formal probate court procedure where every action of the estate is subject to court supervision. Contrasted with unsupervised or limited supervision probate.

tax basis: Taxpayer's tax investment in property, usually the cost *plus* improvements *less* depreciation.

taxable estate: Gross estate less deductions such as marital and charitable deductions, debts, and administrative expenses.

tenancy in common: Co-ownership in property without right of survival: each owner can leave his or her share to whomever they choose.

tenancy in the entirety: Joint ownership limited to married couples that includes right of survival.

term life insurance: Pure insurance coverage only, with no savings component.

testamentary trust: A trust in the deceased's will.

trust: A written and formal agreement that enables a person or institution to hold property and manage it for the benefit of identified beneficiaries in accordance with instructions in the trust agreement.

trust agreement: Document setting out instructions for managing property left in a living trust, including who is to receive each portion of the trust assets.

trustee: Person or institution empowered to manage trust property according to the instructions contained in the trust agreement.

unitrust: Form of charitable trust whereby donor receives at least a minimum annual return based on an annual valuation of assets.

viatical settlement: Insurance payout for those with terminal, or even chronic, illnesses. Essentially, this is an advance draw on insurance proceeds that would ordinarily be paid at death.

will: Basic document for transferring property to successors through probate court.

Index

H-I

Insurance Group of the
Consumer Federation of
America, 49
intangible property
co-ops, 23
personal property, 22
inter vivos (living trusts), 92,
95-96, 101, 222
assets, removing from
wills, 149
funding, 100
irrevocable, 96-99
probate court, 112
revocable, 96
guardianship, 130
interest free loans, gift tax,
185-186
Internal Revenue
Service (IRS)
deferred
compensation, 60
federal estate tax
rates, 176
IRAs (individual
retirement accounts), 58
safe deposit box, 25
tax help line, 170
tax-deferred retirement
plans, 59-60
see also taxes
International Association for
Financial Planning, 11
intestacy, simultaneous
death, 117
intestate, 6, 66, 221
costs, 6
heirs, 67
determining, 67-69
introduction, wills, 77-80
inventory (assets), 16-18
investments, 9
trusts, 101
IRAs (individual retirement
accounts), 57-58, 221

irrevocable living trusts,
96-99
gift giving, 211
irrevocable trusts, 221
gift tax, 186
IRS (Internal Revenue
Service)
deferred
compensation, 60
federal estate tax
rates, 176
IRAs (individual
retirement accounts), 58
safe deposit box, 25
tax help line, 170
tax-deferred retirement
plans, 59-60
see also taxes

J

Joint First-to-Die (whole life
insurance), 46
joint ownership
assets, removing from
wills, 148
with right of survivorship,
marriage, 27-28
simultaneous death, 117
joint tenancy, 221
with right of
survivorship, 19
joint wills, 165
joint-with-survivor pension,
52-53

K-L

Keogh plans, 58
tax deferrment, 59
kiddie tax, 221

law of advancement,
117-118

lead trusts, charitable
donations, 197
legal residence
state taxes, 200-201
wills, 76
legality
anti-lapse law, 86
no-fault divorce law, 141
probate court, 20,
103-104, 222
administrators, 105,
107-110
artificial
insemination, 116
avoiding, 111-112
co-ownership, 111
costs, 110-111
death, medical
definition, 117
law of advancement,
117-118
life insurance, 112
living trusts, 112
marriage, 114-116, 119
murder, inheritance,
119-120
problems form, 118
process, 104-105
supervised, 105-106
surrogate mothers, 116
unsupervised, 105-106
Level (term policy life
insurance), 45
licensed professionals
buy-sell agreement, 155
C corporations, 154
disability insurance, 155
estate planning, 154-155
retirement, 155
liens, wills, 81
life estates, 221
ownership, 20-21
life expectancy, estimating
for pension plans, 56-57

M

Q-R

DATE DUE	BORROWER'S NAME